Field Guide to

HERBS & SPICES

How to Identify, Select, and Use Virtually Every Seasoning at the Market

By Aliza Green

QUIRK BOOKS

PHILADELPHIA

DISCLAIMER
The world of seasoning is wide and varied. While we have taken care to represent a large variety of those available, the author and publisher cannot guarantee this guide addresses every possible herb and spice available worldwide.

Library of Congress Cataloging in Publication Number: 2005930879

ISBN: 1-59474-082-8

Printed in Singapore

Typeset in Adobe Garamond, Franklin Gothic, and Impact

Designed by Karen Onorato
Photography by Steve Legato
Iconography by Karen Onorato
Edited by Erin Slonaker

All photographs copyright © 2006 by Quirk Productions, Inc.,
except photo 7, courtesy istockphoto.com.

Distributed in North America by Chronicle Books
85 Second Street
San Francisco, CA 94105

10 9 8 7 6 5 4 3 2 1

Quirk Books
215 Church Street
Philadelphia, PA 19106
www.quirkbooks.com

Contents

Introduction

Here's a compact, easy-to-carry book that's packed with information to help sort your way through the world of herbs, both fresh and dried, and spices, along with herb and spice mixes. You'll learn how to identify, select, store, and cook with herbs such as Australian lemon myrtle (page 9), French lavender (page 51), and Japanese shiso (page 102) and spices such as Indian ajwain (page 116), African grains of paradise (page 194), and Chinese star anise (page 249). International recipes and menus will be easier to understand because herb and spice names in many languages are included at the beginning of each entry.

Read this book to learn the difference between cinnamon and cassia, green and black cardamom, and white and black mustard seeds. Each listing includes a simple, characteristic recipe that highlights the flavor of that seasoning. A section on herb and spice mixes describes them and includes recipes for creating your own shrimp/crab boil, apple pie spice, Moroccan ras el hanout, homemade chili powder, and more. Recipes, preparation suggestions, and food affinities make it easy to explore new spices and herbs.

While it would take a much larger book to cover all the herbs and spices sold in today's global food market, I have crammed as much information, recipes, and photos as possible into this portable guide.

Please write to me with questions and comments at www.alizagreen.com.

Aliza Green

Herbs

Herbs are the leaves of plants used as flavorings. Fresh herbs may be found loose in small plastic bags, fastened in bunches, growing in a pot, or encased in plastic boxes. No matter how they're packed, choose fresh herbs with vibrant color and aroma, and avoid any that are limp, yellowing, or have black spots. Robust field-grown herbs are generally preferred over more fragile greenhouse-grown herbs. Field-grown herbs will have larger, more fragrant, and hardier leaves, because they've been grown in plenty of sunlight during the day (to produce lustrous deep green leaves) and cool nighttime temperatures (for crispness and sweetness).

To store all fresh herbs, remove any rubber bands or fasteners, spread out the sprigs, and pick out and discard any that are slimy or yellowed. If roots are present, cut them off to prevent the tops from wilting, saving the washed roots to flavor sauces and soups, if desired. Trim the herbs, swish around vigorously in a large bowl of water, scoop out, and drain. Spread them out on towels or spin dry in a salad spinner. Wrap the herbs loosely in paper towels and place them into a zip-top bag, blowing to fill the bag with air as a cushion against bruising. Or place the herbs in an airtight plastic container, taking care to avoid crushing. Store the herbs in the warmest part of the refrigerator.

To freeze fresh herbs without them becoming unpleasant, first surround them with fat, such as olive oil or butter. Use at least 2 cups washed and dried herb leaves for about 1 cup softened butter or olive oil. Tougher leaves like rosemary or oregano should be roughly chopped first. Blend or process the fat and the washed and dried herb leaves. Transfer to a zip-top bag or plastic container marked with the date and contents, squeeze out any air, and freeze up to 6 months.

Dried herbs are useful and convenient, especially for those without ready access to their fresh counterparts. The best dried herbs are the freshest, usually those sold on the branch. Whole leaf herbs are more desirable than crumbled or powdered herbs. Buy dried herbs in small quantities and renew the supply every year. Older herbs lose their complex nuances of flavor and will tend to be bitter. Generally, the greener the dried herb, the livelier and more fragrant it will be.

Above all, learn to use an array of herbs to enhance the pleasure of cooking and eating, to add a bit of fresh greenery to any dish, and to impart the character of a cuisine.

1a–b.   **ANGELICA**

Other Names: *Angélique* (French); garden angelica; herb of the angels.

General Description: *Angelica* (Angelica archangelica) *is one of the most flamboyant-looking herbs, with long, thick, hollow, pale green, celery-like stems supporting huge umbrellas of greenish white flowers above bright green, serrated, flat leaves.* The roots, stems, leaves, and seeds of angelica are all edible and share an earthy, bittersweet, warm flavor reminiscent of licorice and juniper. Angelica is believed to have originated in northern Europe, particularly the area of Lapland, Iceland, and Russia. In Lapland, angelica stalks are stripped off the central stem and eaten as a delicacy. Angelica is grown extensively in Europe, where its stems are commonly candied and used as an attractive light, bright green decoration for cakes, cookies, and ice cream. Candied angelica is especially popular in Sicily, where it is traditional for *cassata*, a cake layered with sweetened ricotta studded with candied fruit and covered with bittersweet chocolate icing. The seeds and roots are the source of an essential oil that flavors ice cream, candy, baked goods, puddings, and liqueurs. French *angélique* liqueur, drunk over crushed ice as a digestive, can also be used for cocktails, sorbets, and desserts.

Season: Fresh angelica is best early in its season, late spring,
    when the shoots are young and softly colored.

Candied angelica will be most easily found in late winter before the holiday baking season.

Purchase and Avoid: There is limited availability of fresh or candied angelica, much of which is exported from France and Italy. Sometimes imitations made of green jelly are passed off as real candied angelica stem, which should have visible strings running through it like celery and a bright vegetal green color. Buy fresh angelica in plant form from herb growers.

Storage: Store candied angelica airtight in a dry place up to 3 years.

Recipe: *Candied Angelica*

1.   **Working in dry weather, start with about 2 pounds young, tender angelica stalks and stems. Cut them into even lengths and put them into a glass or ceramic bowl. Bring 2 cups water and 2 tablespoons salt to a boil and pour over the angelica, weighting with a plate so it's fully submerged. Cover and let soak 2 hours. Drain the angelica, peel off and discard the stringy outer celery-like layer, then rinse under cold water.**

2.   **Make sugar syrup by bringing 3 cups sugar and 3 cups water to a boil. Simmer the angelica in the syrup for 20 minutes, or until tender and transparent. Remove and drain, reserving the syrup. Spread**

the angelica in a single layer on a wire rack and leave
to drain and dry for 4 days. Boil the angelica in the
syrup again for 10 minutes, adding water if the syrup
is too thick, and drain on a wire rack for 4 days longer.
Dust with granulated sugar and store in an airtight
container, cutting into decorative bits as needed. This
recipe may also be used to candy fennel stalks.

Serving
Suggestions:

Press decorative bits of candied angelica into the tops
of shortbread cookies before baking. • Burn angelica
seeds to perfume a room. • Make angelica and mint
sandwiches by combining chopped candied angelica
and mint leaves with enough mayonnaise to bind and
spreading it on whole-grain bread.

Food
Affinities:

Absinthe, apricot, Bénédictine, candied citron, chocolate, cinnamon, cloves, eggs, gin, lemon, orange, pineapple, rhubarb, ricotta cheese, strawberry, vermouth.

2a–b.

ANISE HYSSOP AND HYSSOP

Other Names:

Anise hyssop: Anise mint; giant hyssop; licorice
mint. **Hyssop:** Blue hyssop; *esov* (Hebrew); *issopos*
(Greek); pink hyssop; white hyssop; *zoufa* (Farsi); *zufa
otu* (Turkish).

General
Description:

Anise hyssop (Agastache foeniculum) *has large, soft,
aromatic, anise-scented leaves and long spikes of nectar-*

rich purple flowers. Native to North America, anise hyssop was used by Native Americans as a breath freshener, tea infusion, cough medicine, and natural sweetener. The plant was brought to Europe by bee-keepers, who collect a light, fragrant honey made from the flower nectar. Korean mint (*A. rugosa*), a close relative of anise hyssop, is used in Asian medicine. The two plants cross-pollinate easily, but anise hyssop smells like licorice while Korean mint instead smells of mint.

Hyssop (*Hyssopus officinalis*), related to anise hyssop, has aromatic, mintlike, slightly bitter leaves and lovely flowers, usually dark blue but sometimes pink or white, that make a beautiful garnish. The spiky, narrow leaves may be used as an alternative to sage and added to bouquet garni (page 279), a bundle of herbs used to season soups, stews, and braises.

Hyssop's pungent, peppery flavor goes best with robust dishes such as potato or bean soup and beef, veal, or chicken stew. It's also distilled for use in perfumes and in making liqueurs, especially Chartreuse.

Season:	Anise hyssop and hyssop are at their best in summer, from June to October, when they are in bloom. Hyssop blooms profusely during this period.
Purchase and Avoid:	Look for anise hyssop and hyssop with fragrant, lively leaves and full, deep-colored blossoms.

Recipe: *Anise Hyssop Sauce*

 1.   **Combine 3 tablespoons sugar, 6 tablespoons apple cider vinegar, and ½ cup water in a small pot and bring to a boil. Add ½ cup coarsely chopped anise hyssop leaves and flowers and return the mixture to a boil.**

2.   **Turn off the heat and allow the mixture to steep for 30 minutes. Pour through a sieve, pressing the leaves to extract all the liquid.**

3.   **Combine 2 teaspoons cornstarch and 2 tablespoons water in a small bowl. Whisk into the strained liquid. Bring the mixture to a boil, while whisking, to thicken the sauce. Makes 1 cup sauce. Serve with roast lamb or veal.**

Serving
Suggestions: Cream honey with unsalted butter and chopped anise hyssop blossoms to serve on pancakes, waffles, or toast. • Use anise hyssop leaves or blossoms to make tea and to flavor drinks, such as lemonade. • Use hyssop instead of sage when seasoning duck, veal, turkey, sausage, or pork. • Add young hyssop leaves to salads.

Food
Affinities: **Anise hyssop:** Butter, chicken, cream, cucumber, fish, honey, lemon, rhubarb, veal. **Hyssop:** Beans, beef, cranberry, duck, pork, potato, sausage, turkey, veal.

3a–b.

AUSTRALIAN NATIVE HERBS

General
Description:

Australia's unique, intensely flavored native herbs are now being raised commercially as part of the growing movement to develop a native Australian cuisine. Aniseed myrtle (*Backhousia anisata*), also known as Australian leaf aniseed, is a tree indigenous to the subtropical rain forest of Australia; its delicately flavored leaves are the country's alternative to anise seed, with a sweeter, more subtly aromatic flavor. It is one of the most concentrated sources of anethole, a compound that gives the leaves a distinctive licorice-like flavor and sweet aftertaste, so it should be used sparingly. Widely used in cooking and for herbal teas, aniseed myrtle can flavor pasta, seafood, stocks, sauces, breads, cookies, sweets, ice cream, and liqueurs.

Lemon myrtle (*B. citriodora*) has dark green, highly aromatic, lemon-scented leaves resembling bay leaves, with a fragrance and flavor that combines lemon verbena, lemongrass, wild lime, and a hint of eucalyptus. It grows in the subtropical and tropical coastal rain forest areas of Queensland and northern New South Wales. The leaves are used fresh or dried and either whole or ground and have the ability to hold their flavor and aroma considerably longer than other lemon-flavored herbs.

Forest berry herb (*Eucalyptus olida*), also called strawberry gum or manna gum, which grows in northeast New South Wales, has a refreshing, berrylike flavor and an aroma that's a mix of passion fruit and berry with a savory hint of caraway and cumin. The natural berry and fruit flavor of forest berry herb works well with most fruits and desserts.

Native mint (*Prostanthera incisa*), or cut-leaf mint bush, is a shrubby bush that grows in northern New South Wales. Its leaves taste similar to peppermint with a trace of eucalyptus. Native mint is quite potent, so a little goes a very long way.

River mint (*Mentha australis*, hence its other name, Australian mint) is a creeping herb with pale green, serrated, pointed leaves and flowers at the leaf junctions. It's found along waterways and in wetlands and moist forests in Australia. It has a wonderfully pungent fresh spearmint aroma and is used for mint tea.

Purchase and Avoid:
Aniseed myrtle is available as whole dried leaves, essential oil, and a powder. Lemon myrtle leaf is sold whole or powdered; when stored well, the coarse, pale green powder maintains all the character of the green leaf. Forest berry herb is sold ground. Native mint is sold as a fine, free-flowing, dark green powder. River mint is rarely found for sale; it's gathered from the wild or from gardens.

Recipes:
Aniseed Myrtle–Marinated Feta

 1. Heat ¹⁄₄ cup olive oil to 110°F, or until just warm to the touch, and remove from the heat. Add 2 tablespoons

ground aniseed myrtle, allowing it to infuse as the oil cools.

 2. Add the warm oil to 1 pound drained, cubed feta cheese, adding more oil to cover. Cover and refrigerate for at least 2 days.

3. Add the cheese to salads and sandwiches, or use it to top grilled eggplant and mushrooms. Or use it to stuff artichokes.

Australian Lemon Myrtle and Yogurt Panna Cotta

 1. Soften 1 ½ tablespoons powdered gelatin in ¼ cup cold water. Bring ¾ cup water to a boil. Remove from the heat and stir in 2 teaspoons ground lemon myrtle. Whisk the gelatin mixture with the hot water so the gelatin dissolves and is clear. Cool and then refrigerate until just starting to gel.

 2. Whip 1 ½ cups chilled heavy cream until it begins to thicken. Sprinkle in ¾ cup confectioners' sugar and continue beating until the cream is stiff.

3. Place 1 cup plain whole milk yogurt in a large mixing bowl. Gently fold in the sweetened whipped cream.

 4. Fold 1 cup of the cream mixture into the gelatin to temper. Whisk the gelatin quickly and thoroughly

into the remaining cream mixture. Transfer to an oiled
6-cup mold or a serving bowl and refrigerate, covered,
for 2 hours, or up to overnight, until set. Unmold if
desired. Accompany with sliced mango and kiwi.

Serving
Suggestions:

Sprinkle aniseed myrtle on fish, chicken, or vegetables
before or after cooking. • Add lemon myrtle to fish,
seafood, or vegetables. • Sprinkle ground forest berry
herb on fruit or green salads. • Use native and river
mint in mint sauce for lamb.

Food
Affinities:

Aniseed myrtle: Almond, apricot, bread, chocolate,
feta cheese, peach, seafood, smoked meat. **Lemon
myrtle:** Bread, candy, cheese, cookies, kiwi, mayonnaise, poultry, seafood, tea. **Forest berry herb:** Apricot,
blueberry, cherry, guava, mango, papaya, peach, raspberry. **Native and river mint:** Bread, butter, butterscotch, lamb, lemon, mustard, pesto, vinegar.

4a–h.   **BASIL**

Other Names:

Albahaca or *alfábega* (Spanish); anise basil; *bai krapao*
(Thai holy basil); *barbar, subja,* or *tulsi* (Hindi); *basilic*
or *herbe royale* (French); *basilico* (Italian); bush basil;
cinnamon basil; Genovese basil; holy basil; *hung que*
or *rau que* (Vietnamese); lemon basil; lettuce-leafed
(or curly) basil; opal basil; purple ruffled basil; sweet
basil; Thai basil.

**General
Description:**   *Sweet basil* (Ocimum basilicum) *is one of the most
beloved of all herbs because its sweet, clovelike aroma is
so appealing.* Basil originated in Iran, Africa, and India
and was well-known in ancient Egypt, Greece, and
Rome. In Italy basil symbolizes love—a woman
would leave a pot of basil in her window to indicate
to her lover that he was welcome. However, for the
early Greeks and Romans, basil was a symbol of
hatred. Basil is said to derive its name from its use as
a magical cure against the terrifying basilisk, a mythi-
cal Greek half lizard, half dragon creature with a fatal
piercing stare. The herb is still considered a cure for
venomous snake bites in parts of Europe and Britain,
and in Africa it's believed to protect against scorpions.

Sweet basil has an ineffable flavor reminiscent of
anise, clove, and mint. Although its aroma is heady,
the flavor of most varieties is mild and sweet enough
that it can be used in abundance. Dried basil loses
much of the sweet delicacy and subtlety of its fresh
counterpart, with a spicier, clove-mint flavor that
works best in long-cooked sauces.

There are more than 50 species of basil, differing
in size, color, appearance, and flavor, and even more
cultivars. Large-leafed sweet basil is the variety most
commonly used in the kitchen. Holy basil (*O. sanctum*)
has an intense, pungent aroma and attractive, deep
purple blossoms. Sacred in India, it is often planted
around Hindu shrines. Genovese (or bush) basil (*O.
minimum*) has small leaves with mild flavor and is used

for classic pesto. The highly aromatic basil napoletano is grown in the region of Naples, Italy, and has large, rounded, light green, crinkled leaves; a sweet fragrance; and a mellow, rich flavor. Purple ruffled basil (*O. basilicum 'Purple Ruffles'*) has a mild, pleasing flavor and deeply colored ruffled leaves that are attractive in a salad or as garnish. Strikingly beautiful dark opal basil (*O. basilicum 'Purpureum'*) is deep purple with smooth leaves and a minty flavor.

Thai basil (*O. basilicum 'Thai Queen'* and others) has slender oval leaves with purple stems and blossoms. Because only cooking fully releases its exotic peppery flavor, this type is not eaten raw, but added in generous amounts to stir-fries and spicy soups. Cinnamon basil (*O. basilicum 'Cinnamon'*) has a distinct cinnamon fragrance that complements Southeast Asian dishes. Refreshing lemon basil (*O. citriodora*) and lime basil (*O. americanum*), both from Thailand, and anise-scented basil (*O. basilicum 'Anise'*), from Persia, may be found. Curly (or lettuce-leafed) basil (*O. crispum*) has leaves almost as large as lettuce and may be added to salad or used to wrap fish before steaming.

| Season: | Basil is best in summer months, when field-grown basil is available. Hothouse basil is available and satis-factory most of the year. Look for Thai holy basil in Southeast Asian stores and at farmers' markets. Look for flavored basil plants at garden stores or buy fla-vored basil in bunches at farmers' markets. |

**Purchase
and Avoid:**

For powerfully fragrant basil that will last, choose field-grown basil. It may be very sandy and should be washed thoroughly. In hot weather, basil can become bitter and harsh, especially after flowering.

Sometimes local basil is sold roots and all; this type may be replanted in soil. For kitchen use, cut away the roots, wash the branches, and spin dry before storing.

Hothouse basil is more tender, less fragrant, and more fragile than field-grown, but makes the brightest green pesto because its leaves crush easily. Avoid basil that is wilting or that has dark spots, a sign of over-chilling, or slimy dark-colored leaves, a sign that the leaves have spoiled.

Storage:

Basil is quite tender and perishable. To store, trim the stems, pull off any lower side leaves, and stand the bunch in a jar with enough cool water to just cover the base of the stems. Leave at room temperature for 2 to 3 days, changing the water daily. Alternatively, wrap the basil in paper towels and place in a plastic bag. Refrigerate in the warmest part of the refrigerator—usually under the light or on the top shelf—for 1 to 2 days.

Note:

Basil blackens easily when bruised or cut, especially if the knife is dull or made from carbon rather than stainless steel.

Recipe: ***Emerald Basil Pesto***

1.   **In the bowl of a food processor or blender, combine 1 cup pine nuts, 1 tablespoon chopped garlic, and 3/4 cup extra virgin olive oil, and process to a smooth paste.**

2.   **Add the washed and dried leaves of 1 large bunch basil (about 1 cup) in small handfuls alternating with 1/2 cup crushed ice until all the basil and ice have been incorporated.**

3.   **Transfer to a bowl and stir in 1 cup freshly grated hard cheese (such as pecorino Romano).**

4.   **Cover with a layer of oil, then press plastic wrap directly onto the surface. Refrigerate up to 3 days, scraping away and discarding any darkened (oxidized) pesto from the top before use.**

Serving
Suggestions: Make basil chiffonade (shredded basil) by layering washed and dried leaves, rolling into a cylinder, and slicing crosswise into thin strips using a sharp knife. Toss with olive oil, diced ripe yellow and red tomatoes, red onions, and fresh mozzarella, heat gently, and toss with capellini. • Add torn Thai basil to pad thai, a noodle dish with shrimp, bean sprouts, and toasted peanuts. • Process together softened butter with chopped garlic and basil. Spread on split Italian bread, wrap in foil, and bake to make garlic bread.

Food Affinities: Carrot, chicken, fish, garlic, goat cheese, lemon, mozzarella, olive oil, sweet corn, tomato, veal, zucchini.

BAY LEAF AND CALIFORNIA BAY LEAF

Other Names: **Bay leaf:** Bay laurel; cooking bay; *dafni* (Greek); *defne* (Turkish); Greek laurel; *laural* (Spanish); laurel; *laurier* or *laurier noble* (French); *lauro* (Italian); *llor* (Catalan); *louro* (Portuguese); Mediterranean bay leaf; poet's laurel; *rand* or *waraq ghaar* (Arabic); sweet bay; Turkish bay leaf; victor's laurel. **California bay leaf:** California laurel; Oregon myrtle; pepperwood.

General Description: *Bay leaves come from the ancient Mediterranean bay laurel tree* (Laurus nobilis) *and are one of the most widely used culinary herbs in Europe and North America.* The bay laurel tree has been cultivated since the beginning of recorded history. The term *baccalaureate* (and *bachelor*) for academic degrees is derived from *baccalaureus* (laurel berry), because of the ancient Greek and Roman practice of honoring scholars and poets with garlands of bay branches. The plump, oval-shaped bay laurel leaves, which are shiny, medium green, and sturdy with slightly rough edges, have a sweet, full-bodied aroma. The fresh and dried leaves, dried berries, and leaf oil are used for flavoring, while the wood is used as an aromatic smoke flavoring. The berries' robust taste marries well with venison and potatoes.

California bay leaves come from an evergreen tree (*Umbellularia californica*) related to bay laurel that is common in coastal forests of western North America. The leaves are long, narrow ovals that, unlike their Mediterranean counterparts, are smooth-edged and dark grayish green. They're highly aromatic with a potent resinous character. Use California bay leaves the same way as Mediterranean bay leaves but in half the quantity, because they're much stronger.

Season: Dried leaves are more common, but fresh Mediterranean bay leaves can occasionally be found in summer months. California bay leaves are sold fresh and dried throughout the year.

Purchase and Avoid: Dried bay leaves may be purchased as whole leaves, broken bits, or a powder. Whether buying fresh or dry, choose whole leaves with the brightest green color and strongest aroma you can find. Purchase pliable fresh California bay leaves that are deep green, not faded gray. For best flavor, bay leaves should not be used more than 1 year after harvest.

Recipe: ***Red Onion Marmalade with Bay Leaves***

 I. **In a large nonreactive skillet, sauté 3 sliced red onions in 3 tablespoons butter until softened but not browned. Add ½ cup red wine, 1 tablespoon balsamic vinegar, 3 bay leaves, 1½ teaspoons chopped fresh thyme (or**

½ teaspoon dried thyme), 2 teaspoons honey, ½ teaspoon ground coriander, ¼ teaspoon ground allspice, and salt and black pepper to taste.

2. Bring the mixture to a boil, reduce the heat, and simmer about 30 minutes, or until the liquid is syrupy, stirring occasionally. Serve hot as a topping for sautéed calves liver, grilled steaks or hamburgers, or pasta with gorgonzola cheese sauce. Makes about 3 cups.

Note: Both fresh and dried Mediterranean and California bay leaves have sharp edges that can actually tear your inner organs, so be sure not to eat them. Use them to flavor foods, and remove the leaves before serving. California bay leaves should be used with care because the leaves contain umbellulone, which can cause convulsive sneezing, headaches, and sinus irritation when inhaled deeply.

Serving Suggestions: Add bay leaves to slow-cooked sauces and stocks or when poaching fish or seafood. • Poach pears in red or white wine syrup with bay leaves, peppercorns, and a strip of orange or lemon zest. • Add a pinch of ground bay leaf to a Bloody Mary.

Food Affinities: Artichoke, beet, celery root, chicken, corned beef, fish, potato, roast duck, roast pork, tomato sauce.

BORAGE

Other Names: Beebread; *borragine* (Italian); *borraja* or *rabo de alacrán* (Spanish); *borretsch* or *gurkenkraut* (German; also used for dill); *bourragé* or *bourraio* (Provençal French); *bugloss, burrage,* or *hodan* (Turkish); *lisan athaur* (Arabic); *llanwenlys* (Welsh); star flower (blossom).

General   *Borage* (Borago officinalis) *is a versatile plant valued*
Description: *for its cool cucumber aroma and flavor.* This annual has large, hairy, oval leaves with robust stems and five-pointed, sky blue, star-shaped flowers surrounding black stamens. Borage, thought to have originated in the area of Aleppo, Syria, was probably brought to Europe by the Romans; it is most popular in Great Britain, central Europe, Spain, Italy, and Greece. British summer drinks like Pimm's cup and claret cup, a red wine and brandy punch, are traditionally garnished with a stem of borage, complete with leaves and flowers. The lovely blue flowers can be preserved, candied, simmered in syrup, or used as garnish. In Spain, the succulent stalks are boiled and fried in butter. In Liguria, Italy, borage and other wild spring greens are gathered to fill *pansotti al sugo di noci*, triangular pasta served with a creamy walnut sauce. The flower corollas can be used to color vinegar blue. Both leaves and flowers are brewed for tea, and the flowers yield a honey much appreciated in New Zealand.

Season:	Borage greens are most tender in spring and may be found wild in many places or purchased at local farmers' markets. The flowers bloom in midsummer.

Purchase and Avoid:	Look for the most tender, least hairy borage if you'll be using it as an uncooked herb. The flowers should be sparkling blue and wide open. If using borage as a cooking green, larger, older leaves are acceptable.

Recipe:	***Crystallized Blue Borage Blossoms***

1. Start with absolutely dry blossoms, preferably picked on a dry, sunny morning so the flowers are fully opened. Beat 1 egg white lightly without allowing it to become frothy, and pour into a shallow bowl. Have another bowl ready with 1/4 cup superfine granulated sugar.

2. Using tweezers, dip the blossoms first into the egg white and then into the sugar. Use a fine paintbrush to get the sugar into the folds.

3. Shake off any excess sugar, lay the blossoms on a wire rack, and leave to dry overnight in a warm, dry place. Use to garnish cakes and desserts.

Serving Suggestions:	Freeze borage blossoms (without the inedible calyx) in ice cubes and use to chill summer drinks or punch. • Briefly boil older leaves, steam like spinach, or dip in batter and deep-fry.

Food
Affinities: Butter, champagne, cream, cucumber, dill, fennel,
mint, nutmeg, scallion, sour cream, spring herb
mixes, sugar, walnut.

6.   **CALAMINT**

Other Names: **Calamint:** Common calamint; mountain balm. **Large-
flowered calamint:** Beautiful mint; *calament à grandes
fleurs* (French); mint savory; showy calamint; showy
savory. **Lesser calamint:** Field balm; *nepitella* (Italian).

General
Description: *Calamint* (Calamintha sylvatica) *is an herb with a
strong aromatic fragrance somewhere between mint and
marjoram that's characteristic of Roman cooking.* This
herb is used when stewing zucchini, artichokes, and
other vegetables in olive oil and garlic. Some southern
Italian cheeses are flavored with calamint, which is
gathered in the wild in Tuscany, Sicily, and Basilicata.
Niebita (*Calamintha sp.*), another type of calamint
with attractive light lavender flowers, is indispensable
for Italian bean and mushroom dishes. Lesser
calamint (*C. nepeta*), an herb with a more pungent
taste than calamint, grows all over Tuscany and is
used extensively in Tuscan cooking; it's especially delicious cooked with wild mushrooms. Large-flowered
calamint (*C. grandiflora*) has a pleasing minty fragrance and is used as a seasoning or for tea.

Season: Calamint is in season in summer; the blossoms appear in midsummer.

Purchase and Avoid: Calamint will be available in its plant form from herb growers.

Recipe: ***Shrimp with Calamint, Garlic, and Red Chiles***

1. **In a large, heavy skillet, heat 4 tablespoons extra virgin olive oil. Add 2 pounds large, unpeeled, deveined shrimp, 4 cloves thinly sliced garlic, and 2 seeded and thinly sliced red jalapeño or pasilla chiles and cook until the shrimp are opaque and the garlic is light brown.**

2. **Pour in ½ cup dry white vermouth, add 2 tablespoons chopped calamint, and turn the shrimp over to cook 1 more minute. Season to taste with salt and pepper, toss to combine the flavors, and serve.**

Serving Suggestions: Brown wild mushrooms with garlic and calamint and use to top grilled fillet of beef. • Add calamint to rabbit dishes. • Add calamint to the boiling water for cooking artichokes.

Food Affinities: Beef, eggplant, fresh pasta, garlic, goat, mushroom, rabbit, shrimp, tomato, white wine, zucchini.

7. 　　**CANNABIS**

Other Names: *Bhang* (or *bang*), *charas* (hashish), or *ganga* (Hindi); *cáñamo índico, grifa,* or *hachís* (Spanish); *canapa indiana* (Italian); *chanvre indien* (French); *da ma* (Chinese); grass; hash or hashish; *hashish qinnib* (Arabic); *hind kinnabi* (Turkish); Indian hemp (British); *kannabisu* (Japanese); *kif, qinnib, shâhdânag,* or *sharâneq* (Moroccan); *maconha* (Portuguese); *marihuana* or *marijuana* (Mexican); Mary Jane; pot; weed.

General Description: *Marijuana is the leaves, buds, and flowers of* Cannabis sativa, *popularly used as a spice, herb, and mild hallucinogen.* Cannabis has a long history of use in religious ceremonies, in traditional customs, for medicinal use, and as a culinary herb. Cannabis is used medically for stimulating the appetite and reducing pain for cancer patients, and for helping those with glaucoma.

There are three types of cannabis used in India. *Bhang,* a Sanskrit term referring to cannabis from Bengal, is one of the most ancient forms. It is made from the leaves and stems of uncultivated plants blended into a liquid, sometimes served with yogurt and sweet spices. *Ganja,* more potent than bhang, is made from the resinous tops of cultivated plants. *Charas,* similar to hashish, is obtained by scraping the resin from the leaves of cultivated plants.

Cannabis is mixed with dried fruits, nuts, and spices to make the Moroccan candy called *majoun,* "love potion" in Arabic. Marijuana is considered an essential herb in Jamaica's Rastafarian cooking. Cannabis seeds may be toasted and used as a condiment, ground and brewed as a coffee substitute, made into cakes, or fried. In Japan, the seeds, called *asanomi*, are one of the ingredients in the spice mixture shichimi togarashi (page 286).

Season: This easily grown plant is in season year-round; much of it is grown in hothouses.

Purchase and Avoid: The possession and growing of marijuana for private use are illegal in the United States. Many European countries have either decriminalized cannabis or have stopped enforcing laws against it.

Recipe: *Moroccan Majoun*

1. **Remove stems and seeds from ¼ ounce of marijuana tops, then dry and crumble the leaves. In a dry skillet, toast the leaves over very low heat until the aromas are released.**

2. **Mix the leaves with ½ cup raisins, ½ cup walnuts, 1 teaspoon ground nutmeg, 1 teaspoon ground anise, 1 teaspoon ground ginger, ½ cup honey, and ½ cup water, adding more water if the mixture is too dry and crumbly.**

3. **Simmer together until the mixture is soft and thick. Mash by hand or transfer to a food processor and blend, using several short pulses.**

4. **Stir in 2 tablespoons butter, spoon into a jar, and refrigerate for storage. Spread on crackers or plain cookies, or use as a filling for stuffed cookies. Majoun will keep for 2 to 3 months refrigerated.**

Serving Suggestions: Fresh green marijuana leaves may be dipped into melted butter, sprinkled with salt, and eaten. • The seeds can be added to bread dough.

Food Affinities: Almond, cardamom, cayenne, cinnamon, cumin, dates, ginger, nutmeg, rose water, sesame, sugar, yogurt.

8. CHERVIL

Other Names: *Apo perexil* (Basque); *cerafolio* or *perifollo* (Spanish); *cerbel, französische petersilie,* or *gartenkerbel* (German); *cerfeuil* (French); *cerfoglio* (Italian); French parsley (British); *Frenk maydanoz* (Turkish); garden chervil; *san lo po* (Chinese).

General Description: *The delicately lacy herb chervil* (Anthriscus cerefolium) *is a member of the Apiaceae (parsley) family.* A cousin to carrots, whose leaves it resembles, chervil combines a light anise fragrance with parsley's cleansing freshness. Chervil is France's most elegant herb because its tiny fernlike leaves make a lovely garnish, while its delicate flavor goes well with subtle and refined foods. The fresh leaves are chopped and added to soups, salads, and fish dishes. Herbal vinegars usually contain a few leaves of chervil. If cooked at all, the leaves should be cooked briefly so as not to dissipate the aromas. In Carinthia, Austria's southern region, large ravioli-type pasta are stuffed with cottage cheese, boiled potatoes, and fresh herbs, especially chervil. The related herb cicely, or Spanish chervil (*Myrrhis odorata*), which has a stronger, aniselike aroma, is often substituted for chervil in northern European countries.

Season:

Chervil is not as commonly found in supermarkets as other herbs, but if you do find it, it will likely be in cooler weather. In hot weather, chervil tends to turn white.

Purchase and Avoid:

Look for chervil in farmers' markets and specialty stores. Avoid chervil that's faded or has brown spots. Look for sprightly, light green, feathery chervil with a noticeable aroma somewhere between celery and licorice.

Recipe:

Cream of Carrot Soup with Chervil

1. **Sauté 1 pound peeled and sliced carrots, 1 cup sliced shallots, and ½ cup chopped chervil stalks in ¼ cup butter until the shallots just begin to soften. Add**

2 quarts chicken or vegetable stock and simmer until the carrots are soft.

 2.   Puree in a blender. Add 1 cup heavy cream and 2 tablespoons finely chopped chervil and reheat to boiling. Season with salt, pepper, and nutmeg and serve garnished with a dollop of unsweetened whipped cream and a sprig of chervil.

Serving
Suggestions: Make French *sauce vierge* (virgin sauce) with diced tomatoes, diced shallots, olive oil, and chopped chervil and serve over thinly sliced raw fish or baked fish or seafood. • Add chopped chervil to scrambled eggs or buttered garden peas. • Add chervil to the pan juices when making chicken gravy.

Food
Affinities: Asparagus, butter, carrot, chicken, crabmeat, cream sauces, eggs, garden peas, scallops, shrimp, tomato, spinach, sugar snap peas, white wine.

9a–e.   ## CHIVES AND CHINESE CHIVES

Other Names: **Chives:** *Aglio ungherese* (Hungarian garlic) or *erba cipollina* (Italian); *cebolinha* (Portuguese); *cebollana* (Spanish); *chibu* (Japanese); *ciboulette* (French); *gräslök* (grass-leek; Swedish); *ha la* (Vietnamese); *kucai* (Malay); *schinopraso* (rushlike leek; Greek); *schnittlauch* (cut leek; German). **Chinese chives:** Chinese

leek; *chiu* or *feng pen* (Chinese); garlic chives.
Flowering garlic chives: *Gau choy fa* (Chinese).
Yellow chives: *Gau wong* (Chinese).

General
Description:

Chives (Allium schoenoprasum) *have long, thin, deep green, pointed, hollow leaves with a mild herbal onion flavor.* Chives have been around so long that their origin is unknown. The most delicate member of the onion family, chives are mostly used fresh because they lose much of their flavor by drying, though they are often freeze-dried. Curly chives or German garlic (*A. senescens* var. *glaucum*) has attractive, greenish blue, curled stems.

Chinese chives (*A. tuberosum*) are flat, narrow, green stalks with a sharp, herbal garlic flavor. Originally from Southeast Asia, these chives marry especially well with Chinese and Japanese foods. Yellow chives are Chinese chives kept from light while growing so that they are soft, mild, and tender. These chives are a springtime delicacy. Species related to Chinese chives are used in the cuisines of China, Tibet, and parts of Southeast Asia. In Nepal, *jimbu* or Himalaya onion (*A. wallichii*), with star-shaped purple blossoms, flavors dal, a soupy dish made from split mung beans. Jimbu leaves are usually dried, then fried in ghee to release their flavor.

Season:

Chives are best when tender and green in spring. Look for blossoming chives in late spring. When chives are blossoming, their stalks are too tough to use. Chinese chives are best in winter, especially after a few frosts. Yellow chives are in season in late winter and early spring.

Purchase and Avoid:

In hot or wet weather chives spoil quickly, so sniff before buying and avoid chives with an off smell or yellowed, slimy stalks. Commercially freeze-dried chives are best used for cooking rather than garnishing. The thinner and brighter green the chive, the more delicate. Later in the season, as they grow larger, chives get more oniony. Avoid chives that have dried out and turned brown in hot weather. Young Chinese chive leaves will be milder than older ones.

Storage:

Chives freeze and rot easily, so store them in the warmest part of the refrigerator, generally on the top shelf. Don't plan on storing chives for more than 3 to 4 days unless they are in exceptionally fine condition.

Preparation:

• **Make a bundle out of the chives and thinly slice crosswise. Or, using scissors, snip chives directly over the dish before serving. Chopping chives bruises them.**

• **If the chives are thin and young, stick 3- to 4-inch chive tips into any soft food to make an attractive, edible garnish.**

Serving Suggestions:

Serve American-style baked russet potatoes with sour cream and chives. • Pull chive blossoms away from their green calyx and sprinkle over eggs, salads, rice, pasta, or fish, or stick whole blossoms into the center of a dish for a garnish. • Stir sliced Chinese chives into Asian stir-fries and rice and noodle dishes just before removing from the heat.

Food Affinities: **Chives:** Asparagus, butter, chicken, cream, cucumber, eggs, fish, leek, potato, seafood. **Chinese chives and yellow chives:** Bean sprouts, beef, bok choy, fish, pork, salads, water chestnut, yard-long beans.

10a–c.

CILANTRO, CULANTRO, AND VIETNAMESE CORIANDER

Other Names: **Cilantro:** Arab parsley; Chinese parsley; *cigánype-trezselyem* (Hungarian); *cilantrillo* (some Caribbean islands); *gad* or *kusbara* (Hebrew); Indian parsley; *pak chi met* or *phak hom* (Thai); *wanzendill* (German); *yuen sai* (Chinese). **Culantro:** *Alcapate* (El Salvador); black benny; *cilantro extranjero* or *cilantro habanero* (Mexico); false coriander; fitweed; Mexican coriander; *ngo gai* (Vietnamese); *pak chi farang* (Thai); Puerto Rican coriander; *racao* or *recao* (Puerto Rico); saw leaf herb; sawtooth coriander; sea holly (British); *shado beni* (Trinidad); spiny coriander. **Vietnamese coriander:** Laksa plant; *laksa yip* (Chinese); *chan chom*, *hom chan*, *pa pao*, or *pak pai* (Thai); *rao ram* (Vietnamese); smartweed; Vietnamese mint.

General
Description:

Cilantro (Coriandrum sativum) *has soft green leaves with cut edges, an assertive sage-citrus flavor, and a pungent aroma.* The whole cilantro plant is aromatic and edible, from its rounded lower and feathery upper leaves and white summer flowers to its fruits (usually called *seeds*), tender stems, and potent roots. Cilantro's unmistakable aroma may be considered either addictively wonderful or abhorrently fetid. It is popular throughout Asia (except Japan), the Middle East, and Latin America. Chinese, Thai, and Indian cuisines use cilantro extensively. Note that in the United States, *cilantro* refers to the herb leaves, while *coriander* (page 172) refers to the seed of the same plant.

Culantro (*Eryngium foetidum*) is native to Latin America and the Caribbean and is related to cilantro. It has tall, stiff, serrated leaves with a prominent central ridge and a more penetrating aroma than cilantro. Culantro is used extensively in Southeast Asia and parts of the Caribbean, especially Cuba and Puerto Rico. In Asia, culantro is most popular in Thailand, Malaysia, and Singapore, where it is commonly used with or instead of cilantro for soups, noodle dishes, and curries. The Vietnamese use it to wrap other foods. Candied culantro seeds were popular in eighteenth-century Britain as a tonic, a cough remedy, and an aphrodisiac.

Vietnamese coriander (*Polygonum odoratum*) is a member of the buckwheat family and has smooth, oval leaves with a less pungent, more lemony aroma than cilantro. This herb, which is always used fresh, gives Vietnamese food its unique flavor, though it is also used in Malaysia and Singapore, where it is a common garnish for many kinds of foods, especially the soupy noodle dish called *laksa*, which comes from Singapore.

Season: For the mildest flavor, buy young cilantro, culantro, and Vietnamese coriander in spring or hothouse-grown cilantro year-round.

Purchase and Avoid: Drying destroys most of cilantro's fragrance, so only buy it fresh. When purchasing either cilantro or culantro, be on the lookout for leaves that are yellowing or rotting. Look for culantro in Caribbean and Vietnamese groceries. Be especially vigilant when either herb has been picked in wet weather. Vietnamese coriander may be found in Vietnamese, Thai, or Malaysian markets. The leaves should be sprightly and bright.

Storage: Store cilantro, culantro, or Vietnamese coriander wrapped in paper towels and then in a plastic bag in the warmest part of the refrigerator, generally near the light. Field-grown cilantro sold with roots will keep best in a jar filled with water to maintain moisture. This type of cilantro can be quite sandy, so wash carefully and spin dry.

Recipe: *Mole Verde*

1. Peel off the papery skin from 1 pound of tomatillos and cook in 2 cups boiling salted water for about 10 minutes. Drain, reserving the cooking water.

2. Blend the tomatillos, 2 seeded jalapeños, the leaves from 1 bunch cilantro, 2 cloves garlic, and 1 coarsely chopped white onion with about ½ cup of the cooking water until smooth. Transfer to a bowl.

3. Toast 1 cup raw pumpkin seeds in 1 tablespoon lard or oil. Blend with 1 cup chicken stock until smooth. Combine both mixtures.

4. Melt 2 tablespoons lard or oil and fry the tomatillo–pumpkin seed mixture for 3 minutes, or until bubbling hot. Season to taste with salt. Serve with chicken enchiladas or tacos. Makes 1 quart sauce.

Serving Suggestions: Make Mexican pico de gallo by combining chopped tomatoes, green chiles, onion, lime juice, and plenty of chopped cilantro. • Season Cuban black beans and Puerto Rican pink beans with culantro. • Add Vietnamese coriander at the last minute to Vietnamese soups and Malaysian noodle dishes.

Food Affinities: **Cilantro:** Avocado, beef, ceviche, chicken, chiles, ginger, lime, onion, pork, pumpkin seed, shrimp, tomato, turkey. **Culantro:** Annatto, black beans, chiles, garlic, ginger, lemongrass, scallion, sesame oil, wild lime leaf. **Vietnamese coriander:** Bean sprouts, celery, chicken, chiles, coconut milk, crab, seafood, shrimp paste.

11. **CURRY LEAF**

Other Names:
Bursunga, kari patta, katneem, or *meetha neem* (Hindi); *karapincha* (Sinhalese); *pindosin* (Burmese); sweet neem leaves.

General Description:
The curry tree (Murraya koenigii), *in the Rutaceae (citrus) family, has small, oval leaves with a pleasing aroma that hints of tangerine and anise.* On this tropical tree native to India, the leaflets, which are dark green on top and pale below, run in pairs up the smaller branches. The leaves give off a strong, warm, savory aroma when bruised or rubbed. They are essential to the vegetarian cuisine of southern India and Sri Lanka and are also used in northern India. Curry powder (page 280) is a British invention meant to imitate the flavor of Indian cooking and may have once contained curry leaves. The leaves, which lose much of their fragrance within days, are eaten fresh (or frozen), though they may be briefly oven-dried, toasted, or quickly fried in ghee (clarified butter). In southern India, curry leaves are mainly combined with vegetables and legumes and used to flavor fillings for savory pastries

like samosas. In Sri Lanka, coconut-based chicken and beef curries are flavored with curry leaves.

Purchase
and Avoid:

Look for fresh or frozen curry leaves in Indian groceries. Choose fresh shiny leaves that show no signs of yellowing or wilting. Dried curry leaves are also available but have a much diminished flavor.

Storage:

Curry leaves shouldn't be removed from the branches until needed. They can be stored refrigerated, wrapped first in paper towels and then a plastic bag, up to 2 weeks, or they may be frozen.

Recipe:

Sri Lankan Lamb Curry

1. **Mix 2 pounds lamb cubes with 1/4 cup vinegar and marinate for 30 minutes at room temperature.**

2. **Process 1 coarsely chopped onion, 3 cloves garlic, and a peeled, sliced 2-inch section of ginger to a paste. Fry in 2 tablespoons oil in a large pan over medium-high heat until fragrant.**

3. **Add 1 tablespoon ground coriander, 2 teaspoons paprika, 1 teaspoon cayenne, 1 teaspoon turmeric, 1 teaspoon ground cumin, 1/2 teaspoon ground fenugreek seed, and 1 whole sprig curry leaf. Stir-fry for several minutes. Remove from the pan and set aside.**

4. Drain the lamb, reserving the marinade. Add 2 tablespoons more oil to the pan. Add the lamb cubes, working in batches if necessary, and brown lightly. Add 1 13.5-ounce can unsweetened coconut milk along with the reserved marinade and bring to a boil. Lower the heat, and simmer 1 hour uncovered, or until the lamb is tender. Season to taste with salt, black pepper, and a sprinkle of curry powder. Discard curry leaf sprig before serving.

Serving Suggestions: Mix chopped curry leaf with potatoes for a samosa filling. • Add to vegetable curry dishes at the last minute. • Mix with lentils for sambar or dal.

Food Affinities: Cauliflower, chutney, coconut milk, cumin, fenugreek, green beans, lentils, potato, samosas, turmeric.

12. DILL

Other Names: *Aneth odorant* or *fenouil bâtard* (French); *anitho* (Greek); *gurkenkraut* (German); *koper ogrodowy* (Polish); *krip* (Ukrainian); *krop* (Yiddish); *shamir* or *shevet rehani* (Hebrew); *stinkende vinke* (Dutch); *ukrop* (Russian).

General Description: *Dill* (Anethum graveolens) *has feathery, bright green fronds of long, soft, needlelike leaves with a flavor between anise, parsley, and celery.* Dill originated in central Asia, and it has retained its popularity in

Georgia's famous spice mixture khmeli-suneli (page 283) and in Iran's boiled beans with dill. Dill shows up in Greek and Turkish vegetable casseroles, stuffed vegetables, and yogurt sauces. Today, dill is one of the most commonly available fresh herbs in northern Europe and is especially popular in Poland, Russia, Germany, and, above all, Scandinavia, where it is an essential seasoning. It is also prominent in Ashkenazi Jewish cookery, where it goes into chicken soup and kosher dill pickles.

Dill leaves, especially when fresh, are sweeter and more aromatic than the dried fruits (often misnamed *dill seeds*), which are sharper and more pungent. In Europe, dill fruits are mostly used to flavor breads and fresh or pickled cucumbers. In Poland and Russia, dill is popular in the pickled vegetables that provide freshness during the long cold winters, and it's one of the few herbs used regularly in the Baltic region. Scandinavian cooks depend on dill to flavor fish and shellfish dishes.

Purchase and Avoid:
Look for young, sprightly, bright-colored leaves with no wilting, slime, or yellowing. Dill tends to spoil quickly because the leaves are fine and feathery.

Recipe:
Salmon and Dill Gravlax

1. **Combine ¼ cup kosher salt, 3 tablespoons light brown sugar, 2 teaspoons crushed coriander, 1 teaspoon**

crushed white pepper, 1 large bunch chopped dill including tender stems, and 2 tablespoons aquavit or vodka.

2. **Spread this seasoning mixture over both sides of 1 skin-on fillet of salmon, about 3 pounds. Wrap in plastic, weight with a board and a heavy can, and place inside a pan to contain the drippings.**

3. **Cure the salmon in the refrigerator for 2 to 3 days, turning over and reweighing every day. Continue curing in the refrigerator. The salmon is ready when firm to the touch.**

4. **Drain and wipe off excess coating. Slice thinly and accompany with Mustard-Dill Sauce: Whisk together $1/4$ cup Dijon mustard, $1/4$ cup vegetable oil, $1/4$ cup finely chopped dill, 3 tablespoons sugar, and 2 tablespoons cider vinegar.**

Serving Suggestions:

Top hot beef borscht or cold vegetarian borscht with sour cream and chopped dill. • Add dill to mayonnaise-based potato, egg, chicken, or turkey salad. • Season Greek mixed-vegetable casseroles with dill.

Food Affinities:

Beans, beet, bell pepper, chicken, cucumber, fish, green beans, mustard, pickles, smoked salmon, sour cream, yogurt.

13. **EPAZOTE**

Other Names: *Ambrosia* or *farinello aromatico* (Italian); *ambroisie du Mexique* or *thé du Mexique* (French); *erva-de-santa-maria* or *erva-formigueira* (Portuguese); hedge mustard; *hierba* (or *yerba*) *de Santa Maria* (Spanish); Jerusalem parsley; Jesuit's tea; *mastruço* or *mentruz* (Brazilian Portuguese); Mexican tea; *paico* (Peruvian); skunkweed; Spanish tea; sweet pigweed; West Indian goosefoot; wormseed.

General Description: *Epazote* (Chenopodium ambrosioides), *a strong-tasting resinous herb in the Chenopodiaceae (goosefoot) family, has large, matte, spiky, dark green leaves and a turpentine-like smell.* Epazote is native to Mexico and the tropical regions of Central and South America, where it is commonly found wild. It is also widely naturalized throughout the world and the United States, especially California. In Mexican cooking, epazote is always added to the pot when cooking black beans for its natural carminative (gas-preventing) properties and because its potent aroma cuts the heaviness of beans. It is unsurpassed in quesadillas and wild mushroom dishes and also appears with corn, chile sauces, and stews.

Purchase and Avoid: Epazote is available fresh in supermarkets in Texas and other parts of the southwestern United States, but it's more often found dried in Mexican markets.

Storage:

Epazote dries easily and will keep quite well. Dry in a low (200°F) oven for several hours, or until brittle, then store in a glass jar or tin in a cool, dark place.

Recipe:

Mexican Black Beans with Epazote

1. **Soak 1 pound dried black beans overnight in cold water to cover. Drain and rinse.**

2. **Preheat the oven to 300°F. Place the beans, 3 cups each chicken stock and water, and 2 large sprigs fresh epazote (or 2 tablespoons dried) in a Dutch oven. Bring to a boil on the stove top, skim off foam, then cover and bake for 1 ½ hours.**

3. **In a large, heavy skillet, brown ½ pound chopped fresh chorizo sausage. Remove the chorizo, leaving the fat in the pan. Add 1 diced onion, 2 diced carrots, 2 diced celery stalks, and 1 tablespoon chopped garlic to the pan and cook over medium heat until the vegetables become soft.**

4. **Remove the pot of beans from the oven and stir in the vegetables and chorizo, along with 1 tablespoon ancho or New Mexico chile powder, 1 tablespoon ground cumin, and salt to taste.**

5. **Cover and bake for 1 hour, or until the beans are soft.**

Serving Suggestions:	Add epazote to quesadilla or tamale fillings. • Add epazote to black bean salad and black bean soup.

Food Affinities:	Beef, black beans, corn, cumin, garlic, hot chiles, onion, pinto beans, pork, wild game, wild mushrooms.

---

14.   **FILÉ**

Other Names:	Augue tree; *fenchelholzbaum* (German); filé powder; *sasafrás* (Arabic), *sasafrás* (Spanish); *sassafras* (Dutch, English, French, Russian); *sassafrás* (Portuguese); *sassafrasso* (Italian); *sassafurasu* (Japanese); *szasszafrász babérfa* (Hungarian).

General Description:	*Filé is made from the dried leaves of the sassafras tree (Sassafras albidum), which grows wild along the east coast of the United States.* Filé powder is an important ingredient in the Creole and Cajun cookery of Louisiana, a veritable gumbo of French, Spanish, African, and Native American cuisines. True gumbo, a thick tasty soup made of seafood, poultry, sausage, game, and okra, must be made with filé. Immediately before serving, it's stirred in to thicken the gumbo and impart a mild lemon-anise flavor as well as a woodsy, balsamlike flavor reminiscent of root beer. In fact, root beer, which dates back to the nineteenth century in America, was traditionally flavored with sassafras root, though it's now made with other spices

and herbs, since sassafras root has been demonstrated to be carcinogenic.

Purchase and Avoid:	Buy filé powder in small quantities because it loses its flavor when stored for long periods. Look for filé powder from Cajun food suppliers in Louisiana.
Storage:	Store filé powder in the refrigerator.
Recipe:	***Homemade Filé Powder***

1. **Cut small branches from a sassafras tree in fall before the leaves start turning color.**

2. **Wash the leaves. Hang the branches in a cool, shady place to dry slowly. Don't dry the leaves in bright sunlight, which can cause fading.**

3. **Remove the dried leaves from the stems, discarding the stalks.**

4. **Crush the leaves by hand, then grind in a clean coffee grinder until a fine, green powder is formed. Sift the powder and store the filé powder refrigerated in a well-sealed jar.**

Note:	Remove any dish from the heat just before adding filé, because it becomes stringy with cooking.

Serving
Suggestions:

Add filé powder to gumbo recipes. • Thicken gumbo z'herbes (green gumbo), featuring as many cooking greens and herbs as desired, with filé powder.

Food
Affinities:

Alligator, andouille, celery, duck, garlic, onion, rabbit, scallion, spinach, squirrel, tasso ham, thyme, turkey.

---

15. 📷 **HIBISCUS BLOSSOM**

Other Names:

African mallow; *afrikanische malve* (German); *bissap* (Senegal, western Africa); *cabitutu* (Panama); *flor de Jamaica* (Mexico, Central America); Florida cranberry; hibiscus tea flower; Indian sorrel; Jamaica flower; Jamaica sorrel; Jamaica tea flower; *karkade* (Egypt, Sudan, Switzerland); *malvatee* or *oseille de guinée* (French); pink lemonade flower; red sorrel; red tea; rosella; rosella-tee; roselle or rozelle; *rosellhibiskus* (Swedish); royal roselle; sour-sour; wild roselle.

General
Description:

Hibiscus (Hibiscus sabdariffa), *a plant native to the region stretching from India to Malaysia, is cultivated for the large, ruby red, refreshingly sour, fleshy calyxes of its blossoms.* A cousin of okra, which has similar blossoms, hibiscus was brought at an early date to Africa. From there it reached Jamaica at the beginning of the eighteenth century through the slave trade. Although hibiscus has a tartness similar to sorrel and is often called red sorrel, it is not related to that plant.

Hibiscus has a pleasantly tart and sour taste with a raspberry, rhubarb, and plum character and a floral, berrylike aroma. Because of its vibrant red color, it livens up refreshing teas and other cooling drinks. Hibiscus is used fresh for making wine, jelly, syrup, chutneys, gelatin desserts, beverages, puddings, and cakes. Dried hibiscus is used for tea, jelly, marmalade, ice cream, sherbet, flavored butter, fruit tarts, and other desserts.

In Central America, ruby red hibiscus drinks are important at Christmastime. The tender leaves and stalks are added to soups and curries and, in Latin America, eaten as salad with chile sauce. The seeds, brewed like coffee, have been used as an aphrodisiac. *Jus de bissap*, a cold hibiscus drink often called the national drink of Senegal, is also popular in neighboring parts of West Africa.

Chinese hibiscus (*H. rosa-sinensis*) has flowers that are eaten raw or steamed, or used for coloring foods such as preserved fruits and agar-agar jellies. The young leaves are sometimes eaten like spinach. The edible flowers of rose of Sharon (*H. syriacus*) are used as a tea substitute.

Purchase and Avoid: Fresh hibiscus may be found in markets in Central America, Mexico, and the Caribbean, especially Jamaica. Dried calyxes may be found in Central American, Mexican, and Caribbean groceries.

Recipe: ***African Hibiscus Punch***

1. **Combine 1 cup dried hibiscus blossoms with 4 whole cloves, a piece of cinnamon stick, and a section of vanilla pod in a large pot. Add to 2 quarts boiling water and boil for 1 minute, stirring. Turn off the heat, sweeten with ¹/₂ cup honey or ³/₄ cup sugar, and steep for 1 hour.**

2. **Strain, pressing the blossoms to extract all the juices. Serve hot or cold.**

Serving Suggestions: Add rum and a squeeze of lime to African Hibiscus Punch (recipe above) for a rose-colored Caribbean cocktail. • Steep hibiscus blossoms in the custard for ice cream (strain out before freezing).

Food Affinities: Apricot, basil, cinnamon, cloves, custard, ginger, ice cream, honey, lemon, lime, peach, red currant, vanilla.

16. **HUACATAY**

Other Names: *Aymara wacataya* (Peruvian Quechua); black mint; Mexican marigold; Peruvian black mint.

General Description: *Huacatay* (Tagetes minuta)*, a native Peruvian herb related to marigold and tarragon, has a pungent aroma somewhere between mint and basil.* Among thousands of native herbs, huacatay has given Peruvian seasoning its unique zest from Incan to contemporary times. The herb's spicy-fresh flavor is beloved by the Andean peoples of Bolivia and Peru, who use it to season boiled and roasted dishes, fish and seafood, and the native capybara (an animal like a guinea pig). Jars of huacatay mint paste from the Peruvian rain forest are an acceptable substitute for the fresh herb. Because this herb has such a special flavor, there really is no substitute, though a combination of mint and coriander comes closest.

Purchase and Avoid: Huacatay is commonly sold in small jars in puree form. It is sold fresh in Peru and Bolivia.

Recipe: *Peruvian Huacatay Sauce*

1. **In a blender or food processor, puree ¼ cup fresh lime juice, ¼ cup vegetable oil, 3 tablespoons huacatay paste, 3 tablespoons shredded mint, 2 cloves garlic, and salt to taste.**

2. **Spoon over grilled tuna, swordfish, or Chilean sea bass or serve with ceviche.**

Serving Suggestions: Serve Peruvian Huacatay Sauce (recipe above) with boiled and then fried yuca (manioc) sections garnished with crumbled *queso añejo* (aged white cheese). • Make shredded duck confit empanadas and serve with a sauce made from sour oranges, fresh huacatay (or huacatay puree), vinegar, olive oil, and mirasol chiles.

Food
Affinities: Chilean sea bass, chiles (especially Peruvian amarillo, rocoto, and mirasol), corn, duck, potato, sour orange, swordfish, tuna, vinegar.

17.   **INDONESIAN BAY LEAF AND INDIAN BAY LEAF**

Other Names: **Indonesian bay leaf:** Alam leaf; *daeng klua, dokmaeo, mak,* or *proh hom* (Thai); *daun salam, kelat samak,* or *serah* (Malay); *Indonesisch laurierblad* (Dutch); *manting* (Indonesian); *san thuyen* (Vietnamese). **Indian bay leaf:** Cassia leaves; cinnamon leaves; *laurier des Indes* (French); *talishapattiri* (Tamil); *tamaal patra* (Gujarati); *tejpat* (Hindi); *thitchabo* (Burmese).

General
Description: *Indonesian bay leaf* (Eugenia polyantha) *is an herb that resembles Mediterranean bay leaves in shape, but not flavor, while Indian bay leaf* (Cinnamomum tejpata) *smells like a combination of cinnamon and cloves.* Indonesian bay leaf grows wild from Burma to Malaysia and in western Indonesia. The leaves, which are aromatic and slightly sour, may be used fresh or dried; when dried, they are nearly black. Quite mild in flavor, the leaves develop more flavor after a light frying in fat. They're used as seasoning, especially for meat, in Indonesia,

particularly Sumatra, Java, and Malaysia. Although their flavors are different, Mediterranean or California bay leaf makes the best substitute.

Indian bay leaf comes from a tree related to cinnamon and has a strong, spicy aroma. Indian bay leaf resembles an elongated, large bay leaf with three distinct lengthwise veins. These tough leaves are most commonly used in India and Sri Lanka. In regal Moghul cuisine, liberal use is made of sweet spices such as Indian bay leaves; two specialties are complex rice dishes called *biriyanis* and *kormas*, in which meat is slowly braised in a rich, fragrant sauce thickened with ground almonds and scented with Indian bay leaf. Ground Indian bay leaf appears in the northern Indian spice mixture garam masala (page 283).

Purchase and Avoid:
Fresh and dried Indonesian bay leaves are available in Indonesia, as well as in places with large Indonesian communities, such as the Netherlands. Fresh and dried Indian bay leaves are available at Indian groceries.

Recipe:
Chicken Korma with Indian Bay Leaves

1. **Marinate 1 cut-up chicken in a mixture of 1 cup whole milk yogurt, 1/2 cup chopped onion, 1 tablespoon chopped garlic, 1 tablespoon chopped ginger, and 1 teaspoon sweet paprika for at least 2 and up to 24 hours, in the refrigerator.**

2. **Sauté ½ cup chopped onion and 1 teaspoon chopped garlic in 2 tablespoons butter until soft. Add 1 teaspoon each ground coriander, ground cumin, ground cardamom, ground turmeric, and ground hot chile pepper and 2 tablespoons poppy seeds (white preferred).**

 3. **Add chicken and its marinade along with 2 Indian bay leaves and salt to taste, then cover and simmer about 45 minutes or until chicken is tender, adding a little water if needed to keep moist. Sprinkle with chopped cilantro and serve with steamed basmati rice.**

Serving
Suggestions:
Add Indonesian bay leaf to Indonesian curries, rice dishes, and noodle dishes. • Use Indian bay leaf to flavor soups, stews, vegetables, and meat.

Food
Affinities:
Indonesian bay leaf: Chiles, coconut, galangal, garlic, lemongrass, long pepper, tamarind, turmeric. **Indian bay leaf:** Almond, cardamom, cinnamon, cloves, coriander, cumin, lamb, rice, turmeric.

18. **LAVENDER**

Other Names: *Alfazema* (Portuguese); English lavender; *espígol* (Catalan); French lavender; *khuzaama* or *lafand* (Arabic); *lavanda* (Italian, Spanish); *lavande* (French); *levanta* (Greek); *rabenda* (Japanese); spike lavender.

General Description:	*Lavender* (Lavandula angustifolia) *is a highly aromatic plant with a floral yet pinelike aroma that is characteristic of the French Provençal kitchen.* This type of lavender, commonly called English lavender, has bluish green leaves and blue-tinted, rather than purple, blossoms. Lavender originated in the western Mediterranean and is grown commercially for lavender oil in France, Hungary, and Bulgaria. It is a main ingredient in herbes de Provence (page 282), the special resinous dried herb seasoning used extensively in Provençal cuisine. Use lavender with care and in small quantities because its flavor quickly becomes overbearing. It's especially suited to lamb and goat and makes a delicious flavoring for ice cream. It marries well with honey, especially lavender blossom honey, which is golden with an extremely smooth, almost buttery, texture. Several other species of lavender are found elsewhere in the Mediterranean. Spike lavender (*L. latifolia*) has long leaves and violet blossoms. French (or Spanish) lavender (*L. stoechas*) has dark purple flowers and narrow, long, grayish green leaves. Both buds and leaves are used in the kitchen.
Season:	Lavender blooms in summer and may be found in farmers' markets and herb markets.
Recipe:	***Lavender-Scented Fruit Parfait***
1.	**To make lavender sugar: Process 1 cup granulated sugar and 1 tablespoon dried lavender buds together**

until the sugar is purple-tinged and the lavender
pieces are very fine.

2. In a large bowl, prepare a combination of diced stone
    fruits (such as peaches, plums, cherries, or nectarines)
    and berries (such as raspberries, blackberries, or
    strawberries).

3. Beat 1 cup heavy cream with 4 tablespoons lavender
    sugar in a chilled bowl until it holds soft peaks.

4. In 4 tall parfait glasses, spoon a layer of flavored
    whipped cream into the bottom, cover with a layer of
    crumbled amaretti biscuits, then a layer of the fruit,
    and then repeat. End with a layer of the whipped
    cream. Chill for 30 minutes before serving garnished
    with a sprig of flowering lavender.

Serving
Suggestions:

Use Lavender Sugar (see above) for sweetening lemonade, tea, iced tea, or plain baked goods such as shortbread, sponge cake, or pound cake. • Add lavendar
leaves, petals, and flowering tips in small amounts to
salads, vinaigrettes, hearty soups, and lamb stews. •
Add a sprig of lavender to herbal vinegar, honey, and
fruit jellies.

Food
Affinities:

Apple jelly, butter, cream, custard, dark chocolate,
goat, goat cheese, honey, lamb, sugar, tea, vinegar.

19. 📷   LEMON BALM AND BERGAMOT

Other Names:

Lemon balm: *Badranjbuye* (Farsi); balm (British); *balsamita maior* or *toronjil* (Spanish); *baume, citronell, herbe citron,* or *mélisse* (French); *citronmelisse* (Danish, Dutch); *citrounelo* or *pouncirado* (Provençal French); *erva-cidreira* (Portuguese); *hashisha al-namal* (Arabic); *herztrost* or *zitronenmelisse* (German); *limon nanesi, limon otu,* or *melisa otu* (Turkish); *matochina* (Bulgarian); *melissa* (Greek); *melissa limonnaya* (Russian); *seiyō-yama-hakka* (Japanese). **Bergamot:** Bee balm; *bergamota* (Spanish); *bergamote* or *thé d'Oswego* (French); *bergamotto* (Italian); *blumenmelisse* or *goldmelisse* (German); *monard* or *munardah* (Arabic); Oswego tea; *taimatubana* (Japanese).

General Description:

Lemon balm (Melissa officinalis) *is a perennial herb in the mint family with pale green, deeply veined, downy leaves shaped like plump diamonds.* Since classical times, lemon balm has been considered a cure for melancholy. It flavors herbal liqueurs such as Chartreuse and Bénédictine. While more common as a medicinal herb than in the kitchen, lemon balm's fresh and pure lemon taste makes it a good substitute for fresh lemongrass. In central Europe, lemon balm is used as a flavoring for sweet drinks. It can be used in any dish flavored with lemon juice to accent the lemony flavor.

Bergamot (*Monarda didyma*), not to be confused with the unrelated bergamot orange (page 167), is related to lemon balm and is also in the mint family. Native to North America, its leaves taste like lemon and orange and have a stronger flavor than lemon balm. Its shaggy heads of edible scarlet, deep pink, or purple flowers are minty in aroma and flavor. One American name for bergamot, Oswego tea, came from the Oswego Indians, who brewed it into tea. American colonists drank this tea as a patriotic gesture because it was locally grown and not subject to the British tax on imported tea.

Purchase and Avoid:

Lemon balm's lemony aroma is more pronounced in fresh leaves than in dried. Although the decorative blossoms of bergamot have only a light fragrance, they are the preferred part of the plant. Use only brightly colored blossoms with no wilting or browned edges and full, green leaves.

Recipe:

Strawberry and Lemon Balm–Infused Rosé Wine

1. **Trim, wash, and slice 1 quart strawberries. Wash and shred 4 tablespoons lemon balm leaves.**

2. **Mix strawberries, lemon balm, 4 tablespoons superfine sugar, and 1 bottle rosé wine.**

3. **Cover and refrigerate for 2 days, shaking occasionally. Strain and serve chilled, garnished with a sprig of lemon balm and additional sliced strawberries.**

Serving Suggestions: Use lemon balm to flavor fruit-based desserts and fruit salad. • Use fresh or dried lemon balm leaves and flowers to make an aromatic tea. • Add bergamot to soups, fish, and yogurt, or to fruit, vegetable, and green salads.

Food Affinities: **Lemon balm:** Apple, fish, fruit salad, poultry, salads, sweet drinks. **Bergamot:** Butter, eggs, fish, honey, ricotta cheese, sauces for fish or chicken, soups, yogurt.

LEMON VERBENA AND MEXICAN OREGANO

20a–b.

Other Names: **Lemon verbena:** *Cedron* or *hierbaluisa* (Spanish); lemon-scented verbena; *limonete* (Portuguese); *lipia limonit* or *luisa* (Hebrew); *louïza* or *verbena* (Greek); *remonbabena* (Japanese); *verveine citronelle* or *verveine odorante* (French); *zitronenverbene* (German).
Mexican oregano: Lipia; Mexican wild sage; Puerto Rican oregano; redbrush; scented lippia; *té de pais* (Spanish; also used for lemongrass); Tex-Mex oregano.

General Description: *Lemon verbena* (Lippia citriodora), *native to South America, has long, narrow, rough-textured, apple-green leaves with an intense, clear, lemony floral fragrance.* One hundred years ago, lemon verbena was a common ornamental in European gardens; it is just now being revived as a culinary herb by creative chefs who use it to steam lobster, poach salmon, and flavor veal tenderloin. The leaves are best used fresh, though they may be dried. Because its bright lemon taste emphasizes fruit flavors, lemon verbena has a strong affinity with fresh fruits. It also makes a relaxing and soothing tea, which is served after meals in Chile and Mexico.

Mexican oregano (*L. graveolens*), a close relative of lemon verbena, has an intense aroma of oregano combined with the sweetness of licorice. The ridged leaves are slightly elongated and oval in shape with a somewhat hairy texture. Mexican oregano should be consumed with care because it contains camphor, which is toxic in large quantities. In Mexico, where it's preferred over Mediterranean oregano, it's used in *pay de queso* (cheesecake made with cream cheese and condensed milk) and to flavor tomato-based sauces, stews, and beans. *Kosere* is an Amharic name for *L. adoensis*, another species in the verbena family, which is native to East Africa. It has a sweet aroma and is used in Ethiopia's rich spice mixtures.

Season: Lemon verbena is occasionally found in markets in
☼   the United States in hot summer months. Mexican
             oregano is found fresh in Mexico and in the southwestern United States, especially Texas.

Purchase   Look for lemon verbena with brightly colored, fragrant, and lively leaves. Tips are preferable. Look for
and Avoid: Mexican oregano with full, unblemished leaves.

Storage: Lemon verbena wilts quickly, so store it refrigerated, wrapped in damp paper towels inside a plastic bag.

Recipe: *Lemon Verbena Butter*

1. **Combine ¹/₂ pound softened unsalted butter with 1 cup each lemon verbena and Italian parsley leaves in a food processor and blend until a green paste forms. Pour in the juice of 2 lemons, the zest of 1 lemon, and salt and freshly ground black pepper to taste and process again until creamy and smooth.**

2. **Scrape the butter out of the processor, wrap in plastic, and form into a log. Refrigerate up to 2 weeks or freeze up to 3 months.**

3. **Slice and use to top grilled or steamed shrimp or mild-tasting fish like red snapper, sea bass, or grouper just before serving.**

Serving Suggestions: Add lemon verbena to fruit salads, fruit jellies, cold drinks, and salad dressings. • Use lemon verbena to flavor creamy desserts like panna cotta and custards. • Sprinkle chorizo with Mexican oregano. • Season Texas-style chili con carne and fajitas with Mexican oregano, or add to enchilada sauce.

Food Affinities: **Lemon verbena:** Chicken, cream, fish, guava, mango, nectarine, papaya, raspberry, seafood, strawberry, sugar. **Mexican oregano:** Allspice, beef, chiles, chili powder, chorizo, cumin, garlic, lime, tomato sauce.

21.   **LEMONGRASS**

Other Names: *Bai mak nao* (Khmer); *caña de limón, te de limón,* or *zacate de limón* (Spanish); *cimbopogone* (Italian); *cha krai, soet kroei, squinant,* or *takrai*; (Thai); citronella; *essef limon* (Hebrew); *hashisha al-limun* (Arabic); *remongurasu* (Japanese); *sa chanh* or *xa* (Vietnamese); *sera* (Sinhalese); *serai dapur* (Malay); *sereh* (Indonesian); *si khai* (Laotian); *verveine des Indes* (French).

General
Description: *Lemongrass (Cymbopogon citrates), a grass that resembles pale, tender bamboo, is used for its lemony aroma.* Native to India and Sri Lanka and thriving in the tropical climates of Southeast Asia and Latin America, lemongrass is best known for its use in Thai and Vietnamese cuisine. Its penetrating aroma comes from citral, an essential oil used in aromatherapy and for insect repellent. Lemongrass is sold as long, woody stalks with white root ends; it's formed of layers that wrap around each other. The tips and leaves are light green with a brittle and dry texture. Lemongrass has a more subtle, delicate flavor than lemon or lime and imparts its flavor very quickly, especially when added to a marinade or simmered in a clear broth. Because of its tough texture, lemongrass is usually added to

recipes whole, then removed and discarded before serving. The inner portion of the stalk can be eaten if finely chopped.

Season:
Available fresh year-round at Asian markets and many grocery stores.

Purchase and Avoid:
Look for moist, fragrant lemongrass stalks that are firm, full, and pale green—the pale color indicates freshness. Avoid woody-looking, overly large, or dried-out, leathery stalks. The bottom of the stalk may be woody, but it shouldn't be shriveled.

Storage:
Wrap lemongrass stalks tightly with foil or plastic wrap and store up to 2 weeks in the refrigerator, or freeze, chopping first if desired.

Preparation:

- **Wash thoroughly, peel off and discard the tough outer leaves, and trim the ends with a sharp knife. Use only the heart of the stalk—the bottom 4 to 6 inches up to the point where the leaves branch out. If the lemongrass is dry, soak in warm water to rehydrate.**

- **Before using, smash lemongrass with a meat mallet or the side of a heavy knife to release the oils.**

Serving Suggestions:
Blend Thai fish sauce, lemongrass, and chiles to make a sauce for chicken or fish. • Add a stalk of lemongrass to the water used to steam fish or seafood. • Blend

chopped lemongrass with coconut milk and Thai holy basil to make a sauce for shellfish and chicken.

Food Affinities: Cardamom, chiles, cilantro, fish, fish sauce, holy basil, honey, lemon, seafood, tamarind, Thai curry paste, tomato, wild lime leaf.

---

22.   **LOVAGE**

Other Names: *Ache de montagne, céleri perpetual, gaya à tige simple,* or *vivèche* (French); *apio de montaña* or *ligústico* (Spanish); bladder seed; garden lovage or love parsley (British); *levístico* (Portuguese); *levistiko* (Greek); *ligustico, sedano di montagna,* or *sedano di monte* (Italian); *maggikraut* (German); *maggiplant* (Dutch); *me-na-ri* (Korean); *selâm otu* (Turkish).

General Description: *Lovage* (Levisticum officinale) *looks like extra-large celery leaves on long, hollow stalks.* Lovage's potent celery flavor is accompanied by a warm, spicy fragrance. It was one of the most prominent flavors in classical Roman cookery but later fell from favor. Today it is used in abundance in Liguria, where it is used to season tomato sauces, often in combination with oregano and sometimes with rue. Though the leaves are the most commonly used part, the root and fruits have the same taste, although more concentrated, and may also be used. The fruits (often called *seeds*) come in pairs and

resemble caraway seeds. In northwestern Italy, lovage
seed is sometimes used instead of fennel or anise.

Season:

The earlier in the season, the more tender and mild
the flavor. Lovage from late summer, after blooming,
tends to be overly strong and fibrous.

Purchase
and Avoid:

Lovage is in season in late spring and early summer.

Recipe:

Pennsylvania Dutch Chicken-Corn Soup with Lovage

1. **Place a large stewing chicken in enough cold water to cover and simmer for 1 hour, skimming as necessary. Add 1 large unpeeled onion studded with 4 whole cloves, 1 large carrot, and 2 outer stalks of celery. Simmer 1 hour more. Add 1/4 cup lovage leaves and half a lemon. Continue to cook until the chicken is soft enough to come away from the bones, about 30 minutes longer.**

2. **Strain the stock, discarding the solids. Add the cut kernels from 12 ears of young white corn; the "milk" obtained by scraping the cobs; 1/2 teaspoon crumbled saffron; 1 pound chicken breast, cut into small dice; and 2 cups egg noodles. Cook 3 to 4 minutes or until the chicken is opaque and the noodles are tender.**

3. **Stir in the a small handful of light-colored celery leaves, 2 tablespoons chopped Italian parsley, and salt and pepper to taste. Makes about 2 quarts.**

Serving Suggestions:	Top stuffed or baked pasta, such as ravioli or cannelloni, with crunchy, fried lovage leaves. • Add lovage leaves to slow-cooked stews in place of or in addition to celery. • Use lovage fruits to flavor sour pickles and aromatic vinegars.

Food Affinities:	Beef broth, clams, corn, eggplant, garlic, horseradish, oregano, pork, rabbit, ricotta cheese, tomato, vinegar.

 23a–c.

MARJORAM

Other Names:	**Marjoram:** *Almáraco* or *mejorana* (Spanish); *kekikotu* or *mercanköşk* (Turkish); knotted marjoram (British); *maggiorana* (Italian); *măghiran* (Romanian); *majoran* or *wurstkraut* (German); *majoránna* (Hungarian); *mardaqoush* or *marzanjush* (Arabic); *marjolaine* (French); *matzourana* (Greek); *mayoram* (Hebrew); *mejram* (Swedish); sweet marjoram. **Pot marjoram:** Cretan oregano; *rigani* (Greek); Turkish oregano. **Za'atar:** Bible hyssop; Syrian oregano.

General Description:	*Marjoram (Majorana hortensis) is a sweeter, milder cousin of oregano (wild marjoram), with small, velvety, grayish green, rounded leaves.* Marjoram is native to the eastern Mediterranean and is now widely cultivated in Georgia, Turkey, Lebanon, Syria, Jordan, Israel, and central and eastern Europe. Marjoram is a good all-around herb often combined with sage in poultry

seasoning; it goes especially well with turkey, rabbit, or chicken. Either fresh or dried, marjoram is well-suited to starchy or strong-flavored vegetables, such as beans, split peas, potatoes, Brussels sprouts, chestnuts, and cabbage. Dried marjoram is important in commercial food processing and is much used, together with thyme, in spice mixtures for sausage. It shows up often in Scandinavian recipes and is also common in the Caucasus Mountains, where it is one of the herbs characteristic of the complex Georgian spice mixture khmeli-suneli (page 283). In the colder climate of northern Europe, marjoram is apt to be used dried, while in the warmer southern Europe it's used fresh. Warm climates develop its specific aroma; dried marjoram loses some of its subtlety. Gold-tip marjoram has curled, gold-tipped, green leaves.

Since smaller pot marjoram (*Origanum onites*) grows well indoors, it can provide fresh aromatic leaves all winter long. It has a strong thymelike aroma and is used to flavor red meats and even Turkish delight candy. The seeds or fruits of this plant flavor dressings, liqueurs, soups, sausage, and cured meat.

In Jordan, Lebanon, and Israel, a highly aromatic local marjoram, za'atar (*M. syriaca*), is a common flavoring for grilled lamb and flatbreads. It tastes and smells like a combination of thyme, marjoram, and oregano, and it's often mixed with sumac to spread on pita bread. In areas where no za'atar grows, the same name is used for related herbs.

Season: Fresh marjoram and za'atar are in season in summer.

Purchase   Avoid marjoram with any blackened leaves. Because
and Avoid: dried marjoram loses its flavor easily, buy it in small
quantities and often.

Storage: Marjoram freezes easily, so store it in the warmest part
of the refrigerator—under the light or on the top shelf.

Recipe: ***Asparagus in Lemon-Marjoram Cream***

1.   **Cook 1 pound trimmed asparagus in plenty of
boiling salted water for 3 minutes, or until brightly
colored. Drain and immediately rinse under cold
running water to stop the cooking and set the color.**

2.   **In a small saucepan, simmer 3/4 cup heavy cream over
medium heat for about 10 minutes, until thickened.
Transfer to a skillet and toss with the asparagus,
2 tablespoons chopped marjoram, the juice of 2 lemons,
and the grated zest of 1 lemon. Season to taste with
salt and freshly ground pepper. Cook for 1 to 2 minutes to reheat the asparagus. Serve immediately.**

Serving   Sprinkle marjoram over fried potatoes. • Add crum-
Suggestions: bled marjoram to stuffing for chicken, duck, goose, or
turkey, or rub the skin and insides with the herb. •
Add marjoram to clam chowder, turtle soup, black or
white bean soup, split pea soup, or oyster stew.

Food
Affinities:

Beef, black beans, broccoli, chicken, clams, duck, goose, onion, oysters, peas, pork, tomato, white beans.

MEXICAN NATIVE HERBS

General
Description:

There are many native Mexican herbs that give characteristic flavors to the regional dishes of this complex cuisine. Chaya (*Cnidoscolus chayamansa*) is a large, fast-growing leafy perennial shrub found naturally only on the Yucatán peninsula. The leaves of this nonflowering herb have long been used in Mayan cuisine. In addition to its traditional place in tamales and pumpkin seed sauces, it is used to make modern Yucatecan dishes, such as *crepas de chaya*. Raw chaya leaves are poisonous, but just a minute of boiling destroys most of the toxic acid.

Chepil (*Crotalaria longirostrata*), a drought-resistant plant from Central America, is an important ingredient in the celebrated cooking of Oaxaca. There, the tiny leaves are tucked into *tamales de chepil*. Their pronounced flavor, similar to green beans, adds a delicious touch to white rice, and they can be ground with garlic and brushed on bread.

Corteza de maguey is the outermost layer of leaves of the maguey cactus (*Agave americana*) and is similar to parchment paper in thickness, use, and consistency. Its traditional use is as a cooking wrapper for meat and poultry in bundles called *mixiotes*. This use of maguey is now illegal in Mexico because stripping the young leaves kills the plant. *Aguamiele*, the sweet sap from the flowering stem, can be drunk fresh or fermented into *pulque*, a white, viscous, slightly acidic alcoholic beverage popular in the Mexican countryside.

Hierba de conejo (*Castilleja lanata*), an herb with small, silvery gray leaves covered with fine hairs and bright red flowers, grows wild in desert areas of the United States and Mexico, where it is known as Indian paintbrush. It is frequently added to a pot of beans or rice, or cooked and eaten as a side dish like mustard greens.

Hierba santa (*Piper sanctum*), in the same botanical family as peppercorns, is abundant in the south-central region of Mexico; it has palm-sized, velvety, crinkled leaves, an anise scent, and a sassafras or root beer flavor. It is used to make fragrant wrappers for grilled or steamed fish dishes, such as the *pescado en hoja santa* (fish in holy leaf) of Veracruz.

Hojas de platano, the huge leaves of the banana plant (*Musa paradisiaca*), are used as tamale wrappers. Banana leaves are sold fresh and frozen in Latin American and Asian markets and are becoming more widely available in big-city supermarkets. Hojas de aguacate are the leaves of the avocado tree (*Persea americana*); they have a licorice-like aroma and are used fresh and dried to season *mixiotes*, beans, soups, and fish dishes. Hojas de maíz, the green or dried husks of corn (*Zea mays*), are used as tamale wrappings. They can also be used to wrap foods to be cooked on a grill, imparting their own sweet flavor to the foods inside.

Papalo (*Porophyllum ruderale*) is a distinctly pungent herb used in salsas; it has a flavor somewhere between arugula, cilantro, and rue. In Spanish it's called *mampuitu* (skunk), because of its penetrating aroma.

Pepicha (*Porophyllum tagetoides*) is a warm-weather annual with a taste much like very strong cilantro; it's used in green salsas and in cooking corn and squash. Quintoniles (*Amaranthus hybridus*), a variety of leaf amaranth most popular in Oaxaca, is a wild herb similar to spinach, with long, wrinkled, oval leaves and green flowers. Tila (*Tillia americana*) has fragrant flowers, usually sold dried, that are used in salads or brewed into tea; it is the source of prized linden honey.

Recipe: **Grilled Chile Salsa with Papalo Leaves**

 1. **Preheat a grill. Rub 6 ripe plum tomatoes, 1 red bell pepper, 1 quartered red onion, 2 poblano chiles, and 1 jalapeño chile with a little oil. Grill well on all sides. Alternatively, broil on high, turning once, until the skin is blackened. Peel off most but not all of the blackened skin from the vegetables. Trim and seed the bell pepper and chiles.**

2. **For the best chunky texture, prepare the salsa by grinding all the vegetables in a meat grinder. Alternatively, use a food processor or chop well by hand.**

3.   **Add ¹/₄ cup lime juice, 2 tablespoons chopped papalo
leaves, and salt to taste. Serve with tortilla chips, tacos
filled with guacamole or pork carnitas, or Mexican-
style chile-marinated pork sandwiches (cemitas).**

Serving
Suggestions:

Use hierba santa to flavor green moles, as a tamale
wrapping, and with chicken and shrimp dishes. • Use
hojas de aguacate, hojas de platano, or hojas de maíz
to wrap roast suckling pig or pork, fish, or chicken
before barbecuing. • Eat papalo raw on *cemitas*, central Mexico's version of the Italian-style sandwich. •
Add quintoniles to *guisado* (stew) made with chipotle
chiles and the small white fish called *charales*.

Food
Affinities:

Chaya: Pumpkin seed sauces, tamale wrapper.
Chepil: Garlic, rice, tamales. **Corteza de maguey:**
Mixiotes (meat or poultry bundles). **Hierba de
conejo:** Beans, rice. **Hierba santa:** Fish, green mole,
pumpkin seeds, tamale wrapper. **Hoja de aguacate,
platano or maíz:** Beans, fish, mixiotes, soups.
Papalo: Guacamole, tacos, salad, salsa. **Pepicha:**
Corn, green salsa, *huitlacoche* (corn fungus), squash.
Quintoniles: Fish, salad, tea.

25a–d.

MINT

Other Names: *Bai sa ra nai* or *min indonesia* (Thai); *hakka*
(Japanese); *hung gioi* (Chinese); *menta* (Italian).

Spearmint: Doublemint; *dyosmos* or *menta* (Greek); green mint or lamb mint (British); *menthe anglaise* (French); *nana* (Arabic, Hebrew); *nane* (Turkish); *rau hung cay* or *rau hung lui* (Vietnamese). **Peppermint:** *Edelminze* or *pfefferminze* (German); *fefermints* (Yiddish); *hierba buena* or *piperita* (Spanish); *menta piperita* (Italian); *menthe poivrée* or *sentebon* (French); *pepparmynta* (Swedish); *pereminde* (Swahili).

General
Description:

Spearmint (Mentha spicata) *has slightly ruffled, pointed, oval leaves with prominently serrated edges, deep green color, and cooling but not pungent flavor.* Mint is found wild in central and southern Europe, but was probably first used in the kitchen in England, where it's the country's most important culinary herb, turning up in mint sauce for lamb, cold soups, and beverages. In the Middle East, spearmint is chopped and added in generous portions to salads such as tabbouleh. In Greece, dried spearmint is sprinkled over *halloumi* cheese and lends its coolness to *tzatziki* (cucumber and yogurt salad). All over western Asia, grilled lamb kebabs are seasoned with mint, and dried mint goes into the Georgian spice mixture khmeli-suneli (page 283). Spearmint oil lends its cool flavor to Bénédictine and crème de menthe liqueurs. Today, most spearmint is used in the chewing gum industry.

Peppermint (*M. piperita*) is a natural hybrid of water mint (*M. aquatica*) and spearmint, with smooth oval leaves, serrated edges, dark green color, and a

potent peppery yet cooling flavor. Peppermint is cultivated in Europe and western and central Asia for the
production of menthol, important in the pharmaceu-
tical industry. Peppermint oil is used for candies and
sweet liqueurs, where its cooling and fresh pungency
balances the sweetness of sugar. Peppermint is an ideal
complement for chocolate.

Curly mint (*M. spicata crispa*) is a type of spearmint
prized for its decorative leaves. Orange, lemon, lime,
and lavender mint (cultivars of *M. citrata*), pineapple
mint (*M. suaveolens*), and complicated crosses like apple
mint, chocolate mint, and ginger mint have fragrances
that bear little similarity to mint and are often used
for herbal teas. Bergamot mint, a variety of water
mint, is used in Chartreuse liqueur. Wild mint (*M.
arvensis*) was used by Native American tribes for baking fish. The flowers of Japanese field mint (*M. arvensis piperascens*) delicately scent tea, and sweet-smelling
Chinese mint (*M. arvensis* ssp. *haplocalyx*) also flavors
tea. Large-leafed horse mint (*M. longifolia*) is used in
Indian chutneys and Afghan cooking, while mentuccia
(English pennyroyal; *M. pulegium*) is essential to *car-
ciofi alla Romana* (Roman-style marinated artichokes).
River mint, native to Australia, is detailed on page 10.

In Asia, mint is most important in Thailand and
Vietnam. Thai varieties are milder than European
peppermint and are always used fresh, usually combined with other herbs. In Vietnam, it's particularly
popular in the Hanoi noodle soup *pho bo*.

Season:	For delicate flavor and attractive appearance, buy or cut mint early in spring, when the new shoots come up. Once mint has flowered, the leaves will become tough.

Purchase and Avoid:	For really aromatic mint, buy it at farmers' markets or grow it fresh. Much packaged mint sold in supermarkets is apple mint grown in hothouses and has softer, ruffled leaves and a light, innocuous aroma.

Recipe: ***Cold Minted Cucumber Soup with Toasted Walnuts***

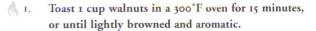

1. Toast 1 cup walnuts in a 300°F oven for 15 minutes, or until lightly browned and aromatic.

2. In a blender or food processor, combine 3 peeled and chopped seedless cucumbers with 1 bunch sliced scallions, a handful each of mint and parsley leaves, 2 cups buttermilk, 2 cups whole milk yogurt (or sour cream), and salt and freshly ground black pepper to taste. Blend until smooth.

3. Add the walnuts and blend again briefly, so that the walnuts stay chunky. Chill before serving.

Serving Suggestions:	Steep mint leaves with green tea and sweeten with sugar to make North African–style mint tea. • Sprinkle crushed mint and olive oil onto fresh white cheese like ricotta or Greek halloumi. • Serve roast lamb British-style, with mint sauce or mint jelly.

	Brandy, bulgur, chocolate, cucumber, dill, garlic,
Food	Brandy, bulgur, chocolate, cucumber, dill, garlic,
Affinities:	lamb, lemon, lime, olive oil, orange, parsley, ricotta,
	scallion, shallot, sugar, tea, tomato, yogurt.

---

26.   **MYRTLE**

Other Names: *Arrayán* or *mirto* (Spanish); *as* or *hadass* (Arabic); *bahar*, *mersin*, *murt*, or *sazak* (Turkish); common myrtle; *hadas* (Hebrew); *hodes* or *mirt* (Yiddish); *kulinaval* (Tamil); *mirto* (Italian, Brazilian Portuguese); *murta* (Portuguese); *myrt* (Russian); *myrte* (French); *nerto* (Provençal French); Roman myrtle; true myrtle.

General   *The ancient myrtle bush* (Myrtle communis) *has glossy,*
Description: *long, narrow, oval leaves that are clear, brilliant green; creamy white flowers; small bluish black berries; and highly aromatic wood.* When pressed or chopped, myrtle leaves emit a pleasant fragrance similar to orange blossom, though their flavor is quite bitter. Myrtle is the only member of its family in Europe; all the others are found in Australia (see lemon myrtle, page 9) and the tropics. Myrtle probably originated in Africa and Asia, but today it grows throughout the fragrant *macchia* (shrubland) forests of Sardinia, Corsica, and Crete, where it is widely used to flavor all sorts of grilled meat. In Corsica, Mirto, a liqueur made from myrtle berries, flavors wild game bird pâté. Myrtle makes excellent firewood, lending a spicy, aromatic

taste to grilled meat and fish. The leaves may be used to wrap meat, or the body cavities of fish or poultry may be stuffed with them. Triloba (sacred myrtle), a form of myrtle with three leaves at every joint instead of two, is esteemed by Jews for use with palm and willow branches in religious ceremonies during the Feast of Tabernacles, the Jewish harvest festival.

Season: Pick flowers in summer, leaves throughout the year, and berries in autumn.

Purchase and Avoid: The plant may occasionally be found at farmers' markets or florists, in season.

Recipe: ***Veal with Myrtle***

1. **Place 1 onion, 1 carrot, 1 celery stalk, and several sprigs of myrtle in a pot of water. Bring to a boil. Generously season a 2-pound lean cut of veal leg or shoulder with salt.**

2. **Immerse the veal in the pot and simmer for 2 hours or until tender.**

3. **As soon as the meat is cooked, drain it and, while still hot, place on a bed of myrtle leaves, cover with another layer of leaves, and wrap tightly with foil.**

4. **Cool, then refrigerate for 24 hours. Remove the leaves and serve the veal thinly sliced, decorated with a few myrtle leaves and a drizzle of olive oil. Duck may be substituted for veal.**

Serving
Suggestions:
Add myrtle berries in small quantities to pâtés and game dishes. • Grill chicken, duck, turkey, pork, or venison over a myrtle wood fire. • Finely crush myrtle berries and heat in a small saucepan with olive oil, lemon juice, diced tomatoes, and sweet onions; sauté black sea bass or other mild white-fleshed fish and spoon the myrtle sauce over.

Food
Affinities:
Bacon, brandy, chestnut, chicken, duck, guinea hen, lemon, olive oil, pancetta, turkey, venison.

27. **NASTURTIUM**

Other Names:
Blomkarse (Norwegian); *blomsterkarse* or *kapuciner karse* (Danish); *cappuccina, nasturzio del Perù,* or *nasturzio indiano* (Italian); *capuchina, espuela de Galán,* or *nasturcia* (Spanish); *capucienerkers* (Dutch); *capucine* or *cresson d'Inde* (French); *chaga seca* (Portuguese); common nasturtium; garden nasturtium; *indejskij kress, kaputsin-kress,* or *nasturtsiya* (Russian); Indian cress; *indiankrasse* (Swedish); *indische kresse* or *kapuzinerkresse* (German); *kova ha-nazir* (Hebrew); *ladan* (Farsi); *lâtin çiçeği* (Turkish); *nabatu al-kabbusin* (Arabic).

General Description:

Nasturtium (Tropaeolum majus) *has peppery-tasting, flat, circular leaves that resemble water lily pads and colorful, open trumpet-shaped blossoms, each ending in a curved, cone-shaped tip that's slightly sweet and peppery.* Nasturtium means "nose twist," referring to its sharp, biting flavor. Although unrelated botanically, nasturtium is often grouped with cresses because their flavors and uses are similar, and in fact, the botanical name for watercress is *Nasturtium officinale*. The colorful, edible, though fragile nasturtium blossoms may be found in colors such as tangerine, salmon, gold, deep red mahogany, scarlet, and cherry red; some are speckled. The young fresh leaves and flowers give bite to savory foods, and the unripe seed pods are pickled as an inexpensive substitute for capers; though larger than capers, they're just as tasty. In Europe and North America, nasturtium is combined with cottage cheese, butter, or cream cheese as a filling for tea sandwiches.

Season:

The plants flower in mid to late summer. The leaves are best when they're young, early in late spring.

Purchase and Avoid:

Nasturtium is always used fresh. Choose lively, brightly colored blossoms without shriveling or brown edges. To avoid pesticides, buy blossoms packaged for eating or garnishing, or from a farmers' market.

Storage:

The blossoms are quite fragile and will keep 1 to 2 days at most after picking. For best results, arrange flowers in a single layer on dampened paper towels and enclose in plastic before refrigerating.

Recipe: ***Risotto with Nasturtium Blossoms and Watercress***

 1. In a medium-sized, heavy-bottomed pot, melt 2 tablespoons butter, add ½ cup chopped sweet onions, and cook over medium heat about 5 minutes, stirring frequently, until tender and transparent but not browned.

2. Stir in 1 cup Arborio rice and cook 2 minutes, stirring constantly, until the rice is shiny but not browned. Pour in ½ cup dry white vermouth and raise the heat to high. Cook until the vermouth has been absorbed, about 3 minutes, and then reduce heat to medium.

3. Stir in 1 cup simmering chicken or vegetable broth and simmer uncovered, stirring occasionally, until most of the liquid is absorbed. Repeat with another cup of broth twice, stirring occasionally, until rice is tender but still firm enough to hold its shape.

 4. Just before serving, stir in 1 cup each chopped watercress leaves and nasturtium blossoms. Stir in ½ cup freshly grated Parmigiano-Reggiano cheese, and season to taste with salt and pepper. Serve immediately, preferably on heated plates, garnishing each portion with a whole nasturtium blossom. Serves 4 to 6.

| Serving Suggestions: | Sprinkle chopped young nasturtium leaves on light vegetable soups, scrambled eggs, or omelets. • Chop the blossoms finely and fold them into softened butter along with chopped shallots, salt, and pepper; use atop grilled fish, chicken, seafood, or vegetables. • Sprinkle nasturtium blossoms on ceviche or thinly sliced raw tuna, salmon, or beef carpaccio. |

| Food Affinities: | Butter, cream cheese, eggs, fish, lemon, peas, ricotta cheese, salmon, shallot, tuna, watercress, vinegar. |

OREGANO

28a–b.

| Other Names: | *Anrar* or *satar barri* (Arabic); common oregano; *diktamos* or *rigani* (Greek); *dost*, *kostets*, or *wilder majoran* (German); *doste*, *marjolaine bâtarde*, *marjolaine sauvage*, *marazolette*, *origan*, *pelevoué*, *thé rouge*, or *thym de berger* (French); *dushitsa* (Russian); *erba acciuga* or *origano* (Italian); *güveyik otu*, *İzmir kekiği*, or *kekikotu* (Turkish); *kungsmynta* or *vild mejram* (Swedish); *orégano* (Spanish); *orégão* (Portuguese); *şovârv* (Romanian); wild marjoram. |

| General Description: | *Oregano* (Origanum vulgare)*, an herb native to the Mediterranean, has dime-sized, often fuzzy, soft green leaves with an unmistakable pungent, robust fragrance.* The ancient Greeks believed oregano was created by the goddess Aphrodite as a symbol of happiness. |

Some confusion surrounds this herb because many related plants are called *oregano* in different countries. There are many species of oregano, as well, but the influence of climate, season, and soil is greater than the differences between the various species, some of which may be closer to marjoram. Italian oregano has narrower leaves, while Sicilian oregano has white flowers and a sweet, pungent aroma. Dittany of Crete (*O. dictamnus*), or hop marjoram, is used as an aromatic in making vermouth. Greek oregano, a special cultivar, is the most common in the marketplace.

The dish most associated with oregano is pizza, which originated with bread bakers in Naples, Italy, who topped their dough with oregano and tomato sauce seasoned with hot red peppers. Throughout the Mediterranean, fresh or dried oregano leaves and blossoms lend their flavor to all sorts of rustic dishes, including beans, thick soups, stews, casseroles, stuffings, and sauces. The fresh leaves and tender shoots of oregano are used as cooking greens in India. In Mexican and Tex-Mex cuisine, it seasons chili con carne and fajitas and is used in chili powder (page 279).

Season: Oregano is in season in summer, with mild, tender
 ☼   leaves early in the season and sharp, biting flavor after
           the plant blossoms.

Purchase   Greek dried oregano on the branch is of excellent
and Avoid: quality and worth seeking out. Buy dried oregano in

smaller quantities to use in long-cooked sauces, where its flavor will have time to develop and mellow.

Storage: Fresh oregano is sturdy and will last up to 1 week in the refrigerator, as long as it doesn't get too cold.

Recipe: ***Swordfish with Sicilian Salmoriglio Sauce***

 1.   **Make the salmoriglio: Whisk 6 tablespoons olive oil with ¼ cup freshly squeezed lemon juice, the zest of ½ lemon, and 2 tablespoons hot water. Add 6 tablespoons chopped Italian parsley, 2 teaspoons finely chopped garlic, and 2 tablespoons chopped fresh oregano (or 2 teaspoons dried oregano).**

 2.   **Preheat a grill or broiler. Brush both sides of four 6- to 8-ounce swordfish fillets, each about 1 inch thick, with some of the salmoriglio and sprinkle sea salt and freshly ground black pepper on both sides. Grill or broil until the fillets are just cooked through, about 5 minutes per side.**

3.   **Transfer to a serving platter. Gently warm the remaining salmoriglio and spoon over the fish.**

Serving Suggestions: Marinate cubes or strips of lamb shoulder with garlic, oregano, red wine vinegar, salt, and pepper, then thread on skewers and grill to make souvlaki. • Sprinkle fresh oregano over a Greek salad. • Season

hearty southern Italian–style tomato sauce and pizza
sauce with oregano.

Food
Affinities:

Anchovy, capers, chicken, eggplant, feta cheese, garlic,
green olives, kalamata olives, lamb, olive oil, pizza,
pork, tomato, tuna, yellow squash, zucchini.

PANDANUS

Other Names:

Pandanus amaryllifolius: *Bai toey* or *toey hom* (Thai);
daun pandan (Indonesian); *dua thom* or *la dua* (Viet-namese); *pandal* or *rampe* (Sinhalese); *pandano* (Spanish,
Portuguese, Italian); *pandanus* (French); *schrauben-baum* (German); screwpine; *taey* (Khmer); *tey ban* or
tey hom (Laotian). **Pandanus tectoris:** *Hala* (Hawaiian).

General
Description:

*Pandanus (Pandanus amaryllifolius) is a tree native to
Southeast Asia with slender, fragrant, shiny, pleated
leaves and a musky, haylike scent reminiscent of aromatic
Jasmine rice.* Called *screwpine* in English because of its
twisted stems, this tree's leaves impart flavor, a distinc-tive aroma, and natural green color to tofu, jellies,
dough, curry, syrup, sauces, coconut rice, and Indo-nesian and Malaysian sweets. Pandanus appears in
Sinhalese yellow rice, northern Indian rice *biriyanis*,
and Indonesian yellow rice. In Thailand, Malaysia, and
Indonesia, rice cooked in coconut milk and flavored
with pandanus leaves is a delicacy, while in Indonesia,

rice is steamed in small baskets made from the leaves. The leaves are especially popular in Bali. In Thailand, iced drinks are made from young coconuts flavored with pandanus leaves; in Indonesia, they appear frequently in sweet puddings or custards of sticky rice and coconut. There are hundreds of species of pandanus, some of which have edible fruits; others have strong leaves, which can be used as plates.

Pandanus blossoms come from a palmlike tree (*P. tectorius*) cultivated in India for its male flowers, which have a delicate scent similar to rose but fruitier. Kewra water, made from these flowers, flavors northern Indian sweets, syrups, betel nut (*pan masala*), and soft drinks. Pandanus trees grow almost everywhere in tropical Asia, but kewra water is mainly a northern Indian flavoring.

Purchase and Avoid:	Look in Southeast Asian markets for fresh pandanus leaves; they may also be found frozen. The leaves lose all their fragrance if dried. The scent of pandanus leaves develops only on withering; the fresh plant has little odor. Many cooks prefer to buy pandan essence, available in Thai groceries. Kewra water, made from pandanus blossoms, is available in Indian groceries.
Recipe:	***Thai Coconut Cream in Kabocha Squash (Sangkaya)***

1. Heat 1 13.5-ounce can unsweetened coconut cream and 1 cup sugar in a saucepan, stirring, until the sugar is dissolved and the mixture is smooth. Cool.

2.   In a bowl, beat 8 eggs well. Mix with the cooled coconut cream and a few drops of kewra water.

 3.   Strain, then pour the mixture into a kabocha squash with the top cut off like a lid and the insides hollowed out, rinsed, and drained. Pour about 1 inch of water into a medium pot with a lid and arrange a steamer basket inside. Place the kabocha squash in the basket and steam, with the top of the squash and the pot lid in place, until the custard is set, about 1 hour, adding water if necessary. Let cool, then slice the squash and custard into wedges as you would a cake.

Serving
Suggestions: Boil pandanus leaves in water, sweeten as desired, strain, and cool for a refreshing beverage. • Add a few pandanus leaves to a rice pot to give the rice a lovely fragrance. • Make rice pudding using coconut milk flavored with kewra water and arrange sliced mangoes and pineapples over the top.

Food
Affinities: Cake, chicken, coconut, ice cream, iced drinks, Indian sweets, kabocha squash, mango, palm sugar, pudding, rice, sugar.

---

29.   **PARSLEY**

Other Names: *Baqdounis* (Arabic); curly parsley; *jaafari* (Farsi); flat-leaf parsley; Hamburg parsley; Italian parsley; *jouver* or *peiresilh* (Provençal French); *julivert* (Catalan); *makedonisi* or *persemolo* (Greek); *maqdounis* (North African Arabic); *maydanoz* (Turkish); *okhrakhushi* (Georgian); *paseri* (Japanese); *perejil* (Spanish); *perrexil* (Basque); *persil* (French); *persilja* (Swedish); *peterselie* (Dutch); *petersilie* or *peterwurz* (German); *peterzili* (Amharic); *petrishke* (Yiddish); *petrosilia* (Hebrew); *petrushka* (Russian); *prezzemolo* (Italian); root parsley; *salsa* (Portuguese); turnip-rooted parsley.

General Description:	*Parsley* (Petroselinum crispum) *is a plant with either flat or curly deep-green leaves that have a cleansing, mildly bitter flavor.* This refreshing, highly adaptable herb is used to enhance practically all European and Middle Eastern foods. Native to the eastern Mediterranean and related to celery, parsley leaves are the basis of green sauces from Italy and France to Germany and Argentina. The two main categories of parsley, flat-leaf and curly, were well-known even to the ancient Greeks. Curly parsley has attractive small, ruffled leaves and is common in English-speaking countries, where it is used as a garnish. Flat-leaf parsley has larger, sturdier, serrated leaves with a more pronounced flavor. Often called Italian parsley, it is a ubiquitous herb in European and Middle Eastern cookery, used in abundance in Middle Eastern dishes like tabbouleh. Neapolitan parsley is larger, with bigger leaves and thicker stems, and can be grown and eaten like celery.

In eastern Europe, Hamburg parsley (*P. crispum* var. *tuberosum*), which has a tender, edible root similar to parsnip, is preferred. The thick, fleshy, creamy-white roots taste like a combination of celery and parsley with a nutty flavor. It is considered essential for soups and stews in that region. It may also be thinly sliced or grated to eat raw in salads, and roasted, mashed, fried, or made into chips. The young leaves are used as soup greens and can also be chopped and added to salads or used as a garnish.

Season:

Curly parsley and Italian parsley are available year-round but are youngest and most tender in spring. In late summer, the leaves may be overly large and tough or spotted. Hamburg parsley is available in fall and winter.

Purchase and Avoid:

In hot weather, parsley tends to spoil quickly, so look for deep green, whole leaves with a pleasant, faintly bitter aroma without any slime or yellowing. Hamburg parsley, sometimes available in supermarkets, is more common in areas with a significant Jewish, Polish, or Russian population.

Recipe:

Argentinean Chimichurri Sauce

1. **In a blender, combine 2 tablespoons red wine vinegar, the juice of 1 lemon, ¹/₂ cup minced red onion, 1 tablespoon hot paprika, 1 tablespoon crushed garlic,**

1 teaspoon finely ground black pepper, 1 teaspoon ground bay leaf, and salt to taste. Pour in 6 tablespoons olive oil and blend again. Add the leaves from 1 large bunch Italian parsley and 2 tablespoons fresh (or 2 teaspoons dried) oregano and blend again, until bright green and smooth.

2. Spoon the sauce over grilled meat and serve extra on the side. Makes about 1½ cups.

Serving Suggestions:
Briefly deep-fry curly or Italian parsley leaves to use as an edible garnish. • Add one or two Hamburg parsley roots when boiling potatoes to make intriguing mashed potatoes. • Briefly boil Italian parsley leaves, drain, and sauté in olive oil and serve as a side dish.

Food Affinities:
Beef, bulgur, capers, carrot, cauliflower, celery, celery root, chicken, clams, eggplant, garlic, olive oil, onion, pasta, potato, shallot, tomato, vermouth, zucchini.

30a–b. **ROSE**

Other Names:
Ätirgül (Kazakh); *bulgarska*, *róża otto*, or *Turecka róża* (Polish); *bussora rose* (British); *gol Mohammadi* or *golesorkh* (Farsi); *gulab* (Hindi); *roos* (Dutch); *ros* (Swedish); *rosa* (Italian, Spanish); *rosa-chá* (Portuguese); *royz* (Yiddish); *roza* (Bulgarian); *vardi* (Georgian); *vered* (Hebrew); *waridi* (Swahili); *gülburnu*, *şam gülü*,

yabanî gül, or *yaği gülü* (Turkish). **Rosa canina:** Briar rose; dog rose; *gülelmasıl* (Turkish); *ruža šípová* (Slovak). **Rosa gallica:** Apothecary rose; French rose; rose de Provence. **Rosa rugosa:** *Hamanasu* (Japanese); *mei gui* (Chinese); rugose rose; tomato rose. **Damask rose:** *Damascenerros* (Swedish); *Damasceńska róza* (Polish); *damasuku-rozu* (Japanese); *măcieş damascen* (Romanian); *rose de Damas* (French); *roza damasskaya* (Russian); *triantafyllo damaskinato* (Greek).

General
Description:

The rose (Rosa) family, while mostly thought of as decorative, is used extensively in the Arab world, central Asia, Iran, and India as an aromatic seasoning for food, especially sweets. The large family of fragrant roses originated in the region that stretches from western Europe to east Asia, with central Asia a center of this plant's diversity. Most European rose varieties stem from *R. gallica*, which grows wild in the Caucasus Mountains. The damask rose (*R. damascena*) is the most important source of rose oil (also known as *rose otto* or *attar*). In France and North Africa, rose oil is obtained from *R. centifolia*. In China, the native rose (*R. rugosa*) has long been used for producing rose-flavored black tea.

Indian rose essence is extracted from small, deep red roses grown specifically for their inimitable fragrance, which is then diluted to make rose water. Northern India is known for its delicious milk-based sweets, many of which hint of rose. Rose preserves made with petals in heavy sugar syrup are sold in

Indian markets, and rose hips jam, packed with vitamin C, is popular in central Europe. In France, red rose petals from Provence are candied and used to decorate cakes and other sweets.

Rose syrup is diluted to make a cool, refreshing drink in the Middle East. Turks dissolve rose-scented *locoum* (Turkish delight candy) into coffee, and in Iran, honey and jams are scented with rose petals. Rose ice cream is enjoyed in many Middle Eastern countries and even tobacco is scented with rose in Turkey.

Season: Roses bloom in summer and are best used in the kitchen in bud form or when newly opened. Rose water, rose syrup, candied roses, and dried rose buds are available all year.

Purchase and Avoid: To avoid toxic pesticides, make sure fresh roses are organic. Look for rose water and rose syrup in Middle Eastern groceries. Look for decorative candied rose petals in markets carrying French gourmet foods.

Note: Use rose water in small amounts to keep your food from tasting like perfume.

Preparation: • **To dry rose petals, collect the roses when the blossoms are fully open. Gather them into a bunch and hang them upside down to air-dry in a dry, dark place. Or, remove the petals and spread them out on a screen, cookie sheet, or any flat surface to dry.**

- When using whole rosebuds, separate the petals from the calyx before using the petals only.

Recipe: ***Mango and Rose Dessert Salad***

1. Slice 4 large, firm, ripe mangoes. Arrange the mango slices attractively on a platter.

2. Combine the juice of 2 limes, 2 tablespoons honey, and 1 teaspoon rose water. Spoon this sauce over the mango slices, sprinkle with rose petals, and serve.

Serving Suggestions: Substitute rose water for vanilla when making pound cake, sponge cake, or shortbread cookies. • Use candied rose petals to decorate a cake iced with dark chocolate frosting. • Add a splash of rose water to apple pie filling, custard sauce, or honey cake.

Food Affinities: Almond, cardamom, chocolate, cinnamon, coffee, cream, lemon, pine nut, pistachio, rice, sugar, tea, vanilla, walnut, yogurt.

ROSE GERANIUM

31a–b.

Other Names: *Attar chia* (Tunisian); scented geranium.

General Description: *Rose geranium and other scented geraniums, which are native to tropical Africa, have small, rounded, decorative, lobed leaves and pink or white flowers.* Rose geranium (*Pelargonium graveolens*) was introduced to Europe in 1690, and has been used since the mid-nineteenth century for flavoring and scenting foods, especially cakes, in the manner of rose water. The leaves (not the flowers) of a number of species have a rose scent; other varieties may smell like lemon (*P. citronellum*); lime (*P. nervosum*); cinnamon, orange, or peach (*P. crispum*); or nutmeg and apple (*P. fragrans*). In Tunisia, an aromatic distilled water made from scented geraniums is popular for flavoring drinks, sweets, and pastries, especially for *makroud,* date and almond paste cookies. Rose geranium adds a pleasing floral note to pound cake, angel food cake, pastry cream, ice cream, fruit salad, and custards.

Season: The plants bloom in summer to fall, with small pink flowers that can be candied.

Storage: The leaves will keep up to 2 weeks, refrigerated; the flowers will last about 2 days refrigerated.

Recipe: **Rose Geranium–Buttermilk Pound Cake**

1. **Preheat the oven to 325°F. Butter and flour a large Bundt pan. Cream ½ pound butter and 2¼ cups sugar until light and fluffy. Beat in 4 eggs, one at a time, then add 2 teaspoons vanilla, the grated zest of ½ lemon, and 2 tablespoons minced rose geranium leaves.**

2.   In a separate bowl, combine 3 cups all-purpose flour, a pinch of salt, and 1 teaspoon baking soda. Starting and ending with the dry ingredients, alternately add the flour mixture and 1 cup buttermilk to the batter.

3.   Pour the batter into the pan and bake for 1 hour and 10 minutes, or until just set in the middle. Cool before removing from the pan, then dust with confectioners' sugar and sprinkle with rose geranium blossoms and garnish with leaves.

Serving Suggestions: Enhance the flavor of fruit jellies, especially apple jelly, by adding rose geranium leaves to the jar just before pouring in the hot jelly. • Sprinkle a few flowers onto a salad, or use them as a garnish. • Brew the leaves into tea.

Food Affinities: Almond, apple, baked fruit, butter, buttermilk, cake, cream, custard, ice cream, fruit jelly, poultry, salads, sauces, sugar, vinegar, white wine.

32a–b.   **ROSEMARY**

Other Names: *Alecrim* (Portuguese); *biberiye, hasalban,* or *kuşdili* (Turkish); *dentrolivano* or *rozmari* (Greek); *ecensier* or *romarin* (French); *eklil kuhi* or *rozmari* (Farsi); *iklil al-jabal* (Arabic); *mi tieh hsiang* (Chinese); old man (British); *ramerino* or *rosmarino* (Italian); *romero* or *rosmario* (Spanish); *rosmarin* (German); *roumanieou* (Provençal French); *rozmarin* (Romanian, Russian, Hebrew, Bulgarian).

General Description:

Rosemary (Rosmarinus officinalis) *has spicy, pungent, rather tough leaves that resemble pine needles in both appearance and aroma.* Native to the Mediterranean region, rosemary is cultivated in nearly all countries around the Mediterranean, as well as England, the United States, and Mexico. Bold though its needles may be, rosemary's lovely blue flowers are sweetly perfumed and delicious sprinkled on salads, rice, or pasta. The blossoms yield a particularly fragrant honey preferred in Spain for making the honey nougat called *turrón*. The use of rosemary is most common in the kitchens of Italy and France. In Greece and some other countries where rosemary grows in abundance, it's not considered suitable for culinary use. Astringent, piney rosemary complements fatty, strong-tasting meats such as lamb, pork, duck, and game. It matches well with garlic and red wine and is especially good for roasted or grilled meat. Trailing rosemary is hardy and winding.

Season:

In late spring, the early part of its season, rosemary will be more tender; by late summer it's more resinous, potent, and tough, so use less and chop finely.

Purchase and Avoid:

Fresh rosemary is always preferable and is widely available throughout the year.

Preparation: •   **Dried rosemary leaves are sharp and pointy, so either**
               chop finely or strain out before serving.

Note: Rosemary is very pronounced, so use it with care, as
               too much can make a dish taste medicinal. Use dried
               rosemary in careful doses and fresh rosemary more
               freely.

Recipe: *Carrot-Currant Salad with Rosemary*

1.   **Whisk together ¹/₂ cup rice wine vinegar and ¹/₂ cup**
       vegetable oil with salt and pepper to taste.

2.   **Mix well with 1 pound peeled and shredded carrots,**
       ¹/₄ cup currants, 2 tablespoons finely chopped shal-
       lots, and 2 tablespoon finely chopped rosemary.

3.   **Marinate for 1 hour before serving. This salad keeps**
       well up to 4 days, refrigerated.

Serving   Use rosemary sprigs to brush olive oil on meat and
Suggestions: poultry when grilling, and sprinkle rosemary stalks on
               the charcoal for extra flavor. • Season diced potatoes
               with rosemary, salt, and pepper and bake. • Stuff
               chicken with rosemary sprigs, a quartered lemon, and
               a handful of garlic cloves when roasting. • Simmer
               rosemary in cream, strain, add lemon juice and lemon
               zest, and serve as a sauce for roasted fish or chicken.

Food Affinities:	Beef, beet, chestnuts, chicken, duck, eggplant, garlic, lamb, lemon, olive oil, onion, orange, pork, potato, rabbit, red wine, tomato, turnip, white beans, zucchini.

33. **RUE**

Other Names:	*Apiganos* (Greek); *arruda* (Portuguese); *fayjan* (Arabic); garden rue; *gartenraute*, *raute*, or *weinraute* (German); herb of grace; *herbe à la belle fille*, *herbe de grâce*, *péganium*, or *rue odorante* (French); *pegam* or *ruta* (Hebrew); *ruda* (Spanish); *ruta* (Italian); *sadab* (Farsi); *sedefotu* or *sezab* (Turkish); *vinruta* (Swedish); *wijnruit* (Dutch). **Fringed rue:** Aleppo rue; Egyptian rue; *taena* or *tena adam* (Amharic); wild rue.
General Description:	*Rue* (Ruta graveolens), *a member of the citrus family, has small, spoon-shaped, fleshy, blue-green leaves whose shape inspired the design of the clubs suit on playing cards.* Rue leaves and berries are most popular today in Ethiopia, where the strong and bitter leaves are used to flavor coffee and are added to the national spice mix, berberé (page 278). The fruits are rarely used in other countries. Pure essential oil of rue taken in large amounts was used to cause abortions, giving us its popular French name, *herbe à la belle fille* (herb of fair maidens). Like many other bitter spices and herbs, rue is popular for flavoring bitters, liquors that stimulate the appetite and help digestion after a rich

meal. Small leaf tips of another variety of rue, *R. chalepensis*, are used in Italy to flavor *grappa con ruta*, the clear liquor distilled from grape skins; they're also added to salads. This type of rue, highly esteemed by the Jews of North Africa, flavors *merguez* (a type of sausage) and the Tunisian egg dish *hajja*. Use fresh rue leaves only in small quantities.

Recipe: ***Ancient Roman–Style Garlic Cheese with Rue (Moretum)***

 1. **Grind 6 cloves of garlic in a food processor, and then add ¹/₂ pound ground pecorino Romano cheese, a handful of cilantro leaves, ¹/₄ cup chopped celery, 2 tablespoons young rue leaves, and 2 to 3 tablespoons extra virgin olive oil, enough to make a smooth paste. Makes about 2 cups.**

 2. **Spread lightly on crostini and broil.**

Note: Rue should never be used by pregnant women because
 it can cause a miscarriage.

Serving   Add a small branch of rue to simmering spicy Italian
Suggestions: tomato sauces; remove before serving. • Because rue's natural bitterness is diminished by acids, it works well in pickled vegetables, herbal vinegars, or salads. • Make a British-style sauce from damson plums cooked with red wine and rue to serve with meat.

Food Affinities:	Bread, capers, cheese, chicken, cream cheese, eggs, grappa, grating cheese, olive oil, pickles, plum, salads, tomato sauce, vinegar.

34a–c.

SAGE

Other Names:	*Adaçayı* (Turkish); *alisfakia* or *faskomilo* (Greek); *chá-da-europa* or *salva-mansa* (Portuguese); *ching chieh* (Chinese); *franse thee* or *salie* (Dutch); *marameeah* (Arabic); *marva* (Hebrew); *salbei* (German); *salbi* (Georgian); *salvia* (Italian, Spanish); *salviya* (Bulgarian); *sathi* (Punjabi); *sauge* or *thé de la Grèce* (French); *sàuvi* (Provençal French); *sezi* (Japanese); *shalfej* (Russian); *yeghesbag* (Armenian); *zsálya* (Hungarian). **Sacred sage:** Diviner's sage; sage of the seers.
General Description:	*Sage (Salvia officinalis) has soft, pebbly, narrow, oblong, gray-green leaves with a slightly bitter, resinous aroma.* Sage, which originated in the Mediterranean and Asia Minor, gets its name from the Latin *salvia*, meaning "to heal," referring to the medicinal value of the plant. Today, this ancient seasoning is most important in the Mediterranean, especially Italy. Sage tea was popular in sixteenth-century England and sage ale was also brewed. The pungency of sage works well to cut the fattiness of meat, so it complements goose, duck, and pork. In Italy, sage is often paired with rosemary in seasoning game, poultry, pork, and veal roasts.

Crispy fried sage leaves are a typical garnish for *fritto misto*, an Italian dish of mixed deep-fried foods. Sage has a particular affinity to poultry; in the United States, it shows up in poultry seasoning and stuffing. Fresh pork breakfast sausages are seasoned with sage and marjoram. Sage works well with starches such as potatoes, dried beans, and split peas. Dried sage, which maintains much of the character of fresh sage, is usually found as grayish green leaves with a wooly, springy texture.

The leaves and seeds of chia sage or Mexican sage (*S. columbariae*) have been important in the diet of desert-dwelling Native Americans for their mucilaginous qualities. Greek sage (*S. triloba*) is quite potent and sought after in Greece and Lebanon. Central American sage varieties have sweet, fruity fragrance and include pineapple sage (*S. rutilans*), peach sage (*S. greggii*), and fruit sage (*S. dorisiana*). Some of these are used for teas; others are grown for their large, brightly colored flowers. Also native to Central America is the only hallucinogenic species in the huge Lamiaceae (mint) family, sacred sage (*S. divinorum*), which was cultivated by Central American Indians for use in religious ceremonies. Variegated and purple sage are also available.

Season:

Fresh sage may be found year-round. Blossoming sage can be found in farmers' markets in late summer.

Recipe: *Saltimbocca alla Romana*

 1. Mash together 2 cloves garlic with salt and pepper to taste (keeping in mind that the prosciutto in the next step is also salty) to form a paste.

2. Spread a little of the paste on 2 pounds of veal (or turkey) cutlets and arrange 3 sage leaves atop each. Cover each cutlet with 2 thin slices of prosciutto. Secure the prosciutto and sage with wooden picks.

 3. In a large, heavy skillet, heat 2 tablespoons olive oil until shimmering. Sauté 2 veal cutlets at a time, prosciutto side down, for about 1 minute. Turn over and sauté 30 seconds, or until the veal is just cooked through.

4. Transfer the cooked saltimbocca to a platter and loosely cover with foil to keep warm. Repeat, adding more oil, until all the cutlets are cooked.

5. Pour off any excess oil from the skillet, then pour in ³/₄ cup dry Marsala wine and deglaze the skillet, scraping up any brown bits. Boil until the liquid is syrupy. Pull off and discard the toothpicks from the cutlets, drizzle the sauce atop, and serve.

Serving Suggestions: Make *paglia e fieno* (straw and hay) by tossing half spinach and half egg fettuccine with cream simmered with sage, nutmeg, matchstick-cut prosciutto, and

green peas, and topping with grated Parmesan cheese.
• Add sage to browned butter and toss with potato
gnocchi, cheese ravioli, or pumpkin ravioli.

Food
Affinities:

Boar, butternut squash, chicken, duck, lima beans,
olive oil, onion, nutmeg, partridge, pork, potato, prosciutto, pumpkin, sausage, turkey, veal, white beans.

35a–b.

SAVORY

Other Names:

Bohnenkraut, kölle, pfefferkraut, or *saturei* (German);
chabyor (Russian); *herbe de Saint-Julien* or *poivrette*
(French); *khondari* (Georgian); *marzeh* (Farsi); *nadgh*
(Arabic); *santoreggia* (Italian); *throubi* or *tragorigani*
(Greek); *za'atar* (Hebrew). **Summer savory:** *Dağ rey-
hanı* (Turkish); garden savory; *sadrèio* (Spanish); *sarriette des champs* (French); *segurelha das hortas* (Portuguese). **Winter savory:** *Ajedrea* or *sabroso* (Spanish);
dağ sateri (Turkish); mountain savory; *pebre d'asé*
(Provençal French); *sajolida* (Catalan); *sarriette de
montagne* (French); *segurelha das montanhas* (Portuguese); *winterbergminze* (German). **Pink savory:**
Barrel sweetener; *kara kekik* (Turkish); Roman hyssop;
satra vruda (Hebrew); thryba; *za'atar rumi* (Arabic).

General
Description:

*Savory comes in two main types: annual summer savory
(Satureja hortensis), with fragrant, tiny, pink or white
blossoms and sparse large, oval, bronze green leaves, and*

perennial winter savory (S. montana), *with lavender or white flowers and small, spiky, dark green leaves.* The two types of savory share an intense flavor and a resinous aroma reminiscent of thyme, though summer savory is milder and more tender. Until world exploration made spices like black pepper more common, savory was the strongest seasoning available in Europe. So for more than two thousand years, this versatile herb has been one of the underlying flavors of European cuisine. The Saxons bestowed the name savory upon this herb because of the spicy, piquant potency it gave their food, and even today we use the word *savory* to denote robust and flavorful nonsweet foods. Savory's Latin name, *satureja*, is said to derive from *satyr*, the mythological half man, half goat with a legendary libido. Indeed, summer savory has a long-standing reputation as an aphrodisiac, while winter savory supposedly decreases desire. Take your pick.

In Germany and Switzerland, cooks use savory (*bohnenkraut* or "bean herb") when cooking beans or lentils, and the Italians, who were probably the first to raise savory as a kitchen herb, use it similarly. In the south of France, savory goes into slow-cooked lamb and daube of beef. Central European cooks season trout, potatoes, and mushrooms with savory. In France, Italy, and the U.S., this spicy, peppery herb seasons sausages and pâtés and is ubiquitous in poultry seasonings.

Pink savory (*S. thymbra*) has small, fragrant, slightly fuzzy foliage with tiny pink flowers. It makes a delicious herbal tea widely consumed in Crete. It's sometimes called *barrel sweetener* because it's used, in a strong infusion, to clean wine barrels before adding the new vintage. Pink savory leaves season brine-cured olives, grilled meat, and braised vegetables, especially in the eastern Mediterranean.

Purchase and Avoid: Choose brightly colored, vigorous bunches. Refrigerate in the package and savory will keep well for 2 weeks.

Preparation: • **Hang savory sprigs to dry, then crumble the leaves into powder. This homemade dried savory will be fragrant and mellow, unlike commercial dried savory, which tends to be overpowering.**

Note: Because both dried and fresh savory are so potent, it's important to use them with a light hand.

Recipe: *Savory Cannellini Bean Spread*

 I. **In a medium sauté pan, cook 1 tablespoon chopped garlic, 4 teaspoons finely chopped fresh savory (or 1 teaspoon dried savory), and ¹/₂ teaspoon crushed red pepper flakes in 2 tablespoons extra virgin olive oil until the aromas are released, about 3 minutes.**

2. **Add 3 cups cooked and drained cannellini beans and cook over medium-low heat until the mixture thickens, 5 to 10 minutes.**

3. In a food processor or blender, puree the bean mixture and another 1 tablespoon extra virgin olive oil until the mixture is smooth. Season to taste with salt and black pepper. Serve warm with crostini, pita chips, or vegetable crudités.

Serving
Suggestions:
Add summer or winter savory sprigs to braised meats, beans or lentils, or venison or rabbit; remove before serving. • Season omelets, scrambled eggs, and deviled eggs with finely chopped summer savory. • Use powdered dried summer or winter savory to flavor crumbs for breading meat, fish, or vegetables.

Food
Affinities:
Beans, brussels sprouts, carrot, cheese, chicken, eggs, kale, lentils, mushroom, olive, turnip, venison.

 36a–b.

SHISO

Other Names:
Bhanjira (Hindi); *chi su, hung sha yao, sugeng, tyu su, yeh su,* or *zi su* (Chinese); Chinese basil; *chinesische melisse* or *schwarznessel* (German); cinnamon plant; *daun shiso* (Indonesian); *egoma* (Japanese); *nag-mon* or *nga-khi-mon* (Thai); perilla; rattlesnake weed; *tia to* or *tu to* (Vietnamese); *tulkkae* (Korean). **Green shiso:** *Ao-shiso* (Japanese); Japanese basil. **Red shiso:** *Aka-shiso* (Japanese); beefsteak plant; crispy shiso; purple mint; purple shiso. **Korean shiso:** Korean sesame leaves; wild sesame; *wilder sesam* (German).

General
Description:

Shiso (Perilla frutescens) *is a Japanese herb with large, ruffle-edged, aromatic leaves that combine elements of cinnamon, anise, basil, and mint.* Shiso's cultivation and use is most important in Japan, although it is also used in China, Burma, the Himalayan foothills, and Korea. There are two types grown in Japan: shiso, with attractive green or red ruffle-edged leaves, and egoma, with flat though serrated leaves, resembling large spearmint or basil. Green shiso has bright green leaves with a cinnamon-like scent and a flavor reminiscent of ginger. Red shiso, with reddish purple leaves and a strong aroma and flavor, is used to impart a purplish red color and special flavor to *umeboshi* (pickled plums), *beni shoga* (pickled ginger for sushi), and *crosnes* (Chinese artichokes). It's also used as a wrapping for *mochi* (sticky rice) sweets. Egoma is valued for perilla oil, extracted from the seeds, which is used for Shinto ceremonies; interest in perilla oil is growing because it has the highest level of polyunsaturates of any oil. Perilla seeds, commonly known as sesame seeds and called *shisonomi* in Japan and *deul gge* in Korea, add their flavor and crunchy texture to soups, pickles, marinades, and sweets in Japan and Korea.

In Vietnam, shiso leaves make a fragrant garnish for noodle soups and spring rolls. Korean shiso is large leafed and green, often called *sesame leaves* or *wild sesame* though unrelated to sesame. It is traditionally eaten raw with rice, cooked with soy sauce and sesame oil as a side dish, fermented into kimchi, or wrapped around meat and fried in batter. Some cultivars have aromas like lemon, cinnamon, or cumin. The ground seeds are also used as a spice, especially in Korea.

Purchase and Avoid:

The leaves are usually used fresh. Frozen leaves can be used for color and flavoring, though not for garnish because they will be wilted and darkened.

Recipe:

Green Tea and Red Shiso Granita

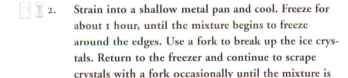

1. **Combine 2 tablespoons green tea leaves, 8 large red shiso leaves, the juice of 1 lemon, and 3/4 cup sugar in a bowl. Add 3 cups boiling water, stir to dissolve the sugar, and steep for 10 minutes.**

2. **Strain into a shallow metal pan and cool. Freeze for about 1 hour, until the mixture begins to freeze around the edges. Use a fork to break up the ice crystals. Return to the freezer and continue to scrape crystals with a fork occasionally until the mixture is frozen and grainy, about 5 hours.**

3. **Scoop into serving bowls and serve topped with cherries and sliced apricots.**

Serving Suggestions:

Garnish sashimi with shiso leaves. • Batter and deep-fry shiso leaves for tempura or garnish tempura with the raw leaves. • Use the larger Korean shiso leaves to wrap foods such as spring rolls. • Use red shiso to make pink vinegar, or make pink rice by mixing in a few chopped leaves just before serving.

Food
Affinities:

Fish, ginger, kimchi, meat, miso, noodle soup, raw fish, rice, salads, sesame oil, soy sauce, spring rolls, tofu, umeboshi.

37a–b. 📷

SORREL

Other Names:

French sorrel: *Acetosa* (Italian); herb patience; *oseille* (French); round leaf sorrel. **Garden sorrel:** Belleville sorrel; broad-leafed sorrel. **English sorrel:** Greensauce (British); sour dock; sour grass.

General
Description:

Sorrel is the name for a group of plants of the genus Rumex, *in the buckwheat family and native to Eurasia, known for their pleasantly acidic leaves, which contain oxalic acid.* Sorrel is shaped like elongated spinach leaves and ranges in color from pale to dark green. It gets its name from an ancient Germanic word meaning "sour"; all other European names for this plant also mean "sour." Sorrel grows wild throughout Europe, Asia, and North America and has been eaten as a salad and cooking green since ancient times because it's stimulating to the appetite and balances rich foods. Laplanders use sorrel in place of rennet to curdle milk when making cheese. Though the French usually tame sorrel's acidity by cooking it in butter or cream, they also utilize the herb's acidity by stuffing spring shad with a puree of sorrel so that the acid softens and supposedly helps dissolve the numerous bones. Garden sorrel (*R. acetosa*), indigenous to Britain and most of Europe, is a slender plant about two feet high, with juicy stems and leaves and whorled spikes of reddish green flowers. Eventually French sorrel (*R. scutatus*), with larger, milder, more succulent leaves, became most popular in Britain.

Season: Fresh sorrel is available in limited supply year-round, with a peak season in spring.

Purchase and Avoid: Choose sorrel with whole, bright green leaves and avoid woody-looking stems or yellow or wilted leaves. Gourmet food stores sometimes carry cooked sorrel in jars and cans. Sorrel is not sold in dried form.

Storage: Refrigerate fresh sorrel in a plastic bag up to 3 days. Cook sorrel briefly and freeze it for use as a sauce.

Note: Avoid using aluminum or cast-iron cookware for sorrel; its high level of acidity will react with the pot, lending a metallic flavor and a grayish color to the food.

Recipe: ***Schav (Chilled Polish Sorrel Soup)***

1. **Wash ¹/₄ pound sorrel, leaving the water on the leaves.**

2. **Shred the leaves and place them in a nonreactive soup pot. Add 6 cups boiling water, 1 teaspoon paprika, and salt to taste. Simmer, covered, for 5 minutes, or until the sorrel is quite soft.**

3. **Pour the hot soup over 3 beaten eggs, whisking vigorously so the soup thickens. Strain, cool, and refrigerate. Serve chilled and garnished with dollops of sour cream.**

Serving
Suggestions:
Add a few chopped young leaves to salad for zesty flavor. • Stir shredded sorrel into creamy potato and leek soup just before serving. • Fill an omelet with sorrel cooked in butter with shallots.

Food
Affinities:
Butter, chicken, cream, eggs, goose, lamb, leek, pork, potato, salmon, scallion, shad, shallot, sour cream, sweetbreads, veal.

38a–b.

TARRAGON

Other Names:
Ai hao (Chinese); *dragoncello* (Italian); *drakebloed* (Dutch); *drakontio* or *tarankon* (Greek); *estragāo* (Portuguese); *estragon* or *herbe dragonne* (French); *estragon* (Russian); *estragon* or *tarragona* (Spanish); *tarhon* (Romanian); *tarhun* or *tuzla otu* (Turkish); *tarkhun* (Arabic).

General Description:	*Tarragon* (Artemisia dracunculus) *has long, thin, tender, dark green leaves and a sweet aromatic flavor combining elements of fennel, anise, and licorice.* Tarragon is popularly linked to dragons, perhaps because of its coiled, serpentine root system and the widespread belief that tarragon could not only ward off serpents and dragons but also heal snake bites. There's some confusion about tarragon because the most aromatic cultivar, French tarragon (*A. dracunculus* var. *sativa*), is difficult to find and grow, while the more common Russian tarragon (*A. dracunculus*), often sold to home gardeners, has little flavor. Supermarkets usually sell French tarragon. This sweetly spicy herb is a special favorite in France. It is well suited to chicken, eggs, or mushroom dishes. Tarragon sprigs are commonly used to flavor white wine vinegar.
Season:	Tarragon is at its best in spring. Later in the season, when the weather gets hot, tarragon bleaches out or spoils quickly.
Purchase and Avoid:	Fresh tarragon is best, but if you use dried, make sure its color and aroma haven't faded.
Storage:	Tarragon is quite tender and freezes easily, so store it in the warmest part of the refrigerator, generally on the top shelf, or place in a vase of water, as for a bouquet of flowers.

Recipe: ***Béarnaise Sauce***

1. Heat ³/₄ pound butter until barely melted and set aside.

2. Combine 2 tablespoons white wine, 3 tablespoons chopped fresh tarragon (or 1 tablespoon dried tarragon), 2 chopped shallots, 2 tablespoons tarragon vinegar or red wine vinegar, and salt and black pepper to taste in a small nonreactive pot. Boil slowly until almost all the liquid has cooked away, leaving a moist paste. Cool.

3. Transfer the paste to the top of a double boiler with boiling water in the bottom portion. Whisk in 4 egg yolks and 2 tablespoons water. Heat, whisking constantly, until the mixture is fluffy and thickened.

4. Remove the top of the double boiler from the heat and beat in the melted butter very slowly, whisking constantly. Correct the seasonings and keep the sauce warm over steaming water until ready to serve over chicken, fish, or steak.

Serving Suggestions: Whisk together red wine or tarragon vinegar with olive oil, Dijon mustard, chopped tarragon, salt, and pepper for a French vinaigrette. • Add chopped tarragon to tartar sauce for fried fish. • Julienne carrots and turnips and toss with lemon juice, olive oil, and chopped shallots and tarragon.

| Food Affinities: | Asparagus, beef, carrot, cauliflower, chicken, fish, lamb, mayonnaise, mushroom, mustard, olive oil, shrimp, sour cream, tomato, vinaigrettes. |

39a–b. 📷

THYME

Other Names:
Common thyme: *Cimbru de cultură* (Romanian); English thyme; French thyme; garden thyme; *koranit* or *timin* (Hebrew); *mashterka gradinska* (Bulgarian); *taimu* (Japanese); *thym ordinaire* (French); *thymari* (Greek); *thymian* (German); *timo* (Italian); *timyan* (Yiddish); *tomilho* (Portuguese); *tomillo* (Spanish); *za'atar* (Farsi); *zatr* (Arabic). **Wild thyme:** *Awishan shirazi* (Farsi); creeping thyme; *kryptimian* (Norwegian); *kwendel* or *wilde tijm* (Dutch); mother of thyme; *serpillo* (Italian); *serpolet* (French); *serpoleto* (Spanish); *zhumbricë* (Albanian).

General Description:
Thyme (Thymus vulgaris) *has tiny grayish green leaves and is an essential herb throughout much of Europe, the Middle East, the United States, and the Caribbean.* Thyme's concentrated spicy, clovelike aroma is highly adaptable and blends well with the foods of many cuisines; in fact, many chefs feel that thyme is the most indispensable herb in the kitchen. Because of thyme's versatility, it is a foundation herb in seasoning mixes from Turkey to the Caribbean. New Orleans's Creole cuisine uses thyme extensively and Cajun seasoning

(page 279) typically contains thyme, as does Jamaican jerk seasoning. In central Europe, thyme seasons soups, fish, meat, poultry, and eggs, and in Britain, thyme is the most popular culinary herb besides mint. Thyme leaves tend to be woody and must be finely chopped before using. Dried thyme is very strong and works best with spicy foods, particularly meat dishes. Fresh thyme has a softer, less smoky flavor and won't overpower fish, seafood, or vegetables.

The flowers of wild thyme (*T. serpyllum*), which grows in the mountains of temperate Europe, flavor Bénédictine, a liqueur that originated during the Renaissance. The flavor of lemon thyme (*T. citriodorus*) complements fish especially well. Potent Mediterranean conehead thyme (*T. capitatus*) is used for the pickled thyme sold in Middle Eastern groceries, and nectar from its blossoms yields the famed Mount Hymettus honey from Greece. Caraway thyme (*T. herba-barona*) has a strong caraway-like fragrance.

Season:	Thyme is in season in the summer, though available fresh year-round at supermarkets. Thyme flowers in June, so that's a good time to buy it. For the largest variety, including lemon and other scented thymes, look for fresh thyme at farmers markets.
Purchase and Avoid:	Look for thyme with bright-colored leaves. Avoid blackened or dried-out thyme. Variegated yellow and green lemon thyme may occasionally be found.

Storage: Thyme keeps quite well in the refrigerator up to 2 weeks, becoming desiccated and darker as it ages.

Recipe: ***Gratin of Potatoes with Sweet Onion and Thyme***

1. **Preheat the oven to 400°F. Scald 1 quart heavy cream combined with 1 tablespoon finely chopped fresh thyme and salt, pepper, and nutmeg to taste.**

2. **Peel and thinly slice 3 pounds russet potatoes. Peel and slice 1 large sweet onion.**

3. **Toss the potatoes and onion with the scalded cream. Transfer to a baking dish just large enough to hold the mixture. Sprinkle 2 ounces grated Parmesan cheese over the top.**

4. **Cover with aluminum foil and bake about 45 minutes, until the potatoes are almost soft and the mixture is bubbling. Remove the foil and bake about 15 minutes longer, until browned on top. Cool slightly before serving.**

Serving Suggestions: Simmer French green lentils with thyme and use as a bed for sautéed or grilled salmon. • Use lemon thyme with oily fish like salmon, tuna, and Chilean sea bass. • Add orange or lemon thyme to seafood stews and marinades for grilled chicken.

Food Affinities:	Anchovy, chicken, clams, cream sauce, eggs, fish, lamb, lentils, mussels, onion, pork, potato, salmon, seafood, tomato, turkey, zucchini.

40. **WILD LIME LEAF**

Other Names:	*Bai makrut* or *makroot* (Thai); *chanh sac* or *truc* (Vietnamese); *daun jeruk purut* (Indonesian); *daun limau purut* (Malay); ichang lime; kaffir lime; *khi hout* or *kok mak* (Laotian); *kobumikan* (Japanese); *kraunch soeuth* (Khmer); makrut lime; *mav naus* (Hmong).
General Description:	*Wild lime leaves* (Citrus hystrix) *are the highly perfumed leaves of a Southeast Asian citrus fruit that's not actually a true lime.* The glossy, dark green wild lime leaves look like two leaves joined end to end. Their common name, kaffir lime, derives from a word of Arabic origin for "nonbeliever" and was used in southern Africa as a derogatory term for black Africans; it has fallen out of favor. Grown in Southeast Asia and Hawaii, the wild lime tree produces small, pear-shaped fruit with bright yellowish green wrinkled skin. Wild limes are valued for their zest and very sour juice, but mostly for the heavenly perfume of their leaves. The leaves are especially popular in Thailand, where they appear in soups, stir-fries, and curries, and in Indonesia (especially Bali) where they appear in fish and chicken dishes. Dried wild lime leaves are used in the same way as bay leaves.

Purchase and Avoid:	Look for fresh or dried wild lime leaves in Southeast Asian markets. Fresh leaves, which have a more intense fragrance, are sometimes available and are preferable. Frozen leaves are fine for flavor, if not appearance.
Storage:	Fresh leaves will keep for several days, or can be frozen. Store dried leaves in a sealed container in a cool, dry place for several months.
Recipe:	***Thai Shrimp and Chayote with Wild Lime and Red Curry Sauce***

1. **Prepare sauce: In a sauce pot, melt 2 tablespoons butter, add 2 chopped shallots, 4 lightly crushed wild lime leaves, 2 tablespoons chopped ginger, and 1 tablespoon curry powder. Cook, stirring, for 2 to 3 minutes or until fragrant. Stir in 2 tablespoons Thai red curry paste, 3 tablespoons frozen orange juice concentrate, 1 tablespoon grated orange zest, and 3/4 cup unsweetened coconut cream. Simmer about 5 minutes, or until thickened. Strain and keep warm.**

2. **Prepare shrimp: In a large skillet, heat 2 tablespoons vegetable oil and add 2 chayote squash (peeled, seeded, and cut into matchsticks). Cook 3 minutes or until crisp-tender. Add 1 1/2 pounds large shrimp (peeled, deveined, and with tail shell left on) and cook 3 minutes longer or until shrimp are opaque.**

3. **Toss shrimp mixture with sauce, season to taste with salt, reheat briefly, and serve over steamed Jasmine rice garnished with wild lime leaves. Serves 4 to 6.**

Serving Suggestions:
Add whole lime leaves during cooking to scent white rice, fish, or stock. • Shred or tear the leaves and add to Thai curries and hot and sour soups. • Make wild lime aioli by pureeing the deveined leaves with a little lime juice and mixing with mayonnaise.

Food Affinities:
Basil, chicken, chiles, cilantro, coconut, crabmeat, fish, galangal, garlic, ginger, lemongrass, pork.

Spices

A spice is an aromatic part of a plant with highly concentrated flavor, used to season foods. It may be a root (ginger and horseradish), bark (cinnamon and cassia), pod (vanilla and cardamom), fruit (chiles and kokam), seed (poppy and sesame), resin (asafetida and mastic), berry (barberry and wolfberry), or flower (capers and saffron). The search for spices was a powerful force in world history. Starting as long ago as the second millennium B.C., Arab traders brought rare and costly spices, especially pepper, cloves, and nutmeg, from the Spice Islands of the Pacific through India to the West, keeping their places of origin secret. Starting in the fifteenth century, Europeans set out to find a shorter way to the spice-laden world of the East and on the way discovered the New World, with spices including vanilla, chiles, and allspice.

Today, spices of all kinds are available. The trick is to learn how to use them with a confident but measured hand so that they enhance foods without overwhelming them. Because spices are so varied, each kind of plant part requires a different kind of use. Some are added at the beginning of cooking, others just before serving. Some need advance preparation; others are ready to use as is.

Using spices in the kitchen will liven up food, make it more fragrant (and therefore more appetizing), and provide flavor without adding fat.

41.   📷   **AJWAIN**

Other Names: *Ajowan* (English, French, Italian, Spanish); *ajvain, carom,* or *omum* (Hindi); ajwan; bishop's weed; *adiowan, Indischer kümmel,* or *königskümmel* (German); *kamun al-muluki* or *taleb el koubs* (Arabic); *nanavva* or *zenian* (Farsi); *netch azmud* (Amharic).

General Description: *Ajwain is a popular spice in India, where both fruits and leaves of this pungent plant* (Trachyspermum ammi) *in the parsley family are used.* The small, hard, oval, pale brown fruits (often mistakenly called *seeds*) are grayish and resemble cumin or caraway in shape. Slightly bitter and pungent, ajwain has a musty character somewhere between anise and oregano. Often confused with lovage seed, ajwain is reminiscent of a more aromatic and less subtle thyme because both contain the essential oil thymol.

Ajwain is thought to have originated in the eastern Mediterranean, perhaps in Egypt, and then traveled to India with the Greek conquest of central Asia. Today it's mainly cultivated in Iran and northern India and also commonly used in Egypt and Afghanistan. Ajwain is rarely used raw; it's either dry-roasted or fried in ghee (clarified butter) so it develops a more subtle and complex aroma, similar to caraway but brighter. In India, lentils are commonly flavored with an aromatic butter, called *tadka*, that often contains ajwain. Ajwain is said to reduce the gaseous effects of beans and other legumes.

Purchase and Avoid:	Purchase whole seeds from an Indian, Iranian, or Pakistani grocery, where the turnover will be greatest.

Note: Use raw ajwain seeds judiciously, because even a small amount can overpower other flavors.

Recipe: ***Red Lentil Dal with Spiced Tadka***

 1. **To make the dal: Combine 1 pound dried split red lentils with 1 teaspoon ground turmeric and salt to taste.**

 2. **Add 2 quarts water and bring to a boil, stirring occasionally. Lower the heat, partially cover, and simmer for 30 minutes, or until the lentils disintegrate into a thick, soupy puree.**

 3. **To make the *tadka*: Fry 1 teaspoon each ajwain, dill, and cumin seeds in ¼ cup ghee (clarified butter) until they turn brown and release their aromas. Add 1 tablespoon chopped garlic and 2 tablespoons grated ginger and fry briefly.**

4. **Just before serving, add salt and a squeeze of lemon juice to the lentils. Pour the hot tadka over the dal and sprinkle with chopped fresh cilantro.**

Serving Suggestions: Toast ajwain seeds and add to vegetable curries or steamed cabbage, carrots, potato, or pumpkin. • Cook ajwain in butter or oil and add to slow-cooked dishes for a thyme flavor. • Toast ajwain and add to savory biscuits and Indian breads.

Food Affinities:

Butternut squash, carrot, cauliflower, cheese, curry, eggplant, fish, fritters, green beans, legumes, potato, pumpkin, savory biscuits, turmeric.

42.   **ALLSPICE**

Other Names:

Allehånde (Danish); *aromatopeperi* or *piperi Iamaïkis* (Greek); *bahar* (Arabic); *englisches gewürz* or *piment* (German); *guayabita* (Latin American Spanish); Jamaica pepper; myrtle pepper; newspice; *pepe di Giamaica* or *pimento* (Italian); *pilpel angli* (Hebrew); *piment Jamaïque, poivre de la Jamaïque,* or *toute-épice* (French); *pimenta-da-jamaica* or *pimenta síria* (Portuguese); *pimienta de Jamaica, pimienta dulce,* or *pimienta gorda* (Spanish).

General Description:

Allspice (Pimenta dioica) *is a tree in the Myrtaceae (myrtle) family, originating and still grown mainly in Jamaica, with highly aromatic berries.* Allspice berries, which are cured and dried before use, are dark reddish brown and somewhat larger than a peppercorn, with little aroma until crushed. Their aroma resembles a combination of cloves, cinnamon, and nutmeg with some of the heat of black pepper. The Aztecs spiced hot chocolate with allspice and vanilla, while the

Mayans used allspice to embalm the dead.

The British developed a taste for allspice in the three hundred years, beginning in 1655, that Jamaica was a British colony. In Britain, allspice goes into stews and sauces, and it flavors pickled vegetables and pickled and cured meats; it's used in much the same way in the United States. In Europe, allspice goes into spice mixtures for sausage, and it's much loved in Scandinavia for savory meat pastry fillings. Allspice is well-known in Turkey and Lebanon, where it appears in baharat (page 278). In Africa, the Ethiopian spice mixture berberé (page 278) contains allspice.

Allspice is used extensively in Caribbean cuisine, especially in Jamaica. Fiery jerk seasoning pastes featuring allspice are used to marinate pork, goat, or chicken before barbecuing, preferably over an allspice-wood fire. Meat may also be stuffed or wrapped with allspice leaves, similar to the use of myrtle in the Mediterranean. Jamaican pimento dram is a liqueur made by steeping allspice berries in rum. Fresh allspice leaves, called West Indian bay leaf, are sometimes used for cooking or smoking meat.

Purchase and Avoid:
Whole allspice berries should be even in color, dark reddish brown, and rounded, with a rough surface and no musty smell. Ground allspice should be a rich dark brown with a warm aroma. It should be somewhat oily in consistency, never dry and dusty.

Storage: Store whole or ground allspice in a cool, dark place
with low humidity. Whole allspice will keep up to 3
years before its flavor fades; ground, up to 1 1/2 years.

Recipe: ***Jamaican Jerk-Spiced Chicken***

 1.   **Toast 3 tablespoons allspice berries, 3 crumbled bay
leaves, 1 stick cinnamon, and 2 teaspoons black peppercorns in a dry pan until aromatic. Cool, then grind.**

 2.   **Whisk together 1/2 cup malt or cider vinegar, 1/2 cup
water, 1 or more Scotch bonnet or 2 jalapeño chiles
(seeded and thinly sliced), and 1 bunch thinly sliced
scallions. Stir in the spices.**

 3.   **Mix the marinade with 5 pounds cut-up bone-in chicken
and marinate overnight, covered, in the refrigerator.**

 4.   **Light a charcoal grill. Drain the chicken, pat dry, and
brush lightly with oil. Grill indirectly with the grill
covered for about 20 minutes per side. Alternatively,
roast the chicken at 425°F for 30 to 40 minutes.**

Serving   Season marinated herring, pickled vegetables, pâtés,
Suggestions: and smoked meats with allspice. • Add a few whole
berries (not powdered, which will darken the color) to
poaching liquid for fruit, removing before serving. •
Mix a few allspice berries with peppercorns in a pepper mill for aromatic pepper.

| Food Affinities: | Apple, chicken, chocolate, goat, peach, pear, pickled fish, plum, pork, pumpkin, rum, sausage, tomato. |

43. **ALMOND AND BITTER ALMOND**

| Other Names: | **Bitter almond:** *Almendra amara* (Spanish); *amande amère* (French); *amêndoa amarga* (Portuguese); *bittermandel* (German); *ku wei bian tao* (Chinese); *lawz murr* (Arabic); *mandorla amara* (Italian); *pikromygdalo* (Greek). |

| General Description: | *Bitter almonds are the seeds of the small, light green almond fruits of the bitter almond tree* (Amygdalus communis amara), *with an enticing, bittersweet aroma.* Almond fruits are leathery and can only be eaten when immature, in early spring. Bitter almonds contain hydrocyanic acid, making them poisonous. In the United States, it's illegal to sell bitter almonds; they are sold in Europe, where they're added in small quantities to marzipan, amaretti biscuits, and amaretto liqueur. |

Almonds, the nuts of the almond tree (*Amygdalus communis*), have long been cultivated in the Mediterranean; further north, the trees do not thrive. Due to centuries of cultivation and breeding, sweet almonds are very low in the amygdalin found in bitter almond fruits. However, even sweet almond trees sometimes yield bitter almonds (up to 1 percent), and some sweet almond cultivars contain traces of bitter almond aroma.

Marzipan, a well-kneaded mixture of finely ground almonds and sugar often molded into various shapes, has a long history in Europe and the Arab world. Almond paste is similar to marzipan but is less sweet and coarser in texture; it's used for baking. Bitter almonds and almond extract are used mostly for sweets and, because they are so concentrated, always in small quantities. Delicate and expensive, almond oil is extracted from bitter or sweet almonds and used in baking.

Purchase and Avoid:
"Pure almond extract" derives from bitter almonds, "natural extract" usually contains benzaldehyde produced from cassia bark, and "imitation extract" contains synthetic benzaldehyde.

Note:
The poisonous hydrocyanic acid contained in bitter almonds breaks down when heated, so the poison is unlikely to accumulate when used in any cooked dish. It is unwise to eat raw bitter almonds. Serious almond poisoning is rare in adults, but children may die after eating just a few bitter almonds.

Recipe: **Chinese Almond Cookies**

 1. **Preheat the oven to 300°F. Grease 2 baking sheets.**

 2. **Beat 1 cup (½ pound) lard or vegetable shortening (at room temperature) with 1 cup granulated sugar until creamy. Beat in 1 tablespoon almond extract and a**

pinch of salt, then beat in 3 cups all-purpose flour, a little at a time. The dough will be crumbly.

3. Shape spoonfuls of dough into flat, round cookies about 2 inches in diameter. (The edges of the cookies will have cracks.) Transfer to the prepared pans.

 4. Beat together 1 egg yolk and 2 tablespoons water and brush it atop the cookies. Press a whole blanched almond into the center of each cookie.

5. Bake for 30 minutes, or until lightly golden. Cool slightly, then transfer to a wire rack to cool fully. Store in an airtight container. Makes 4 dozen.

Serving Suggestions: Add pure almond extract to almond custard sauce or ice cream to intensify its flavor. • Use pure almond extract to flavor pound cake, angel food cake, sponge cake, or cookies. • Add a few drops of pure almond extract to fruit salad.

Food Affinities: Apricot, cherry, cream, honey, lemon, nectarine, orange, peach, plum, sugar, vanilla.

44. **AMCHUR**

Other Names: *Aamchur* (Hindi); amchoor; *anbeh* (Farsi); *karino* (Gujarati); *ma mouang* (Thai); *manga* (Portuguese);

mango; *mangue* (French); *manguey* (Spanish); *manja* (Arabic); *mwembe* (Swahili); *thayet* (Burmese).

General
Description:

Amchur, a pale gray to light yellow powder made from dried unripe mangos (Mangifera indica)*, is used as a spice in northern India for its subtle, tart, and slightly resinous flavor and souring capabilities.* The name means mango (*am*) powder (*chur*). To make amchur, the fruit of an unripe mango is cut in slices, dried, and ground to a powder. A bit of ground turmeric is often blended in, giving the powder a yellow tint. Amchur is used for a hint of tartness or when the dark brown color of tamarind, another Indian souring spice, is undesirable. Amchur is mostly used to season vegetables, but it can also be found in spice mixtures for tandoor-barbecued meat, where it also serves as a tenderizer.

Purchase
and Avoid:

Buy preground amchur in small amounts because the flavor will diminish within 1 year.

Recipe: **South Indian Spiced Chickpeas**

 1. **Heat 2 tablespoons vegetable oil, add 1 cup chopped onions, and fry until light brown. Add 2 teaspoons each chopped garlic and ginger, and fry for 2 minutes, stirring.**

2. **Stir in 2 teaspoons ground coriander, ½ teaspoon ground cardamom, and 1 teaspoon amchur. Stir-fry for 2 minutes or until fragrant.**

3. **Add 1 diced tomato, 1 15-ounce can of chickpeas with their liquid, and salt and pepper to taste. Cook 10 minutes longer or until thickened. Serve garnished with thinly sliced red onion and minced green chile.**

Serving
Suggestions:
Substitute amchur for lemon juice in marinades, especially for fish, seafood, vegetables, or chicken, using 1 teaspoon amchur for 3 tablespoons lemon juice. • Use amchur to flavor vegetable curries, chutneys, marinades, dipping sauces, soups, and stews.

Food
Affinities:
Chicken, chickpeas, chutney, coriander, cumin, fish, pickles, seafood, vegetable curry, yogurt.

 45 a–b.

ANARDANA

Other Names:
Anar (Farsi); *anardana* (Hindi); *granada* (Spanish); *granat* (Russian); *granatapfel* (German); *grenade* (French); *komamanga* (Swahili); *melograna* (Italian); *milgraym* (Yiddish); pomegranate powder; *rodia* (Greek); *romā* (Portuguese); *rumman* (Arabic); *shiliupi* (Chinese); *tap tim* (Thai).

General
Description:
Anardana is the dried seeds of varieties of pomegranate (Punica granatum) *too sour to eat as fresh fruit; they have a tangy, fruity flavor.* The wild pomegranate called daru, which grows in the southern Himalayas, is reputed to yield the best anardana. Though used

mostly for vegetables and legumes, anardana also flavors Moghul-style meat dishes. Grenadine, reduced pomegranate juice, is used in India to marinate meat, acting as a tenderizer because of the enzymes it contains. It's not the same as grenadine syrup, a sweet red liquid, all too often artificially colored and flavored, used for many cocktails. Pomegranate molasses is a thick reduction of the juice of a tart variety of pomegranate. In the Middle East, it's used for salads and marinades; in Iran it goes into *fesenjan*, chicken in walnut-pomegranate sauce; in Armenia and Georgia, it's used to make sauces for kebabs.

Purchase and Avoid:
Buy anardana powder for ease of use; buy anardana seeds for texture and good keeping qualities. Pomegranate molasses is available in Middle Eastern groceries.

Recipe:
Mint and Anardana Chutney

1. **Combine 1 cup thick plain yogurt, the juice of 1 lemon, 1 small green chile pepper (seeded and chopped), 1 tablespoon grated ginger, 2 teaspoons ground cumin, and 2 tablespoons anardana powder and blend until smooth.**

2. **Add 1 generous cup each mint and cilantro leaves in two batches and blend until chunky. Season with salt to taste. Refrigerate in a covered jar up to 1 week.**

Serving Suggestions:	Add anardana powder to Indian spiced chickpeas. • Drizzle pomegranate molasses over crepes or gelato. • Marinate shrimp with garlic, ginger, turmeric, lemon, coriander, garam masala, cumin, chiles, fenugreek, and anardana powder, then grill.
Food Affinities:	Apple, beans, bulgur, chicken, chickpeas, cilantro, cream cheese, eggplant, ginger, lentils, mint, parsley, scallion, shrimp, turkey.

46.   **ANISE**

Other Names:	*Anason* (Turkish); *anice verde* (Italian); *anis* (German, Hebrew, Norwegian, Swedish); *anís* (Spanish); *anis verde* (Portuguese); *anis vert* (French); aniseed; *anison* (Greek); *anisu* (Japanese); *cay vi* (Vietnamese); *huei-hsiang* (Chinese); *jinten manis* (Indonesian); *kamoon halou* (Arabic); *saunf* (Hindi); sweet cumin.
General Description:	*Anise* (Pimpinella anisum) *has small sage green to yellow ochre crescent-shaped seeds similar to caraway in appearance, with a distinct sweet though not overpowering licorice flavor.* Anise is native to the Middle East and is widely cultivated in temperate regions of northern Africa, Greece, southern Russia, Malta, Spain, Italy, Mexico, and Central America. Highly regarded in first-century Rome, anise was eaten after the meal in cakes to aid digestion and freshen the

breath. Anise is widely used in the manufacture of sweets, cough drops, and, most importantly, in a variety of liqueurs: Italian anisette, Spanish and Latin American aguardiente, Turkish raki, Greek ouzo, and French Pernod, although in many cases less expensive oil of star anise is substituted for all or part of the anise oil.

In Western cuisine, anise is mostly used for breads, cakes, and cookies. It shows up in Indian curry recipes and Mexican recipes with a Spanish heritage. Though fennel and anise are similar in flavor, in Italy fennel is traditionally reserved for savory foods like fresh pork sausage, while anise goes into all sorts of sweets, such as pizzelle cookies.

Purchase and Avoid:	Anise seed is best purchased whole, as the ground powder quickly loses its flavor.
Storage:	Whole anise seed keeps up to 3 years. Dry-roast anise seeds to heighten their aroma and make them brittle and easy to crush. Store ground anise in a clean, dry jar and use within 6 months.
Recipe:	***Broiled Summer Fruit with Anise-Honey Butter***

  1. Combine ¹/₄ pound softened unsalted butter, 1 tablespoon ground anise seed, ¹/₄ cup honey, and the inner scrapings of 1 split vanilla bean in a food processor. Process until smooth and creamy; set aside.

2. **Prepare an assortment of summer fruit, including quartered figs; sliced peaches, plums, and apricots; pitted and halved cherries; diced mango and papaya; sliced red bananas; halved strawberries; and whole raspberries, blackberries, and blueberries.**

 3. **Preheat the broiler. Spread the fruit out on a metal baking pan. Spoon bits of the butter mixture over, using about half of the butter. (Refrigerate the remainder for another use.) Broil the fruit for 5 to 8 minutes, or until the fruit is bubbling and browned. Serve with pound cake, angel food cake, shortbread cookies, or vanilla ice cream.**

Serving Suggestions: Make biscotti with walnuts, diced figs, and ground anise seeds. • Simmer carrots with a little sugar, butter, ground anise seeds, salt, and pepper until tender. • Toast anise seeds in hot oil and pour over cooked lentils, Indian-style, as a fragrant, sizzling garnish.

Food Affinities: Almond, apricot, black pepper, butter, eggs, fig, honey, lemon zest, orange zest, peach, sugar, walnut, vanilla.

47. **ANNATTO**

Other Names: *Açafroa-do-Brasil* or *anato* (Portuguese); achiote; achote; *achuete* (Tagalog); *annatto* or *orleanstrauch* (German); *anotto* (Italian); *beninoki* (Japanese); *hot dieu mau*

(Vietnamese); *jarak belanda* (Malay); *kam tai* (Thai); *kesumba* (Indonesian); *latkhan* or *sendri* (Hindi); lipstick tree; natural color E1606; *roucou* (French).

General
Description:

The dark red seeds of the annatto tree (Bixa orellana)*, a tropical evergreen, are used mainly for the deep reddish orange color they impart.* Annatto, native to Latin America, is now cultivated in many tropical countries, especially the Philippines. In Europe, annatto was used to deepen the color of chocolate until the seventeenth century. In Mexico, annatto colors stews, sauces, and tacos. In the Yucatán, annatto is combined with other spices to make brick red seasoning pastes: achiote paste and adobo (both page 277). In the United States and Europe, annatto provides natural color for butter and cheeses such as orange Cheddars, English red Cheshire, and the red wax coating for Dutch Edam.

In the Caribbean, the seeds are usually heated in lard or oil to extract their color; the yellowish orange oil is strained and used as a cooking fat. In the Philippines, it goes into *pipian*, a dish of chicken and pork. The Chinese use it to color roast pork. In Vietnam, annatto is added to frying batters and coconut-based curries for its color. A Vietnamese version of Beijing duck (*ga quay mat ong*) uses annatto oil to color the bird's skin.

Purchase
and Avoid:

For simmering in oil, purchase whole annatto seeds that are uniformly dark brick red without any flaky pieces of dried pulp. Purchase ground annatto for mixing into sauces or making seasoning pastes; the whole seeds are quite hard and difficult to pulverize.

Recipe: ***Annatto Oil***

 1. **Toast ½ cup annatto seeds in a dry pan until they just start to smoke.**

 2. **Pour 2 cups mild olive oil or other vegetable oil into a small pot and add the toasted annatto seeds. Heat until the oil just begins to bubble. Remove from the heat and allow to cool.**

 3. **Strain the oil, cool, and store in an airtight container in a cool, dark place up to 3 months.**

Serving Suggestions: Use annatto oil for frying vegetables, fish, poultry, and pork. • Use powdered annatto to color vegetable curries, Chinese-style roast pork, or chicken, vegetable, or pork stews. • Color beer batter or other frying batters with a little powdered annatto.

Food Affinities: Allspice, bitter orange, butter, cheese, chicken, chiles, cinnamon, cumin, garlic, lime, oregano, paprika, plantain, pork, shrimp, sweet potato, taro, tuna, yautia, yuca.

48. **ASAFETIDA**

Other Names: *Anghuzeh* (Farsi); *asafétida* (Spanish); asafoetida; *a-wei* (Chinese); *aza* (Greek); devil's dung; *férule persique* or *merde du diable* (French); *haltit* or *tyib* (Arabic); *hing* (Hindi); *mvuje* (Swahili); *stinkasant* or *teufelsdreck* (German); stinking gum.

General Description:

The notorious asafetida is the strong-smelling, even stinking, dried brownish resin extracted from the root of a plant (Ferula assafoetida) *that grows wild from the eastern Mediterranean to central Asia.* Asafetida gets its name from two languages: *assa* from the Farsi meaning "resin", and *foetidus*, Latin for "stinky" (hence, *fetid*). Fresh asafetida resin is indeed powerful; it can be unpleasant to the uninitiated but stimulating to its fans.

Stone Age nomad tribes may have used the hollow stems to transport fire between their camps. Two thousand years ago, asafetida was used in Greek and Roman cuisines, and it continued to be used though the early Middle Ages in Europe for dishes like roast mutton before disappearing from European cookery. In central Asia, especially India and Iran, asafetida has remained an important culinary spice and herbal medicine. In India, some people don't eat onions and garlic for religious reasons, substituting asafetida instead; however, in northern Indian cooking, asafetida is often combined with either garlic or onion. In southern India, asafetida is even more popular and shows up in the Tamil spice mixture sambar podi (page 280), which generally seasons vegetables, not meats, because vegetarianism is more prevalent in southern India.

Purchase and Avoid: For stronger flavor, buy asafetida resin; for a milder spice that's easier to use, buy powdered asafetida. Yellow asafetida is milder than brown.

Storage: Powdered asafetida loses its aroma after about 1 year, but the resin lasts indefinitely.

Note: Asafetida resin is powerful and must be used in tiny amounts (a pea-sized bit will flavor a large pot of food). Always fry the resin quickly in hot oil so that it dissolves and disperses throughout the food, and to transform the flavor to make it more appealing.

Recipe: *Mushrooms with Asafetida*

 1. **Heat 2 tablespoons vegetable oil in a large pot and add a generous pinch of ground asafetida or a small lump of asafetida resin to the oil and allow it to sizzle and color for a few seconds.**

 2. **As soon as the asafetida darkens, add 1½ pounds trimmed and quartered mushrooms, 2 small dried red chile peppers, ½ teaspoon turmeric, 1 cup crushed tomatoes, and salt to taste.**

3. **Cover, lower the heat, and simmer for 15 to 20 minutes, or until the liquid has been absorbed.**

Serving
Suggestions:

Add a pinch of asafetida to the pan when frying onions and garlic for curry. • Fry a pinch of asafetida and add to lamb, mushrooms, chickpeas, lentils, split peas, or other legumes.

Food
Affinities:

Beans, chickpeas, garlic, lamb, lentils, mushroom, onion, split peas, turmeric.

49a–c. 📷 **AUSTRALIAN NATIVE SPICES**

Other Names:

Wattleseed: *Arrilya, juntala,* or *nyurrinpa* (Aboriginal); colony wattle; prickly wattle. **Akudjura:** *Akatyerre* or *akutjera* (Aboriginal); bush tomato; desert raisin. **Tasmanian pepper:** *Australischer pfeffer* or *Tasmanischer pfeffer* (German); *bergpeper* (Dutch); mountain pepper; mountain pepperleaf; native pepperberry; *poivre indigène* (French).

General
Description:

Australia has a variety of unusual and delicious native spices that season bush food, creative cookery using native Australian foods. Akudjura (*Solanum centrale*), native to Australia's arid regions, yields tiny tomato-like berries that are yellow when fresh. They taste similar to sun-dried tomatoes with an added sweet tone of caramel. The spice is usually sold in its dried form either whole, resembling raisins in size and texture, or as a brownish red powder. Akudjura works well in place of sun-dried tomatoes and is used to flavor sauces for meats and poultry.

Tasmanian pepper (*Tasmannia lanceolata*) is a dark blue to black dried berry that resembles black peppercorns in size and color, with a distinctive woody aroma. Its hot peppery taste is a cross between chile and peppercorn. The berries, hand picked from a shrub that grows in the cool, wet climate of Tasmania, are dried and milled. Their complex flavor is initially sweet, followed by a quick, intense pungency that gives way to a numbness similar to that induced by Szechuan pepper, with a mineral-like aftertaste. Because Tasmanian pepper is quite potent, use only about 10 percent as much as you would black pepper.

Dorrigo pepper (*T. stipitata*) is closely related to Tasmanian pepper and has a unique sharp, hot, spicy flavor reminiscent of black pepper and cinnamon. Dorrigo pepper flourishes in the Dorrigo Mountains of northern New South Wales. For hot flavor, add Dorrigo pepper at the end of cooking; for milder flavor, add during cooking.

Wattleseed (*Acacia victoriae* and *A. murrayana*) comes from several of the more than seven hundred species of *Acacia*—most of which are poisonous—that grow over much of central Australia. It has a flavor that combines coffee, chocolate, and hazelnut. These small brown seeds are in high demand in Australia for their delicious flavor; they appear in pastries, breads, and other desserts and are used to make a coffeelike beverage. To prepare it, wattleseed is roasted in a process similar to roasting coffee and then ground to a dark brown, grainy powder that resembles coffee grounds.

Purchase and Avoid:

Although the color of akudjura can vary according to the amount of rain when it was grown, this has no effect on quality. Look for akudjura with a consistency no softer than a raisin. Purchase Tasmanian and Dorrigo pepper whole, ground, or blended with black and white peppercorns. Wattleseed is relatively expensive because it is mostly gathered from the wild and requires time-consuming processing.

Storage:

Whole akudjura will keep well for several months; buy small amounts of ground akudjura as it is more perishable. Powdered akudjura may form clumps from the oils present; as long as the powder feels dry, it's fine. Whole wattleseed is best used within 2 years; ground wattleseed is more perishable.

Recipe:

Akudjura-Crusted Ribeye Steak

1. **Spread 2 tablespoons ground akudjura combined with kosher salt and black pepper to taste onto both sides of 4 rib-eye steaks or salmon fillets.**

2. **Heat a heavy skillet (preferably cast-iron) until it just begins to smoke. Add a little oil, then place the steaks in the skillet. Sear them on both sides until the akudjura caramelizes, reducing the heat, if necessary, to cook the steaks to the desired doneness. Transfer the steaks to a platter, cover with aluminum foil, and allow to rest for 5 to 10 minutes so the juices are evenly distributed. Remove foil and serve.**

Serving Suggestions: Use wattleseed to flavor cakes, chocolates, and cream desserts, such as panna cotta or crème brûlée. • Add akudjura to tomato sauce, pizza, or tomato soup to enhance the flavor of tomatoes. • Marinate meat with a mixture of crushed Tasmanian pepper and vegetable oil before grilling or frying. • Season long-cooked stews and pasta dishes with Tasmanian pepper just before serving. • Use Dorrigo pepper to season pasta, salty cheeses, vegetable and cheese dips, mustards, pâtés, sauces, and soups.

Food Affinities: **Akudjura:** Antipasto, beef, bread, cheese, pesto, potato, salads, salmon, soups, tomato. **Tasmanian pepper:** Beef, emu, hamburgers, kangaroo, pasta. **Dorrigo pepper:** Cheese, dips, mustard, pasta, pâté, sauces. **Wattleseed:** Brown sugar, chocolate, coffee, cream, custard, hazelnut, praline, sugar, vanilla.

50.   **BARBERRY**

Other Names: *Agracejo* (Spanish); *berberis* (Arabic); berbery; *épine vinette* (French); European berbery; holy thorn; pipperidge bush; sowberry; *zereshk* (Farsi).

General Description: *Barberries* (Berberis vulgaris) *grow in elongated clusters; when dried the bright red berries resemble miniature red currants and are used in cooking for their pleasantly acidic taste and fruity aroma.* There are many species of the genus *Berberis*, some of which are poisonous. Because barberry is host to a type of rust that affects wheat, it has long been unpopular with farmers; it was responsible for famines in early tenth-century Spain. Early American settlers preserved barberries in syrup or vinegar and made them into jelly. *Confiture d'épine vinette*, a celebrated French jam that's a specialty of Rouen and Dijon, is made from a seedless form of barberry; a liqueur is made from this seedless variety, too. In Afghan and Iranian cooking, barberry flavors rice dishes, and in Iran it's used in *kookoo-ye sabzi* (an herb omelet) and *polow* (rice pilaf). In India, pickled barberries are served with curries or used like raisins in desserts.

Purchase and Avoid: Purchase dried barberries only from a reputable merchant, because some species are poisonous. Look for moist, red to dark red dried barberries; the red color darkens with age as they oxidize.

Storage: Store airtight in the freezer to maintain bright color
            and freshness.

Recipe: ***Zereshk Polow (Iranian Chicken and Rice with***
            Barberries)

 1. **Soak 2 cups basmati rice in cold salted water for sev-
            eral hours.**

2. **Season 8 boneless, skinless chicken thighs with salt and
    pepper. In a large frying pan, fry 2 thinly sliced onions
    in 1 tablespoon butter until lightly colored. Remove
    onions from pan and reserve. Add 1 more tablespoon
    butter and sprinkle the chicken with 1 teaspoon
    turmeric. Brown the chicken gently on both sides. Add
    1 cup water and simmer, uncovered, for 20 minutes, or
    until the chicken is tender and the liquid is syrupy.**

3. **Remove the chicken from the pot and cool, separately
    reserving the cooking liquid and onions. Remove the
    chicken meat from the bones, discarding the bones.**

 4. **Soak ¹/₂ teaspoon saffron in a little milk until brightly
    colored, then whisk in ¹/₂ cup plain yogurt, 1 egg, and
    the chicken meat. Set aside.**

 5. **Wash 2 ounces barberries well, drain, and cook in a
    small pan with 2 tablespoons butter and 1 tablespoon
    sugar for several minutes, stirring, or until plump.**

6. **Drain the soaked rice and rinse under cold water. Bring 6 cups salted water to a boil, add the rice, and cook for 5 minutes. Drain and rinse with cold water.**

7. **Preheat the oven to 300°F. Brush a large casserole with 2 tablespoons butter and spread in half the rice. Arrange the chicken mixture over the rice. Combine the barberry mixture with the remaining rice and spread over the chicken. Spoon the reserved onions with liquid over the rice. Cover tightly and bake for 1 hour, or until the rice is fluffy. Remove from oven. Rest the casserole for 15 minutes before serving.**

Serving Suggestions: Add to stewed fruits or to apple pie filling. • Substitute a few barberries for raisins in fruitcakes and pies.

Food Affinities: Almond, apple, chicken, duck, game, lamb, onion, orange, rice, saffron, veal, venison, yogurt.

51. **CAPERS**

Other Names: *Alcaparra* or *tápana* (Spanish); *alcaparras* (Portuguese); caper berries; *cappero* (Italian); *câpre, fabagelle,* or *tapana* (French); *kabar* (Arabic); *kaper* (German); *kapersy* (Russian); *kappari* (Greek); *kappertjes* (Dutch); *kebere* (Turkish); *keipa* (Japanese); *kiari* or *kobra* (Hindi); *lussef* (Egyptian); *mchezo* or *mruko* (Swahili); *tsalaf qotsani* (Hebrew).

General Description:	*Capers are the small, round, pickled or salted unopened flower buds of a spiny plant* (Capparis spinosa) *that grows wild all over the Mediterranean.* Capers are cultivated in France, Spain, Italy, Algeria, Iran, and Greece, and grow profusely in Cyprus. Once cured by salting, brining, or pickling in vinegar, the caper develops its palate-wakening pungent, astringent flavor and spicy fragrance.

Caperberries are the teardrop-shaped pickled fruit of the caper bush with a flavor similar to capers, though stronger. They are most common in Spain, which is also the main producer; they work well for cooked dishes. *Pantelleria* are a prized variety of caper grown on the island of the same name, which lies between Sicily and Tunisia. These extra-large capers, usually cured in salt, are plump, juicy, and highly aromatic. The fruits of the related central Asian species Indian caper (*Capparis aphylla*) are sometimes pickled and used as a flavoring in Afghanistan, Pakistan, and parts of India.

Capers were introduced by the Spaniards to Latin America, where they appear in beef or pork *picadillo*, a highly seasoned mixture of ground meat, capers, green olives, raisins, and spices.

Purchase and Avoid:	The smaller the caper bud, the higher the cost. The smallest capers are called *nonpareilles*, followed in increasing size by *surfines*, *fines*, *mi-fines*, *capucines*, and *communes*. Capers packed in layers of salt, similar to salt-packed anchovies, rather than in brine, are preferred by some connoisseurs, as their full-bodied

fragrance and firm texture are maintained. Very large, inexpensive "capers" are most likely pickled nasturtium buds rather than true capers.

Storage: Once the jar has been opened, it must be refrigerated. Keep capers submerged in their brine, removing them from the jar with a clean stainless steel fork.

Recipe: *Piccata di Pollo (Chicken Cutlets with Lemon and Caper Sauce)*

 1. Heat 2 tablespoons each butter and olive oil in a large skillet until shimmering hot. Meanwhile, season four 3-ounce chicken cutlets with salt and pepper, then dust with flour, shaking off any excess.

2. Brown the chicken on both sides, 1 to 2 minutes per side. Transfer to a plate. Pour off any fat, add ¼ cup dry white vermouth to the pan, and deglaze, scraping up any browned bits. Add ¼ cup chicken stock and cook until syrupy.

 3. Add 1 thinly sliced, seeded lemon and 2 tablespoons drained capers and cook for a few minutes, until the sauce has thickened slightly.

 4. Season to taste with pepper and a bit of salt (capers are salty), then swirl in 2 tablespoons unsalted butter and sprinkle with chopped Italian parsley. Return the

**chicken to the pan for 1 to 2 minutes to reheat, then
serve immediately.**

Serving Suggestions:	Use capers to flavor Italian puttanesca sauce for pasta or French rémoulade for vegetables, meats, or fish. • Garnish smoked salmon with chopped red onion, capers, and chopped hard-boiled egg. • Make Montpellier butter with anchovies, capers, and blanched tender herbs such as tarragon, chervil, and chives and use to top fish and poultry.
Food Affinities:	Anchovy, butter, chicken, cured black olives, eggs, garlic, olive oil, orange, parsley, pork, red onion, red wine, salt cod, smoked salmon, tarragon, thyme, tomato, veal, white wine.

CARAWAY

Other Names:	*Alcaravea* or *carvi* (Spanish); *alcaravia* (Portuguese); *caro* or *carvi* (Italian); carvies; *cumin des prés* or *grains de carvi* (French); *hom pom* (Thai); *karawiya* (Arabic); *karo* or *karvi* (Greek); *karvia* (Hebrew); *kiml* (Yiddish); *kisibiti* (Swahili); *kümmel* (German); *saksankumina tmin* (Russian); *shia jeera* or *vilayati jeera* (Hindi); wild cumin; *yuan sui* (Chinese).
General Description:	*Caraway* (Carum carvi) *has tiny, crescent-shaped fruits (commonly called* seeds*); their color is warm brown with*

pale yellow edges. Caraway seeds have a warm, earthy, robust flavor with an edge of sharp bitterness and a hint of anise. Caraway is the most typical spice of northern, central, and eastern Europe, found in the cooking of Germany, Holland, Hungary, Russia, Sweden, and the former Yugoslavia. Caraway was believed to prevent lovers from straying, and for this same reason it was fed to homing pigeons to encourage them to return to their coops.

Caraway seeds are commonly sprinkled on top of Jewish-style rye bread and are used to flavor kümmel, a German sweet liqueur, and Scandinavian aquavit. Caraway gives southern German and Austrian foods, from breads and cheeses to roast pork and vegetables like turnips and potatoes, their characteristic flavor; it's used in similar ways in Scandinavia and the Baltic states. Caraway is best suited to savory foods, though it's also sprinkled on spice cakes and added to cookie dough. The use of caraway jumps from central Europe to North Africa, especially Tunisia, skipping southern Europe, where it is practically unknown. In Tunisia, caraway is essential to harissa (page 282), a fiery chile and garlic paste.

Purchase and Avoid: Dutch caraway is considered to be of top quality. Most caraway is sold as whole seeds; if a recipe calls for ground caraway, grind the seeds in small amounts using a clean coffee grinder.

Recipe: ***Cabbage Borscht with Caraway***

1. Place 3 pounds chopped top rib of beef (or beef shin) in a large soup pot. Cover with 2 quarts chicken stock and 1 quart cold water and bring to a boil. Reduce the heat to low, skim as necessary, and simmer 1 hour.

2. Add 2 cups chopped onions; 1 tablespoon chopped garlic; 1 (2½ to 3 pound) green cabbage, cored and shredded; 1 15-ounce can chopped plum tomatoes; and 1 tablespoon ground caraway. Bring back to a boil, then reduce heat again and simmer 2 hours, covered.

3. Remove the beef from the soup. Cool and then pick the meat from the bones, discarding the bones, fat, and any connective tissue. Shred the beef and add it back to the soup along with ¼ cup fresh lemon juice and 2 tablespoons dark brown sugar. Season to taste with salt and pepper.

4. Cool and then refrigerate the soup overnight. The next day, remove and discard the hardened fat from the top of the soup. Reheat, seasoning if necessary with a little more salt, lemon juice, and sugar.

Serving Suggestions: Season sauerkraut dishes with caraway seeds. • Serve Muenster cheese sprinkled with caraway seeds.

<table>
<tr><td>Food
Affinities:</td><td>Apple, bacon, beef, butter, cabbage, duck, garlic,
Muenster and Gouda cheese, potato, red chiles, rye
bread, sausage, sour cream, turnip, vinegar.</td></tr>
</table>

53a–b.

CARDAMOM

Other Names:

Green cardamom: *Bach dau khau* (Vietnamese); *cardamome* (French); *cardamomo* (Italian, Portuguese, Spanish), *elaichi* (Hindi); *grüner cardamom* (German); *hal* (Arabic); *hamama* or *kakule meyvesi* (Turkish); *hel* (Farsi, Hebrew); *kakoules* or *kardamo* (Greek); *kapulaga* (Indonesian); *kardemomme* (Danish, Norwegian); *kravanh* (Thai); *pai-tou-k'ou* (Chinese). **Black cardamom:** *Badi* or *kali elaichi* (Hindi); bastard cardamom; brown cardamom; *cao guo* (Chinese); *cardamome du Népal* or *cardamome noir* (French); *cardamomo negro* (Spanish); *cardamomo nero* (Italian); false cardamom; greater Indian cardamom; *hal aswad* (Arabic); large cardamom; Nepal cardamom; *schwarzer cardamom* (German); winged cardamom.

General
Description:

Green cardamom (Elettaria cardamomum) *is a seed generally sold enclosed in its fibrous lantern-shaped pod.* The outer pods of green cardamom may be light green or white, depending on whether they've been bleached; the inner seeds are small, angular, oily, and brownish black. Called "queen of the spices" in India, cardamom is native to the mountains of southwest

India and to Sri Lanka and was not grown elsewhere until about one hundred years ago, when German immigrants brought cardamom to Guatemala, now the largest producer. Because cardamom pods ripen at different times, they must be picked by hand, making it the world's third-most-expensive spice after saffron and vanilla. Cardamom has a delicately fragrant, slightly astringent, warming quality with notes of pungent camphor and eucalyptus.

There are two different varieties of green cardamom. Malabar, a small round capsule with a high percentage of delicate flowery compounds, develops its best flavor when the pods have begun to turn from green to off-white. Mysore cardamom, a larger, three-angled capsule with more resinous pine and eucalyptus notes, is often sold green.

In Scandinavia, cardamom is used in cookies, sweet breads, pastries, and sausage. Elsewhere in Europe, cardamom is rare, though it does flavor cookies like German *lebkuchen*. In northern India's Moghul cuisine, the pods are fried and added to rice *biriyanis* and mild meat dishes. In Sri Lanka, the pods are added to fiery beef or chicken curries, while cardamom-flavored sweets are found all over the Indian subcontinent.

Bedouins have special coffeepots that hold a few cardamom pods in their spouts, flavoring the coffee as it trickles through the pods. In Ethiopia, coffee is toasted immediately before use, often with spices such as cardamom. Cardamom is a popular spice in northern and eastern Africa, and it appears in Moroccan ras el hanout (page 286) and Ethiopian berberé (page 278). Cardamom is frequently added to northern Indian garam masala (page 283), and Indian chai masala (tea spices; page 283).

Black cardamom, the seed of a cardamom relative (*Amomum subulatum*) that grows in the eastern Himalayas, is enclosed in large, oblong, dark brown pods that are ribbed on the edges (the ribs are sometimes called *wings*). Black cardamom may also refer to several cardamom-related plants grown in the mountains from central Africa to Vietnam, such as Siam cardamom (*A. krervanh*). Black cardamom is much stronger than green cardamom, with a bold, resinous, and smoky flavor; much of the crop is smoke-dried, and the seeds are rich in penetrating aromatics. Black cardamom is used in India in spicy and rustic dishes, in western Asia in savory dishes and to season pickles, and in Sichuan province in central China, where it goes into slow-simmered beef stews.

Purchase and Avoid:

Purchase whole cardamom: The seeds lose their flavor quickly when ground; even whole cardamom loses about 40 percent of its essential oil per year. Choose green cardamom pods that are lime green, not pale or washed out. Note that some green cardamom is bleached for sale, although this practice is dying out. Avoid powdered cardamom unless it has been recently ground. If you buy ground cardamom, it should be dark pearl gray; light-colored and fibrous cardamom is ground from the whole pods, not the seeds alone. The whole inner seeds are sold in Indian groceries.

Recipe: *Mashed Sweet Potatoes with Ginger, Cardamom, and Honey*

1. Steam 2 pounds of peeled and diced sweet potatoes with 1/2 pound of peeled and diced baking potatoes until quite soft, about 20 minutes.

2. Meanwhile, in a small saucepan, combine 2 tablespoons honey, 1/4 cup grated ginger, 4 tablespoons unsalted butter, 1 teaspoon ground cardamom, and salt and black pepper to taste. Heat to simmering.

3. Drain the potatoes and mash them together, gradually beating in the honey mixture.

Serving Suggestions: Flavor Danish pastry dough, cakes, cookies, and fruit desserts with cardamom. • Sprinkle grapefruit halves with brown sugar mixed with cardamom, then broil. • Make Arabic cardamom coffee by boiling together freshly roasted, finely ground coffee with several bruised green cardamom pods.

Food Affinities: Apple, banana, chicken, cinnamon, cloves, coffee, cream, curry, honey, lamb, lemon, lime, mango, milk, orange, peach, pear, plum, rice, sugar, tea, vanilla.

54a–b. 📷 **CELERY SEED**

Other Names: *Aipo* (Portuguese); *ajmoda* (Hindi); *apio* (Spanish); *céleri* (French); *chin* or *kan-tsai* (Chinese); *karafs* (Arabic); *kin chai* (Thai); *sedano* (Italian); *selderij* (Dutch); *sellerie* (German); *serori* (Japanese); smallage; *syel' derey* (Russian); wild celery.

General Description: *Celery seeds are light brown to khaki in color with a penetrating, haylike aroma reminiscent, not surprisingly, of freshly cut celery stalks and with a strong, bitter, warm, lingering, and penetrating astringent flavor.* The seeds are gathered from the ancient, hardy marsh plant known as smallage or wild celery (*Apium graveolens*). Celery seeds marry perfectly with tomato and are essential to mixed vegetables juices. Many popular commercial spice blends for poultry and meat rely on celery seed. The dried or young fresh leaves of cultivated celery sold as celery flakes can be added to salads, sandwiches, and soups for a mild celery flavor.

Celeriac or celery root (*A. graveolens rapaceum*) is grown for its enlarged roots, which can be dried and ground with salt as another type of celery seasoning. Leaf celery (*A. graveolens secalinum*) closely resembles wild celery, and its abundance of erect-growing leaves can be cut like parsley and used to flavor soups and stews.

Purchase and Avoid: Because of their tiny size, celery seeds are generally used whole, and it is best to purchase them in that form. Ground celery seed quickly loses its aromatic notes, leaving a bitter flavor in their place. Celery salt is made of 3 parts salt and 2 parts ground celery seed, and the blend may include herbs such as parsley and dill.

Recipe: ***Sweet and Sour Celery Seed Salad Dressing***

1. **Grate 1 small sweet or white onion. Whisk in a small bowl with ¼ cup sugar, 6 tablespoons apple cider vinegar, 2 teaspoons celery seeds, and 2 teaspoons dry mustard.**

2. **Beat in 1 cup mild oil, such as grapeseed oil, and salt and black pepper to taste. Use the dressing on spinach salad, grated carrot salad, or potato salad. Makes about 1½ cups.**

Serving Suggestions: Use celery salt in Bloody Marys and to season roast beef, roast pork, and meatloaf. • Add celery seed to the mayonnaise dressing for coleslaw or tuna, turkey, chicken, or egg salad. • Season the boiling liquid for hard-shell crabs or shrimp with either celery seed or celery salt.

Food Affinities: Beef, blue cheese, canned tuna, carrot, cheese, chicken, crab, egg, mustard, parsley, pork, potato, shrimp, tomato, turkey, vinegar.

55a–z. **CHILE PEPPERS**

Other Names: *Ají, chile, guindilla,* or *pimienta* (Spanish); *berberé* or
mitmita (Amharic); *biber* (Turkish); *bisbas* (Arabic);
cabé or *lombok* (Indonesian); *chili-pfeffer* (German);
csilipaprika (Hungarian); *diavoletto* or *peperoncino*
(Italian); *hari mirch* or *lal mirch* (Hindi); *la jiao* or
lup-chew (Chinese); *ot* (Vietnamese); *pilipili hoho*
(Swahili); *pilpel adom* or *tsili* (Hebrew); *piment fort*
(French); *piperi kagien* or *tsili* (Greek); *piripíri*
(Portuguese); *pisi hui* or *prik* (Thai); *Spaanse peper*
(Dutch); *togarashi* (Japanese).

General
Description:
*Chiles are a huge group in five main species of the
Capsicum (pepper) family with thousands of varieties
around the world that all contain capsaicin—a sub-
stance that makes them spicy.* Each type of chile has
subtle flavors besides their heat, which may lie any-
where between tingling and searing. Capsaicin is
found mainly in the spongy white tissue to which the
seeds cling. The Scoville method of measuring chile
heat ranges from Anaheims at 1,000 units to Scotch
bonnets and habaneros at up to 300,000. Generally,
the smaller the chile, the hotter it will be. However,
within varieties, individual chiles vary greatly one to
the next. Capsaicin can irritate or even burn skin and
inner tissues, but it also causes the brain to release
endorphins, creating a sense of well-being and stimu-
lation. People develop a tolerance for the hotness, so

that those who are accustomed to eating chiles can eat much hotter food than novices.

All chiles start out green with distinct heat and herbal, vegetable-like flavor. Ripe chiles may be yellow, red, orange, brown, purple, or almost black. Ripened varieties are generally sweeter, fruitier, and often hotter. Dried chiles are more full-bodied and concentrated with a fruity, raisinlike flavor, which may be accompanied by smoky notes depending on the variety and how it was dried. In Latin America and the Caribbean, the use of specific chile varieties is essential to the character of individual dishes; in Asia and the Indian subcontinent, chiles are simply classified by size and whether they are green or red, fresh or dried.

India is by far the largest grower of chiles in the world. Bedagi karnataka are medium-large deep red chiles with pungent flavor though relatively mild spice. Also from southern India is the rounded, oblong yellow curd chiles, also called tanjore chiles.

The most important chile species economically is *Capsicum annuum*; milder members of this genus are called *paprika* (page 225). In this family, New Mexico chiles have a fairly mild, earthy flavor; they're long and tapered and may be brown, green, red, orange, or yellow. They're commonly dried and sold whole, or sold in powdered form as New Mexico chile powder. Chile pasilla, a popular Mexican chile, is dried for use in mole sauces and has a fruity character with a note of licorice. The smoke-dried, purplish brown ancho is large and shaped like a long, pointed heart. Called *poblano* (*pasilla* in California) when fresh, it has full-bodied flavor and moderate heat. The longer, narrower, dark brown chile mulato is similar to the ancho, and has a smoky flavor. Dark green, oblong jalapeños are the most common hot chile in the United States. Serrano peppers resemble thin jalapeños. Chipotles are tobacco-colored, finger-sized, smoke-dried red jalapeños. They may be found powdered or whole but are commonly packed in small cans in adobo (tomato-garlic sauce). The Pakistani heart-shaped dundicut chile, prominent in Balti cooking, is another cultivar in this species. Vermilion-colored, heart-shaped Spanish piquillo peppers are sweet and slightly piquant with thin-walled flesh and concentrated fruity flavor. Small, round, burgundy red ñora peppers are intensely flavored and sweet fleshed. They are sun-dried and added to stews or soups and used to flavor chorizo; they're much more common in Spanish cuisine than hot chiles. Chile de arbol, meaning "tree chile," comes from a plant with thick woody stems. Bright red in color and slender and tapered in shape, these peppers originated in Mexico, where they are popular. They are also known as rat tail, bird beak, or cow horn chiles. Red Holland chiles are a long, medium-large hybrid variety with a pointed tip that resemble cayenne peppers in flavor and heat. Sold fully ripened and deep red, they are available fresh all year because

Color Plates

Icon Key

SEASON

spring	summer	fall	winter

PREPARATION

bowl	tap water	heat	whisk
strainer	vegetable peeler	knife	blender or food processor
mortar and pestle	plastic bag	paper bag	airtight container

PREPARATION (continued)

refrigerator	frying pan	pot	light
avoid light	scissors	requires waiting	season
paper towels			

MISCELLANEOUS

risk of illness	caution	photograph

1a. **angelica:** fresh

1b. **angelica:** candied root

2a. **anise hyssop**

2b. **hyssop**

3a. lemon myrtle:
a) powder; b) whole leaf

3b. forest berry herb

4a. sweet basil: a) fresh; b) dried

4b. basil: anise

4c. **basil:** genovese

4d. **basil:** holy

4e. **basil:** lemon

4f. **basil:** napoletano

4g. **basil:** purple

4h. **basil:** thai

5a. **bay leaf:** a) dried; b) fresh

5b. **california bay leaf**

6. **calamint**

7. **cannabis:** dried bud

8. **chervil**

9a. **chives**

9b. chives: a) freeze-dried; b) curly

9c. chives: chinese

9d. chives: chinese with blossoms

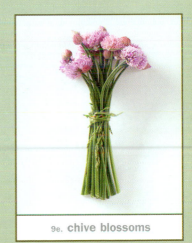

9e. chive blossoms

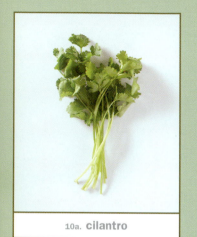

10a. **cilantro**

10b. **culantro**

10c. **vietnamese coriander**

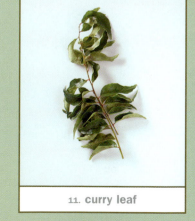

11. **curry leaf**

12. **dill:** a) weed; b) seeds

13. **epazote:** a) dried; b) fresh

14. **filé**

15. **hibiscus blossoms:** dried

16. **huacatay paste**

17. **indian bay leaf**

18. **lavender:** a) buds; b) leaves

19. **lemon balm**

20a. **lemon verbena**

20b. **mexican oregano**

21. **lemongrass:**
a) chopped; b) whole

22. **lovage**

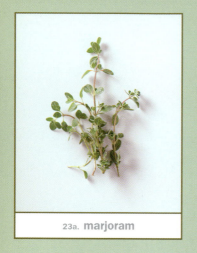

23a. **marjoram**

23b. **marjoram:** a) dried; b) gold-tip

23c. **marjoram:** pot

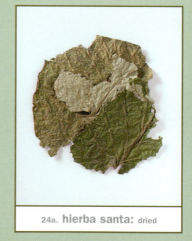

24a. **hierba santa:** dried

24b. **hoja de aguacate:** dried

24c. **hoja de maíz:** dried

24d. **hoja de platano:** frozen

24e. **papalo:** fresh

24f. **pepicha:** fresh

24g. **tila (linden):** dried

a

b

25a. **spearmint:** a) dried; b) fresh

25b. **peppermint**

a

b

25c. **mint:** a) curly; b) chocolate

25d. **pennyroyal (mentuccia)**

26. **myrtle**

27. **nasturtium**

28a. **oregano:** a) dried; b) fresh

28b. **dittany of crete**

29. **parsley:** a) flat; b) curly

30a. **rose:** fresh petals

30b. rose: a) syrup; b) dried petals

31a. **rose geranium**

31b. **lime geranium**

32a. **rosemary:** fresh

32b. **rosemary:** a) dried; b) trailing

33. **rue:** a) dried; b) fresh

34a. **sage:** a) dried; b) fresh

34b. **sage:** pineapple

34c. **sage:** a) purple; b) variegated

35a. **summer savory**

35b. **pink savory**

36a. a) **perilla seed;**
b) **korean shiso leaves**

36b. shiso: ground red

37a. sorrel: english

37b. sorrel: french

38a. tarragon: fresh

38b. **tarragon:** dried

39a. **thyme:** french

39b. **thyme:** lemon

40. **wild lime leaves:** fresh

41. **ajwain**

42. **allspice:** a) whole; b) powdered

43. **almond paste**

44. **amchur powder**

45a. anardana:
a) powdered: b) whole dried seeds

45b. pomegranate molasses

46. anise seed

47. annatto: a) whole seed; b) powder

48. **asafetida:** a) brown; b) yellow

49a. **akudjura**

49b. **tasmanian pepper**

49c. **wattleseed**

50. **barberry**

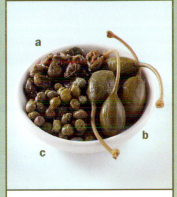

51. **capers:** a) salt-packed; b) caperberries; c) brined

52. **caraway seed**

53a. **cardamom:** a) green; b) black

53b. **cardamom:** a) seed; b) powder

54a. **celery seed**

54b. **baby celery leaves**

55a. **aji amarillo:**
a) paste; b) whole, dried

55b. chile ancho: dried

55c. chile de arbol: dried

55d. chile guajillo: dried

55e. chile mulato: dried

55f. chile pasilla: dried

55g. chiltepíns: pickled

55h. chipotles in adobo

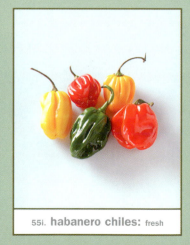

55i. habanero chiles: fresh

55j. red holland chiles: dried

55k. indian red chiles
(bedagi karnataka)

55l. indian yellow chiles
(curd chiles)

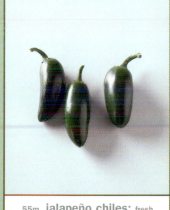

55m. jalapeño chiles: fresh

55n. piquillo peppers: roasted

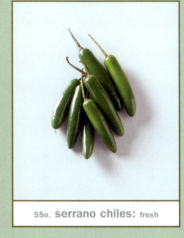

55o. serrano chiles: fresh

55p. thai chiles: pickled

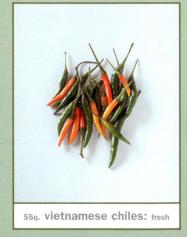

55q. vietnamese chiles: fresh

55r. cayenne pepper hot sauce

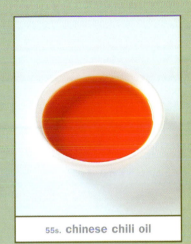

55s. chinese chili oil

habanero chile sauce

55t. habanero chile sauce

55u. rocoto chile paste

55v. **sambal oelek paste**

55w. a) **aleppo pepper**;
b) **chili powder**

55x. **chipotle:** a) flakes; b) powder

55y. **crushed red pepper flakes**

55z. **korean red pepper flakes**

56. **chinese wolfberry**

57a. **soft-stick cinnamon**

57b. **soft-stick (true) cinnamon powder**

57c. cassia cinnamon sticks

57d. cassia cinnamon powder

57e. camphor leaves

58a. citric acid

58b. grated citrus zest:
a) lemon; b) orange; c) tangerine

58c. citrus oil: a) lime; b) orange

58d. a) **candied citron**;
b) **lemon confit**

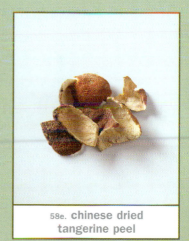

**58e. chinese dried
tangerine peel**

58f. omani dried limes:
a) black; b) white

59. cloves: a) whole; b) powdered

60. coriander seed:
a) microcarpum; b) vulgare

61. a) black cumin; b) **cumin**

63a. fennel:
a) lucknow fennel seed; b) fennel seed

62. elderberry leaves

63b. fennel pollen

64a. fenugreek: whole seed

64b. fenugreek: greens (methi)

65a. galangal: fresh

65b. galangal: dried slices

a

b

66. garlic: a) peeled cloves; b) scapes

67a. **ginger:** a) stem ginger in syrup; b) candied; c) whole, dried

67b. **ginger:** ground

67c. **mioga ginger:** pickled

68. **grains of paradise**

69. **horseradish:** a) prepared; b) root

70. **juniper berry**

71. **kokam:** dried

72. **licorice:** a) liquid; b) roots

73. **mahlab:** whole dried

74. **mastic resin crystals**

75. **msg**

76a. **mustard seed:**
a) yellow; b) black

76b. chinese hot mustard powder

77. nigella seed: whole

78a. nutmeg: whole

78b. mace: whole blades

79a. **onion:** a) minced; b) powdered

79b. **shallots:** freeze-dried

79c. **shallots:**
a) fried asian; b) fresh asian

80a. **paprika:** hungarian hot

80b. **paprika:** spanish sweet

80c. **pimentón:** powder

80d. **espelette:** pepper flakes

81a. **peppercorns:**
a) tellicherry: b) cracked black

81b. white peppercorns:
a) whole; b) ground

81c. green peppercorns:
a) brined; b) dried

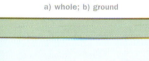

81d. mixed peppercorns

81e. pepper: long

81f. **pepper:** cubeb

81g. **betel leaves**

82. **pink pepper:** freeze-dried

83. **poppy seeds:** a) black; b) white

84. **spanish saffron threads**

85a. **salt:** a) kosher; b) table

85b. **hawaiian salt:**
a) alea pink; b) black lava

85c. **salt:** indian black

85d. **salt:** korean roasted

85e. **salt:** a) maldon; b) australian flake

85f. **salt:** a) peruvian pink;
b) south african sea

85g. **salt:** a) sel gris; b) fleur de sel

86a. sesame seeds:
a) white; b) black; c) natural

86b. sesame paste:
a) lebanese; b) chinese

87. star anise

88a. sugar:
a) dark brown; b) light brown

88b. sugar: brown rock

88c. sugar: chinese rock

a

b

88d. sugar: a) raw; b) sanding

88e. panela: granulated

88f. **panela:** block

88g. **sugar:** a) jaggery; b) palm

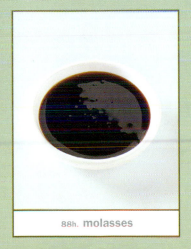

88h. **molasses**

88i. **golden syrup**

88j. **sugar cane**

89. **sumac berries:** ground

90. **szechuan peppercorns**

91. **tamarind:**
a) paste; b) concentrate; c) fresh

92a. truffles:
a) summer; b) chinese; c) winter

92b. truffle:
a) flour; b) breakings; c) paste

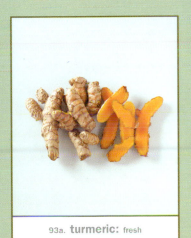

93a. turmeric: fresh

93b. turmeric: a) alleppy; b) madras

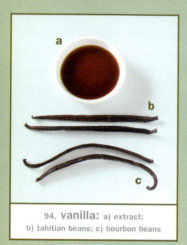

94. vanilla: a) extract;
b) tahitian beans; c) bourbon beans

95. wasabi powder

96. achiote paste

97. baharat

98. **barbecue seasoning rub**

99. berberé

100. **bouquet garni**

101. cajun seasoning

102. **chinese five-spice powder**

103. **cinnamon sugar**

104a. **sambar podi**

104b. **poudre de colombo**

104c. japanese curry powder

105. dukkah

a

b

106. fines herbes: a) dry; b) fresh

a

b

107. gomasio:
a) black sesame; b) white sesame

108. **harissa**

109. **herbes de provence**

110a. **garam masala:** whole

110b. a) **garam masala:**
powdered; b) **chaat masala**

111. **montreal steak seasoning**

112. **old bay® seasoning**

113. **panch phoron**

114. **pickling spice**

115. **poultry seasoning**

116. **pumpkin pie spice**

117. **quatres épices**

118. **ras el hanout**

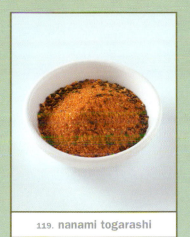

119. nanami togarashi

120. thai curry paste:
a) green; b) red; c) yellow

121. za'atar mix

122. zhoug

they are greenhouse-grown in Holland for export.

After *C. annuum*, the next most common species, *C. frutescens*, generally includes small and hotter types, such as bird's-eye and tabasco peppers. Chile pequín's small, pointed, and glossy fruits start out purple, turning orange and then red, and have a spicy fruit flavor. Chiltepíns are tiny and round, ripening to purple; they're used dried. The Brazilian malagueta pepper, believed to be the wild form of the tabasco pepper, is not to be confused with the same term used for grains of paradise. Vietnamese chiles are fiery hot, about 1½ inches in length, and shaped like a long, thin, pointy cone. Small plastic bags of these fresh mixed green and red chiles are sold in Vietnamese groceries.

The fruity chiles known as *ají* in South America are in the *C. baccatum* species. The most common cultivar is the yellow ají amarillo, referred to as *cusqueño* in dried form. This flavorful species, which has been grown in the southern Andes for thousands of years, is commonly oblong and yellow when ripe. Guajillo or cascabel chiles are dried mirasols, which have a distinctive, relatively mild earthy flavor with plum and raisin notes.

C. chinense, the species that includes the hottest chiles, is most important in the Caribbean. Scotch bonnets are light green, yellow, or red bonnet-shaped peppers. They were used by the Carib Indians for torturing captives and for seasoning pepper-pot stew. Habaneros are cherry-sized, squat, lantern-shaped, orange pods famed for their intense heat and underlying sweet apple-tomato flavor. Rocotillos come from the Cayman Islands and Congo peppers from Trinidad. Take care when handling and eating the above chiles because their exceptional heat makes them extremely potent. The ají panca, a Chilean cultivar, is mild and fruity. Ose utoro in Nigeria and other African cultivars were introduced to Africa by repatriated slaves.

The hardy *C. pubescens* is native to the Andes and, even today, cultivation outside that region is rare. This small group includes the rocoto chile, which is thick fleshed, small, round, and mild enough to be stuffed and baked; the Cuzco chile, an ancient strain from Cuzco, Peru; and the manzano amarillo (yellow rocoto or canario), with rather hot, blocky, long, canary yellow fruits and sweet, crisp flesh.

Hot sauces are made the world over using a huge variety of chiles, sometimes mixed with garlic and other spices and brewed with vinegar. They include American cayenne pepper sauces, Caribbean habanero sauces, African *piri-piri* sauce, and Mexican Cholula® sauce. Tabasco® sauce is made on McIlhenney Island, Louisiana, with almost the entire American crop of tabasco peppers.

Chile pastes like Indonesian *sambal oelek* and Turkish *kirmizi biber* are chiles mashed with garlic and other seasonings and packed in oil. Chile oil is made by steeping the peppers in oil and straining it. Small whole hot chiles, like piri-piri or bird's-eye, may be packed in vinegar and used as a table condiment. Thai chiles (*prik dong* in Thai) are 1 to 3 inches long, slightly curved, and deep green ripening to bright red. When fully ripe, these potent peppers are commonly packed in glass jars. In Asia, dried red chiles are often fried in hot oil until dark brown; the oil is then used to prepare stir-fries.

Chiles that have been dried and crumbled, either with or without seeds, are a convenient way to season food. Aleppo pepper, which originated in Aleppo, the culinary capital of Syria, is coarsely ground red chiles; it's gritty, dark red, earthy, robust, and mildly hot with a rich fruity flavor. Korean pepper flakes are used in huge quantities in Korean cooking; these deep red flakes are made from only the flesh of the pepper. *Pepe rosso picante*, Italian-style crushed red pepper flakes commonly sprinkled on pizzas, include seeds. *Piri-piri* is a general term for chiles in South Africa, Angola, and parts of India. In powdered form, it's generally a blend of very hot red chiles. Chipotles and mirasols can also be made into flakes and powders.

Season:	Many varieties of fresh chiles can be found year-round, with the greatest variety in hot summer months and in areas with a large Hispanic population.
Purchase and Avoid:	The selection of chiles will vary depending on the ethnicity of customers—Asian chiles in Asian markets, Caribbean in Caribbean markets, and so on.

Choose firm, plump, crisp fresh chiles with a shiny skin and fresh smell. For the most flesh, get the heaviest ones for their size. Avoid wrinkled, soft fresh chiles with any mushiness toward the stem end or soft, brown spoiled spots. Look for dried chile peppers that are whole and flexible rather than brittle and cracked. Deeper-colored chile powders are generally ground from the flesh of the chile only; lighter-colored powders may have been ground with their seeds, making for a hotter product.

Storage:

Place fresh chiles in a plastic bag and refrigerate up to 1 week. Store dried chiles out of the light. Store ground chile powders in the freezer.

Preparation: • **Handle fresh chiles with care. Protect your hands from the capsaicin by wearing rubber gloves, or by coating your hands first with oil, as native cooks have done for centuries.**

• **Once your hands or gloves have been in contact with chiles, don't touch your lips, eyes, face, or delicate body parts. To prevent burning those sensitive areas later, scrub your hands and arms vigorously with plenty of hot, soapy water.**

 • **Toast either whole dried chiles or seeded and trimmed chiles in a dry pan over medium heat until the aromas are released.**

• **Soak dried chiles in warm water to soften, then remove the spongy tissue and seeds, if desired.**

 • **Fry small whole chiles in oil before adding other ingredients to the pan; remove before serving.**

Serving Suggestions: Make Mexican salsa by mixing chopped serrano or jalapeño chiles with diced onions, diced tomatoes, chopped cilantro, and salt. • Mix ground chiles with garlic to make a rub for meat. • Make a Thai curry with shrimp or chicken, coconut milk, fish sauce, and thinly sliced hot green chiles.

Food Affinities: Avocado, beans, beef, ceviche, cheese, chicken, chickpeas, Chinese fermented black beans, cilantro, coconut milk, cumin, curry, fish, garlic, ginger, lamb, lemon, lime, mint, mole sauce, olive oil, onion, orange, oregano, pasta, peanut, pork, potato, rice, seafood, sesame, soy, tomatillo, tomato.

56. **CHINESE WOLFBERRY**

Other Names: Boxthorn berry; Chinese boxthorn; *gau gei choi*, *goji*, *gouqizi*, or *ji zi* (Chinese); matrimony vine fruit; red caper.

General Description: *The Chinese wolfberry* (Lycium chinense) *is a deep red, dried fruit about the same size as a raisin with a flavor*

somewhere between dried cranberry and dried cherry.
Wolfberries are moderately sweet, with a hint of bitterness and tartness. They're used in Chinese cooking for their flavor, their beautiful color, and their beneficial properties. Perhaps the most nutritionally dense fruit on the planet, wolfberries have traditionally been regarded as a food of the highest order for longevity, sexual potency, and building strength. Wolfberries grow in protected valleys of Inner Mongolia and Tibet. The berries are never touched by hand; they will oxidize and turn black if touched while fresh. Harvesters shake the large bushes so that the ripe berries fall onto mats, where they are then dried in the shade.

Purchase and Avoid:

Purchase dried wolfberries in Chinese markets, choosing those with bright red color and plump shape; avoid any berries that are very wrinkled and brown. The larger the berry, the more expensive.

Storage:

Store in a cool, dark place with low humidity or freeze until needed.

Recipe:

Chinese Chicken Soup with Wolfberries

1. **Prepare a roasting chicken by cutting off the tail high enough that the two glands on either side are also eliminated. Pull out and discard the fat from the body cavity and remove all the skin except for that on**

the wings. Hack the chicken into about 16 pieces using a cleaver.

 2. Place the chicken in a large, heavy pot, along with 6 slices fresh ginger, 2 sliced scallions, 2 tablespoon rice wine (or dry sherry), 1 tablespoon light soy sauce, 2 tablespoons dried wolfberries, and water to cover.

 3. Bring to a boil, skimming as needed, then lower the heat, cover tightly, and simmer for 1½ hours. Just before serving, strain without pressing on solids, and sprinkle with salt to taste and a few drops of toasted sesame oil.

Serving
Suggestions:
Sprinkle wolfberries over dry cereal or add to bread or muffin batters, just like raisins. • Add wolfberries to stewed pork, beef, chicken, or fish 10 minutes before the meat is done. • Chop and add to vinaigrettes.

57a–e.

CINNAMON AND CASSIA

Other Names: **Cinnamon:** *Canela* (Portuguese, Spanish); *canelle* (French); *cannella* (Italian); *darchini* (Hindi); *echter zimt* (German); *jou kwei* (Chinese); *kanela* (Greek); *kayu manis* (Indonesian); *kerefa* (Amharic); *koritsa* (Russian); *mdalasini* (Swahili); *op cheuy* (Thai); *qinamon* (Hebrew); *que Srilanca* (Vietnamese); *qurfah* (Arabic); *shinamon* (Japanese); soft-stick cinnamon; true cinnamon; *tsimring*

(Yiddish). **Cassia:** Bastard cinnamon; *canela de la China* or *casia* (Spanish); *cannella della Cina* or *cassia* (Italian); *canelle de Chine* or *casse* (French); *cássia-aromática* (Portuguese); *darasini* (Arabic); *kaeng* (Thai); *kassie* (German); *kasia* (Greek); *kayu manis cina* (Indonesian); *korichnoje derevo* (Russian); *kwei* (Chinese); *qassia* (Hebrew); *que don* (Vietnamese); *shinamonkassia* (Japanese). **Vietnamese cinnamon:** Baker's cinnamon; Saigon cassia or cinnamon.

General Description:

Cinnamon is the sweetly scented inner bark of the cinnamon tree (Cinnamomum zeylanicum)*, which is related to the bay laurel.* Cinnamon bark is manually rolled into light reddish brown coils, called quills, that have a warm and spicy yet sweet and delicate flavor. Beloved worldwide, cinnamon is one of the oldest spices in the world. The ancients used it to flavor wine, much as it's used now for mulled wine or sangria.

Cinnamon is used heavily in the fiery curries of Sri Lanka and in *biriyanis*, rice dishes of northern India's Moghul cuisine. Medieval habits of seasoning savory foods with cinnamon persist in the cured meats and sausages of Spain and the *b'stillas* and tagines of Morocco. In Greece, Lebanon, Syria, and Turkey, lamb is always seasoned with cinnamon. In France, cinnamon appears in homey sweets like apple tarts and rice pudding. In Mexico, cinnamon flavors chocolate and mole sauces. In India, cinnamon is used whole: The bark pieces are fried in hot oil until they unroll, releasing their fragrance; the fried cinnamon is generally used as a fragrant garnish. Powdered cinnamon goes into many spice mixes.

Cassia (*C. aromaticum*), or Chinese cinnamon, is similar in flavor to true cinnamon, though thicker and tougher, with a dark brown, rough outer surface. Cassia is reddish brown when powdered, with a pronounced, slightly bitter aroma. Chunks of cassia bark are thick but brittle, and they're often sold in small pieces or irregular shapes. Much "cinnamon" used in the United States is actually cassia, but in Europe, cassia is generally found only in Chinese markets. Cassia is preferred in Asia and goes into Hunan "red cooking" or "red braising" (*hongshao*), wherein food is cooked in a spiced broth or master sauce.

Vietnamese cinnamon (*C. loureirii*) looks similar to cassia, but it is smaller and thinner. Highly esteemed in China and Japan, the bark is high in essential oil and has a sweet, rich, pungent flavor. The unripe fruits are dried and sold as "cassia buds." Indonesian cinnamon (*C. burmannii*) is much thicker than Vietnamese cinnamon and not as breakable. The quills are reddish brown outside, but the inner side of the bark is a much darker grayish brown. It's cultivated in Java and Sumatra and is much used in the Netherlands.

Cinnamon buds, which resemble cloves, are the unripe fruits of the cinnamon tree. They have a mild, pure, sweet flavor, but must be finely ground to release their fragrance. The buds are used in China (where they come from the cassia tree) and India.

The wood of the related camphor tree (*C. camphora*) is used for smoking foods, especially duck, in Chinese cuisine. It's also the source of an essential oil that flavors bitters, candy, and baked goods. In India, very small quantities of crystallized camphor resin, called *kacha karpoor*, are added to milk puddings and sweets.

Purchase and Avoid:	Paler true cinnamon is of better quality because it comes from young cultivated shoots, resulting in quills that are thin and delicately flavored. Ground cinnamon quickly loses its subtle nuances of aroma. For whole cassia, look for reddish brown rather than dark brown quills. Note that in the United States and France, *cinnamon* refers to both cinnamon and cassia; in England and Australia it's illegal to sell "cinnamon" that's actually cassia.
Preparation:	• **Soft-stick cinnamon is soft enough to crumble with your hands and then grind.**
	• **To grind cassia, first crush up several quills with a meat mallet or hammer, then grind the crushed pieces to a rough powder in a coffee grinder, in a blender, or with a mortar and pestle.**
Note:	Add powdered cinnamon shortly before the end of the cooking time, as it becomes slightly bitter with longer cooking.

Serving Suggestions:	Bake acorn or butternut squash with crushed cinnamon stick. • Toss steamed green beans and sliced oranges in a dressing of cider vinegar, whole-grain mustard, honey, cinnamon, and thyme. • Crush cassia or cinnamon sticks, steep in scalded milk overnight, then strain and use the milk to make ice cream, custards, and pastry cream.
Food Affinities:	Apple, beef, black pepper, brandy, brown sugar, cardamom, carrot, cherry, chicken, chocolate, duck, ginger, honey, lamb, nutmeg, peach, pork, saffron, winter squash, yam.

CITRUS SEASONINGS

 58a–f.

Other Names:	**Sour orange:** *Bigarade* (French); bitter orange; Curaçao orange; *daidai* (Taiwan); Seville orange. **Lime:** Key lime; *lima* (Spanish); Mexican lime; Persian lime; West Indian lime. **Tangerine:** Mandarin; satsuma. **Preserved lemons:** *Hamad muraqqad* (Morocco); *qaris baldi* (Tunisia). **Orange blossom water:** Orange flower water; *zhaar* (Morocco).
General Description:	*Citrus fruits are members of the Rutaceae family, which includes lemons, oranges, limes, tangerines, citrons, grapefruits, and many more.* All citrus fruits are native to the region from east Asia south to Australia. The colorful rind of almost any citrus fruit may be used as

a fragrant seasoning, and the juices are a basic seasoning worldwide. Essential oils made from the rinds are also sold, and fragrant orange blossom water is made from the flowers of the bitter orange tree. Citrus fruits have an acidic tang due to the presence of citric acid, known as *sour salt* in powdered form. Sour salt is used for seasoning in parts of the world without easy access to the fruit, such as Russia and Poland.

The lemon (*Citrus limon*) is grown primarily for its acidic juice, but the oil in its perfumed yellow peel is almost as important for use as a flavoring and in the perfume industry. North Africans cure and preserve lemons by soaking them in brine or salting them and layering in olive oil. Lemon juice and zest flavor the popular southern Italian liqueur Limoncello, and lemons and olives are pressed together to make the oil called Limonato.

The Meyer lemon (*C. limon 'Meyer'*), which originated in China, is a cross between a lemon and an orange or a mandarin. Meyers are rounder than lemons and their thin, soft, smooth rind is a rich orangish yellow when fully ripe. A good Meyer lemon has juicy, deep yellow pulp, is succulent and low in acid, and has a highly aromatic rind.

The sweet orange (*C. sinensis*) is a small, round fruit full of tart-sweet, juicy, orange-colored pulp, with a thick, fleshy, orange rind. The bitter orange (*C. aurantium*) has sour juice and aromatic rind and is used for seasoning, especially in Spain and Latin

America, and for making marmalade. It flavors liqueurs, most notably Grand Marnier, Cointreau, and Triple Sec. The blossoms scent tea and are distilled to make an essential oil, neroli, used in perfumery. When the oil is drawn off, the watery portion that remains is orange blossom water. Originating in the Middle East, this liquid lends a delicate perfume to syrups, pastries, and puddings. In Morocco, it flavors salads and tagines; it's also used in Turkish coffee.

Bergamot orange (*C. bergamia*), not to be confused with the herb bergamot (page 53), is a a small pear-shaped fruit with notoriously tough peel that is the source of a potent and aromatic essential oil used to flavor hard candy, cakes, desserts, and Earl Gray tea. The highly acidic juice can be used to replace vinegar or lime in dressings, marinades, and drinks. The flowers are used for fragrant flower water in Morocco.

The small, rounded, yellow-green lime (*C. aurantifolia*) is used for its acidic green juice and the concentrated and somewhat bitter essential oil in its rind. These limes, which predominate in the world beyond the United States, are what Americans call *key limes*. In the United States, the larger dark green Persian or Tahitian lime is most common; it's believed to be a hybrid of the key lime and the citron. *Omani*, dried limes, are widely used in Persian and Gulf cuisine. They range in color from light to dark brown or almost black and add a highly aromatic, fermented flavor that complements fish and chicken dishes. Pierce the dried lime with a skewer or fork before adding it whole to a dish or placing it in the cavity of poultry before roasting. When the cooked lime is soft, squeeze the juice out to release its intriguing flavor.

Tangerines or mandarins (*C. reticulata*) are a group of flattened, sweet, orange-colored citrus fruits with loose, easily peeled, netted skin and sweet-tart, juicy flesh. Called *mandarins* in England and later *tangerines* in the United States, they were first cultivated in China thousands of years ago. Tangerines have soft, oil-rich rinds that are highly perfumed, perfect for use as a seasoning. Chinese dried citrus peel is made from the skins of tangerines; it may be added to braised duck and pork.

The citron (*C. medica*) is cultivated mainly for the thick rind of the fruit, which is commonly candied and used in fruitcakes and other desserts, especially those from Sicily and other Mediterranean islands.

Season: Most citrus fruits are at their peak season in winter months. Peak season for Meyer lemons is November through January. Look for fresh bitter oranges in Latin American markets in winter. Bergamot oranges are available fresh in the Mediterranean region and now in U.S. specialty markets in early winter. Fresh citrons are sold during the Jewish Feast of Tabernacles holiday in early fall.

Purchase and Avoid:	Look for big, plump, firm citrus fruits that are heavy for their size, with even, brightly colored skin that is firm and bumpy. Purchase pure citrus oils in small quantities; because the oil is so potent, substitute only small quantities for fresh grated rind. Look for brightly colored preserved lemons well-covered in brine and without any white mold.
Storage:	Store citrus fruits in a plastic bag in the refrigerator up to 2 weeks.
Preparation:	• **Scrub citrus fruits with soap and water before zesting. Because most citrus fruits are treated with chemical preservatives, it's a good idea to buy organic when you're planning to use the zest.** • **Use a handheld microplane zester or the fine side of a box grater to remove only the bright oil pockets located on the skin of the lemon. The white pith directly underneath is bitter.**
Serving Suggestions:	Make flavored citrus butter by beating softened butter with generous quantities of zest and a bit of the juice. • Use preserved lemons in North African dishes like braised chicken with olives and preserved lemons. • Dice only the rind of preserved lemons and add to lemon mayonnaise or citrus-based salad dressings. • Grind whole dried limes and mix with black pepper for seasoning chicken and fish.

Food
Affinities:

Almond, butter, chicken, duck, fish, fruit desserts, meringue, olive oil, olives, pine nut, pound cake, salads, salmon, seafood, sponge cake.

59. ⬤ **CLOVES**

Other Names:

Cengkeh (Indonesian); *chiodo di garofano* (Italian); *clou de girofle* (French); *clavo de olor* (Spanish); *cravinho* (Portuguese); *ding xiang* (Chinese); *dinh huong* (Vietnamese); *garifalo* (Greek); *gram goo* (Thai); *gvozdika* (Russian); *kabsh qarunfil* (Arabic); *karafuu* (Swahili); *krinfud* (Amharic); *kruidnagel* (Dutch); *lavang* (Hindi); *mikhak* (Farsi); *nejlikor* (Swedish); *nelke* (German); *tsiporen* (Hebrew).

General
Description:

Clove (Syzium aromaticum) *is a dried, unopened flower bud that resembles a small, dark, reddish brown, round-headed nail—the source of its name in many languages.* Cloves are a legendary and exceptional ancient aromatic spice, esteemed by cooks in Europe, North Africa, India, and much of Asia. Very intense, cloves have a sweetly fiery taste that's delicious in small quantities but medicinal if overdone. Cloves are native to the north Molucca Islands in Indonesia, where the Dutch kept a monopoly on this spice until the eighteenth century. Cloves are much loved by the Chinese, play an important role in Sri Lankan cooking, are extensively used in the Moghul cuisine of northern India, and are popular in the Middle East and northern Africa for adding to meat dishes and rice. In Europe, cloves flavor fruit, sweetbreads, rice, and meat stews and soups. They're included in many spice mixtures.

Purchase and Avoid: Whole cloves are rather expensive but keep well and are only used in small quantities. Powdered cloves should be purchased and used in very small quantities; in powdered form cloves can be overpowering.

Recipe: *Kourambiedes (Greek Clove Cookies)*

 1. Beat ½ pound softened unsalted butter with 1 egg, 1½ cups confectioners' sugar, 1 teaspoon vanilla, and 1 tablespoon brandy until creamy and smooth.

 2. Blend in 3 cups all-purpose flour and ½ teaspoon ground cloves. Chill dough until firm, about 1 hour.

 3. Preheat the oven to 350°F. Shape the dough into small, flat crescents. Press 1 clove into the center of each cookie. Bake on ungreased baking sheets for 12 to 15 minutes, or until set but not brown. Cool, then dust generously with confectioners' sugar.

Serving Suggestions: Add a pinch of cloves to tomato sauce. • Add a pinch of cloves to pea soup, potato soup, bean soups, and cream of tomato soup. • Make German *pfeffernüsse*

cookies, Dutch *speculaas* cookies, or Greek *kourambiedes* cookies—all flavored with cloves.

Food
Affinities:

Apple, apple pie, beans, beef, beet, ginger, ham, mulled wine, pear, pickles, prune, quince, red wine, rice, sweet potato, tomato.

60.   **CORIANDER SEED**

Other Names:

Coentro (Portuguese); *coriandolo* (Italian); *coriandre* (French); *coriandro* (Spanish); *dhania* (Hindi); *gad* or *kusbara* (Hebrew); *giligilani* (Swahili); *hu sui* (Chinese); *ketumbar* (Indonesian); *kişniş* (Turkish); *koliandro* (Greek); *koriander* (German); *koriandr* (Russian); *kusbarah* (Arabic); *mellet pak chi* (Thai); *mui* (Vietnamese).

General
Description:

Coriander (Coriandrum sativum) *has tan-colored, ribbed, lightweight fruits, commonly called* seeds, *with a pleasing warm, nutty, and orange- or lemonlike flavor with floral undertones.* Although cilantro and coriander are respectively the leaves and fruits of the same plant, their flavors are totally different. The fruits of the smaller *microcarpum* variety, more common in Europe and the United States, have more floral essential oil than those of the Indian variety, *vulgare*, which are elongated and shaped like tiny lemons.

In the Mediterranean, coriander cultivation dates back to ancient Egypt; coriander is also mentioned in the Bible, where it's compared to manna. Sugar-coated coriander seeds are used as a breath freshener in India. Now out of fashion, in Great Britain the candy-coated seeds were called *comfits*; in the United States they were called *candy marbles*. The herbal-tasting unripe seeds are used in pickles by the Pennsylvania Dutch.

Unlike coriander's pungent leaves, its seeds are an unassuming and versatile spice popular in much of Europe, North Africa, India, Asia, and Latin America. They flavor gin, pickling brines, sausage, hot dogs, Greek-style vegetables (à la grecque), pastries, and cookies, and are often mixed with peppercorns as an aromatic seasoning. Crushed coriander has a thickening property when added to sauces, such as Indian curries. Coriander is an ingredient in Ethiopian berberé (page 278), Indian curry powders (page 280), and Arabic baharat (page 278).

Purchase and Avoid:

Many recipes call for either coarsely crushed coriander or whole seeds, and since the seeds are light and easy to crush, it's best to buy them whole for flavor.

Recipe:

Artichokes à la Grecque

 1.

In a nonreactive pot, combine 1 cup white wine, 1 cup water, 1/4 cup olive oil, and the juice of 1 lemon. Tie 2 bay leaves and 1 teaspoon each peppercorns, coriander seeds, and fennel seeds into a cheesecloth bag and add to the pot. Boil for 10 minutes, then add

¾ pound fresh or frozen artichoke heart wedges. Cover and simmer for 15 minutes, or until the artichokes are tender when pierced.

 2.   Cool in the cooking liquid, then lift the artichokes out of the pan. Cook the liquid down until syrupy before salting to taste. Strain and pour this sauce back over the artichokes and serve at room temperature.

Serving
Suggestions: Toast coriander seeds in a dry pan before grinding to add to Indian, Asian, and North African dishes. • Add ground (untoasted) coriander to cakes, cookies, apple pie, fruit crumbles, and Danish pastry. • Add ground coriander to polenta, as the early Romans did.

Food
Affinities: Apple, artichoke, asparagus, beet, cardoon, carrot, celeriac, chicken, fennel, fish, gin, ginger, leek, lemon, mushrooms, parsnip, polenta, sausage.

61.   **CUMIN AND BLACK CUMIN**

Other Names: *Cominho* (Portuguese); *comino* (Spanish); *cumin blanc*, *cumin du Maroc*, or *faux anis* (French); *cumino* (Italian); *jamda* or *kisibiti* (Swahili); *jeera* (Hindi); *jinten* (Indonesian); *kamoun* (Arabic, Hebrew); *kemun* (Amharic); *kimino* (Greek); *kimyon* (Turkish); *kmin* (Russian); *kreuzkümmel* (German); *kuming* (Chinese); white cumin; *yeera* (Thai); *zireh* (Farsi).

General Description:	*Cumin* (Cuminum cyminum) *has small, curved, khaki-colored fruits (commonly called seeds) with a warm, earthy, lingering aroma and pleasingly bitter, pungent flavor.* Cumin is highly popular in the Middle East, India, North Africa, western and central Asia, Spain, and Latin America. Iran is reputed to produce top-quality cumin seeds. Toasted cumin combined with coriander is characteristic of south Indian and Sri Lankan cuisine, where it flavors dal (thin lentil soup). It's used whole and either fried in ghee (frequently with onion) or dry-roasted. Cumin is essential for northern Indian tandoori dishes and is typical for North African tagines (meat stews) and for many Mexican and Tex-Mex dishes. Although not as common in Asia, cumin is important in Burmese cooking and is also used in Thailand and Indonesia.

Rare and more expensive, black cumin (*Bunium persicum*) grows wild in Iran and Kashmir. Called *royal cumin*, or *kala jeera* in India, the small, dark brown, curved seeds are highly aromatic, with a resinous, astringent flavor that's sweeter and more complex than common (white) cumin. It's preferred for northern Indian meat kormas and shows up in savory dishes of North Africa and the Middle East. It is sometimes confused with the unrelated nigella seed.

Purchase and Avoid:	Cumin will lose its most subtle flavor notes soon after grinding, so buy it in small quantities and choose oily-textured, khaki-colored powder. Look for whole black cumin seeds in Indian groceries.

Storage: Whole cumin seeds will keep for about 3 years.

Recipe: ***Moroccan Charmoula Dressing***

1. **Blend ¹/₂ cup extra virgin olive oil, 2 tablespoons red wine vinegar, ¹/₄ cup fresh lemon juice, and 1 tablespoon chopped garlic until smooth and creamy. Add 2 tablespoons sweet paprika, 2 teaspoons hot paprika, 1 tablespoon ground cumin, and salt and black pepper to taste and blend again.**

2. **Stir in the diced rind of 1 preserved lemon and ¹/₄ cup chopped cilantro. Use to marinate meats, poultry, fish, and vegetables before grilling or roasting. Serve extra on the side. Makes about 1 ¹/₂ cups.**

Serving Suggestions: Sprinkle flatbreads, crackers, and breadsticks with cumin seeds just before baking. • Season Mexican bean dishes with toasted, ground cumin.

Food Affinities: Barbecue sauce, beans, carrot, chicken, chickpeas, cilantro, corn, curries, garlic, lamb, lemon, onion, orange, peppers, tandoori chicken, turmeric.

62. **ELDERBERRY**

Other Names: **Canadian elder:** American elder; common elder; sweet elder (trees). **European elder:** *Bacca di sambuco*

(Italian); *baie de sureau* (French); *baya de sauco* (Spanish); Englishman's grape; *holunderbeere* (German); pipe tree. **Chinese elder:** *Chieu-ku-ts'ao* (Chinese); Chinese elderberry.

General Description:

Elderberries are the small, very dark purple (almost black) berries of the elder tree, found almost everywhere in Europe, western Asia, and North America. In the Middle Ages, legends held that the tree was home to witches and that cutting one down would bring on the wrath of those residing in the branches. In many parts of Europe, the elder is associated with black magic, and gypsies wouldn't burn it in their camp-fires. Elder flowers, very high in vitamin C, are made into teas in Europe, especially as an antidote against colds; they were used in a similar way by Native Americans. Berries from the European elder (*Sambucus nigra*) are used to make elderberry wine and to flavor preserves and pies. The trees grow abun-dantly throughout Italy and both the berries and the white blossoms are infused to make Italian Sambuca liqueur. Chinese elder (*S. javanica*) is used for preserves, teas, and confectionary. Mexican elder (*S. mexicana*) grows in North America's Southwest. Canadian elder (*S. canadensis*) has deep purple fruits.

Elderberries are inedible when raw because they contain small amounts of a poisonous alkaloid and have an unpleasant smell and taste. Cooking or dry-ing brings out the palatable flavors and destroys the alkaloid. In England, the dried berries were made into a ketchup called *pontack*. Scandinavian mixed fruit cups often contain elderberries. Elderberry cordial makes a delicious summer drink, while elderberry wine is a traditional country product. Vinegar is also made from the berries. Europeans have used the blossoms to make elder flower fritters since medieval times; Native Americans also used them in this way. The flowers can be used to flavor cooked fruit and jam by stirring the pan of fruit with a spray of flowers.

Season: The tree flowers in summer months. The purplish black berries follow in early fall.

Purchase and Avoid: To pick your own berries, wait until they are purple and ripe, when the clusters begin to turn upside down. Avoid picking overripe berries. Wash well and strip from the stalks using a fork. Look for fresh elderberries and flowers in farmers' markets. Look for dried elderberries and flowers in home-brewing supply catalogs.

Storage: Refrigerate fresh elderberries and flowers (flowers will keep only 1 to 2 days). Store dried elderberries and flowers in the refrigerator up to 6 months.

Recipe: ***German Chilled Elderberry Soup***

1. **Wash 3 cups of fresh (or 1 cup dried) elderberries (stems removed) and place in a large nonaluminum**

soup pot. Add 6 cups of water and bring to a boil. Reduce heat to low and simmer, covered, for 45 minutes or until the elderberries are soft. Blend and then strain through a sieve. Return the strained liquid to the cleaned pot over medium heat, and add 3/4 cup of sugar.

 2. In a separate bowl, make a slurry by combining 1 tablespoon of cornstarch with 2 tablespoons of water. Whisk the slurry into the pot and bring back to a boil, whisking often.

 3. Add 2 cups peeled and diced tart apples and 1 tablespoon grated lemon zest, and simmer for 5 minutes or until the soup is thickened, smooth, and clear.

 4. Cool the soup and refrigerate to chill. Serve cold topped with crumbled gingersnap cookies and dollops of sour cream. Makes about 2 quarts.

Serving Suggestions: Dry elderberries and use them like currants in apple pies • Combine elderberries with crabapples to produce a delicious and pretty colored jelly. • Mix elderberry juice with honey and use as a spread for toast.

Food Affinities: Allspice, anise seed, apple, cinnamon, cloves, crabapple, jam, jelly, licorice, port wine, red wine, star anise, sugar.

63a–b. 📷 **FENNEL SEED**

Other Names: **Fennel seed:** *Aneth doux* or *fenouil* (French); *fenchel* (German); *finocchio* (Italian); *finokio* (Portuguese); *hinojo* (Spanish); *jintan manis* (Indonesian); *maratho* (Greek); *mellet karee* (Thai); *razianaj* (Arabic); *saunf* (Hindi); *shamari* (Swahili); *shumar* (Hebrew); sweet cumin; *tieu hoi huong* (Vietnamese); *ukrop sladki* (Russian); *xiao hue xiang* (Chinese). **Fennel pollen:** *Polline di finocchio selvatico* (Italian); spice of the angels.

General Description: *Fennel* (Foeniculum vulgare) *has tiny, light green, curved fruits (commonly called* seeds*) with a sweetly refreshing licorice-anise flavor.* Fennel seed is used for meats and poultry, but even more for fish and seafood. In Italy, anise seed is reserved for sweets and fennel for savory dishes. Italians, who first cultivated fennel, use the seeds to season pork, boar, rabbit, fresh sausage, fish, and seafood. It's popular in southern France, where it's often found in the mixture herbes de Provence (page 282). In central Europe, it's used to flavor rye bread and for pickled vegetables and herb vinegar. Fennel is a main component of Chinese five-spice powder (page 279) and the Bengali spice mix panch phoron (page 284), and in Sri Lanka, the toasted seeds go into fiery curries. Fennel seed is much used in Iran, the Arab world, and the Levant. Prized Lucknow fennel seeds, from Lucknow, India, are brighter, smaller, sweeter, and more aromatic than common fennel. In India, they are often served after dinner as a breath freshener and digestive.

Though the leaves of cultivated fennel don't have much flavor, those of wild fennel are quite flavorful. Fennel pollen, an expensive spice with a spicy yet ethereal fennel scent, is used in Italy and is now being produced in California. Fennel pollen should be added just before serving.

Season: Fennel pollen is in season in late summer after the flowers open. Fresh fennel seeds can be picked in late summer.

Purchase and Avoid: Look for dried fennel seeds with bright green color. Specialty producers may offer fennel pollen.

Storage: Store fennel pollen in the refrigerator.

Recipe: **Taralli with Fennel (Italian Boiled Pretzels)**

 1. **In a large bowl, scatter 2 teaspoons dried yeast over a mixture of ¹/₂ cup each warmed white wine and warmed water; leave for several minutes to bubble up, then stir to mix well.**

 2. **Add 3 cups all-purpose flour, 2 cups semolina flour, ¹/₂ cup olive oil, 3 tablespoons lightly crushed fennel seeds, and salt to taste. Mix together, then turn onto an unfloured board and knead until the dough is**

smooth and elastic. Return to a lightly oiled, clean, dry bowl, lightly oil the top, cover with a damp towel, and let rise for 45 minutes or until puffy.

3. Divide the dough into small pieces. Roll each into a long, slim pencil, cut into 3-inch lengths, and pinch the two ends firmly together to form a ring.

4. Preheat the oven to 375°F. Bring a pot of salted water to a rolling boil and drop the taralli in, a few at a time. When the taralli rise, remove and drain on a kitchen towel.

5. Arrange boiled taralli on a greased cookie sheet and bake 15 to 20 minutes, until golden brown and crisp. Makes 4 to 5 dozen.

Serving Suggestions:
Make risotto with tomatoes and thyme and sprinkle with fennel pollen just before serving. • Marinate vegetables and seafood with ground fennel seeds and olive oil. • Use ground fennel seeds to season polenta, fresh pork sausage, tomato-based pasta sauces, and game such as boar, rabbit, and venison.

Food Affinities:
Boar, canned tuna, capers, garlic, lemon, lime, olive oil, orange, oregano, polenta, pork, rye bread, sausage, seafood, thyme, tomato.

64a–b.

FENUGREEK

Other Names:

Fenugreek: *Abish* (Amharic); *alfarva* or *feno-grego* (Portuguese); *alholva* or *fenogreco* (Spanish); *bock-shornklee* (German); *fenugrec, sénegré,* or *trigonelle* (French); *fieno greco* (Italian); *kelabet* (Indonesian); *hilbeh* (Arabic, Hebrew); *hu lu ba* (Chinese); *methi* (Hindi); *moschositaro* or *trigonella* (Greek); *shanbalile* (Farsi); *uwatu* (Swahili). **Blue fenugreek:** *Balsamo, fieno-greco ceruleo,* or *meliloto azzuro* (Italian); *baumier* or *trigonelle bleu* (French); *blauer honigklee, brotklee,* or *hexenkraut* (German); blue melilot; blue-white clover; blue-white trigonella; curd herb; *meliloto azul* (Spanish); sweet trefoil; *trevo-azul* (Portuguese).

General Description:

Fenugreek (Trigonella foenum-graecum) *has small, roughly angular, brownish yellow seeds. The seeds have a bitter yet pleasing flavor and potent aroma, similar to lovage, that is characteristic of curry powders (page 280).* The pebblelike seeds are often toasted to enhance their pungent aroma and have a powerful bittersweet, somewhat acrid taste, so use them in moderation. Westerners unfamiliar with fenugreek sometimes find its flavor unpleasantly "goaty." Fenugreek seeds are most commonly used in Indian, Yemeni, and Ethiopian cookery. In Yemen and Ethiopia, they are soaked and ground for their flavor and their thickening powers to make the thick, souplike *hilbeh,* a national dish in Yemen. Fenugreek leaves appear in the Georgian spice

mixture khmeli-suneli (page 283). In India, the leaves
are eaten like spinach or dried and used as a flavoring,
and in southern India, the dried leaves flavor potato
curries. Fenugreek leaves, along with dried limes, are
used in *ghormeh sabzi*, a thick Iranian vegetable sauce.

The leaves of a related plant, blue fenugreek (*T.
caerulea*) are dried and used in Europe, especially central
Europe, for their aromatic, spicy flavor, similar to but
milder than dried fenugreek. A Swiss specialty cheese,
sapsago, is flavored with blue fenugreek, which imparts
a unique flavor and a pale green color. In the southern
Alpine regions of the Tyrol (in Austria) and the Alto
Adige (in Italy), ground, dried, and fermented blue
fenugreek leaves are used in rye bread dough.

Storage:

Store ground fenugreek in the refrigerator; ground
fenugreek loses its fragrance rather quickly, so check
the quality before you use it. Whole fenugreek seeds
will keep quite well up to 2 years unrefrigerated.

Preparation:

- **Fenugreek seeds tend to have a hard shell, so crush
  them in a mortar and pestle or with a hammer, or
  soak them to soften before mashing.**

Recipe:

Yemenite Fenugreek Sauce

 I. **Soak 4 tablespoons fenugreek seeds in ½ cup cold
water overnight, or until they are soft and have a jel-
lied coating.**

2. **Place the seeds and their soaking liquid in a blender and add 4 cloves garlic, ½ cup cilantro leaves, 2 teaspoons salt, the juice of 2 lemons, and 1 small dried hot red chile (seeded). Blend to a coarse puree. Store in the refrigerator up to 1 week. Serve with falafel or with pita bread for dipping.**

Serving Suggestions: Add a pinch of ground fenugreek to Indian-style curries, lamb, or beef dishes, especially those using ground meat. • Add ground fenugreek to chickpeas, falafel mix, and Indian potato dishes and naan. • Add blue fenugreek to cottage cheese spreads.

Food Affinities: **Fenugreek:** Beef, chickpeas, curry, curry powder, dried lime, falafel, Indian breads, lamb, potato. **Blue fenugreek:** Cottage cheese, potato, rye bread, soups.

 65a–b.

GALANGAL

Other Names: **Greater galangal:** *Adkham* or *khalanjan* (Arabic); *djus rishe* (Farsi); *galang* (Spanish); *galanga maggiore* (Italian); *galanki* (Greek); *gengibre do Laos* or *junça ordinária* (Portuguese); *grosser galanga* or *Siam-ingwer* (German); *khaa* (Thai); *kulanjan* (Hindi); *lam keong* (Chinese); *laos* (Indonesian); *odorant* or *souchet long* (French); Siamese ginger; *son nai* (Vietnamese). **Lesser galangal:** *Ban-ukon* (Japanese); *cekur* or *kenchur* (Malay); China root; Chinese ginger; collic root; East Indian catarrh root; *galanga camphré* (French); *gewürzlilie* or *kleiner galgant* (German); *kencur* (Indonesian); *pro hom* (Thai); resurrection lily; *tam nai* (Vietnamese).

General Description:	*Greater galangal* (Alpinia galanga)*, in the Zingiberaceae (ginger) family, has a gingerlike rhizome (root-bearing underground stem) formed of plump, pale reddish, cylindrical sections divided by reddish brown rings, with a hard, reddish brown, woody interior.* Warm, sweet, and spicy, fresh galangal has a distinct piney fragrance and coarse, fluffy, fibrous texture; dried galangal is spicier and sweeter, somewhere between cinnamon and ginger. Originating in southern China, greater galangal is popular in Thai cooking and is also used in Malaysia, Indonesia, Cambodia, Vietnam, and southern China. In Europe and the United States, galangal is just becoming better known, though it was a valued spice in Europe in medieval times. Fresh galangal is preferred for Thai foods; dried galangal is used only when fresh isn't available. Indonesians frequently use galangal to season *nasi goreng* (fried rice with vegetables and meat) or in Javanese and massaman curries.

Lesser galangal (*A. officinarum*), also in the ginger family, resembles ginger in shape, though it is much smaller, with dark reddish brown skin, a creamy white soft interior, and a strongly aromatic, medicinal flavor. Though native to south India, it is used only in Malaysia and Indonesia, especially Java and Bali.

Purchase and Avoid: Fresh greater galangal can be found in Asian markets and in well-stocked supermarkets sporadically throughout the year. Choose plump, light red roots with smooth, taut skin. Avoid shriveled or moldy galangal. Lesser galangal is nearly unknown outside Malaysia, Singapore, and Indonesia, though it is available in the Netherlands, which has a large Indonesian community.

Storage: Store fresh galangal in the refrigerator for up to 1 week. Fresh galangal may be frozen just like ginger (page 193).

Recipe: *Tom Kha Kai (Thai Chicken Soup with Coconut Milk and Galangal)*

 1. **Bring 4 cups chicken stock, ¼ cup Thai fish sauce, the juice of 1 lime, 2 crushed wild lime leaves, a 2-inch section of lemongrass, and a 1-inch section of galangal to a boil. Simmer 20 minutes. Strain if desired (though left unstrained in Thailand, the lemongrass, lime leaves, and galangal are not meant to be eaten).**

 2. **Add ¼ pound bite-sized pieces of chicken breast, 1 13.5-ounce can coconut milk, and 2 to 10 (to taste) small red chiles, slightly crushed, and return to a boil. Lower the heat and simmer until the chicken is cooked through, about 2 minutes. Garnish with cilantro leaves and serve.**

Serving Suggestions:	Add chopped galangal to Southeast Asian stir-fries. • Use ground galangal in green and red Thai curry pastes. • Add grated galangal to Laotian green papaya salad.
Food Affinities:	**Greater galangal:** Asian chiles, beef, chicken, cilantro, coconut milk, fish, garlic, lemongrass, lime juice, *nam pla*, pork, rice, turmeric, yard-long beans. **Lesser galangal:** Coconut milk, duck, hot green chiles, lemongrass, lime juice, peanut.

GARLIC

Other Names:	*Aglio* (Italian); *ail* (French); *ajo* (Spanish); *alho* (Portuguese); *chesnok* (Russian); *katiem* (Thai); *kesuna* (Indonesian); *knoblauch* (German); *lasun* (Hindi); *ninniku* (Japanese); *sarmisak* (Turkish); *shum* (Hebrew); *skordo* (Greek); stinking rose; *suan* (Chinese); *thoum* (Arabic); *toi* (Vietnamese).
General Description:	*Garlic* (Allium sativum) *is a bulb enclosing individual pearly cloves covered by parchment-paper-like skin that has a notoriously pungent and sharp, earthy flavor.* There are two main types of garlic: the older hardneck or rocambole (*A. ophioscorodon*) varieties and the newer softneck (*A. sativum*) varieties developed by selection. Softneck has a fibrous stem that dries into a grasslike top that can be braided and has a milder flavor; intensely flavored hardneck garlic has a long,

hard, central stem surrounded by firm, easy-to-peel cloves. Peeled garlic cloves, which have had their skin removed by blowing air, are now sold in many supermarkets. Garlic scapes, also known as stems, spears, or tops, are the firm green seedpod stalks that form on hardneck garlic plants in early summer. When young and tender, they will be curled; as they mature, they straighten out and stiffen. A seasonal delicacy, the stalks are best stir-fried and are enjoyed for their herbal garlic flavor and tender-crisp texture.

Garlic may be purchased in many forms, including whole heads, whole peeled cloves, chopped garlic in oil and preservatives, dried garlic powder, granulated dried garlic, garlic extract, garlic granules, fried garlic pieces, and garlic salt.

Season:

Garlic is sold year-round, though new crop garlic is the best choice. Garlic is harvested in mid-summer and hung in sheds to dry. Garlic scapes may be found in farmers' markets and Asian, especially Korean, markets in early summer.

Purchase and Avoid:

Choose bulbs that are large, plump, and firm with a tight and unbroken sheath. Garlic heads with soft or shriveled cloves or with visible green shoots will be bitter. Pass up garlic with dark, powdery patches under the skin, signs of mold. When buying peeled garlic, look for pearly-white, firm cloves with no shriveling and no mold or stickiness.

Supermarket garlic is almost all softneck garlic. Look for hard-neck or rocambole garlic at farmers' markets or markets in areas with large Latino or Mediterranean populations.

Storage:

Store garlic in a cool, dark place with good air circulation away from other foods. Store peeled garlic in its container for up to 2 weeks in the refrigerator. Refrigerate garlic scapes for up to two weeks. Store garlic powder in a cool, dry, dark place.

Preparation:

- **To peel fresh garlic, rub off the loose outer skin, exposing the individual cloves. Pull cloves away from the core and place on a cutting board. Using the side of a heavy knife, smash down each garlic clove to break open its skin. Remove skin from individual cloves.**

- **Use garlic cloves whole, smashed, sliced, slivered, chopped, or pressed through a special garlic press. Chop garlic with a little kosher salt to keep the pieces from jumping around. Chopped garlic quickly oxidizes, darkening and becoming bitter, so chop no more than is needed.**

Serving Suggestions:

Steam new potatoes then sprinkle generously with persillade, parsley chopped with garlic. • Make Cuban cucumber salad: Thinly slice peeled and seeded cucumbers and toss with lime juice, chopped garlic, salt, and hot red pepper flakes. • Roast chicken quarters with peeled garlic cloves and chunks of new potatoes seasoned with chopped rosemary.

Food Affinities: Garlic, both raw and cooked, is used extensively with almost every savory food, cooked or raw, in almost all hot-weather cuisines of the world.

67a–c.

GINGER

Other Names: *Adrak* (Hindi); *chiang* (Chinese); *gember* (Dutch); *gengibre* (Portuguese); *gingembre* (French); *gung* (Vietnamese); *imbir* (Russian); *ingber* (Yiddish); *ingefær* (Danish, Norwegian); *jamveel* (Farsi); *jengibre* (Spanish); *khing* (Thai); *piperoriza* (Greek); *tangawizi* (Swahili); *zangvil* (Hebrew); *zanjabil* (Arabic); *zenzero* (Italian); *zinjibil* (Amharic); *zinziya* (Japanese).

General Description: *The knobby, hand-shaped rhizomes of ginger* (Zingiber officinale) *have a peppery, slightly sweet flavor and pungent, spicy aroma.* Ginger root ranges in color from pale greenish yellow to ivory; it may contain inconspicuous to prominent fibers, depending on age and variety. Ginger has been indispensable to Chinese cooking for 2,500 years and was probably introduced to Japan from there more than 2,000 years ago. In Japan, mioga ginger (Z. mioga) is used for its young buds and stems, rather than the rhizomes. It is pickled as a condiment for sushi.

Babylonians, ancient Egyptians, and Persians used ginger in cooking; the ancient Greeks of about 2400 B.C. made gingerbread similar to that we still eat today. Arab traders introduced ginger to the Mediterranean world in the first century A.D., and it's mentioned in the Koran. In the Middle East and North Africa, ginger is used dried even today, because historically drying was the only way it could arrive unspoiled on the lengthy voyage from Asia and India. The Spaniards planted ginger in Jamaica to avoid the long voyage from the Far East; today the spice is used in Jamaica to make ginger beer. Portuguese slaves cultivated ginger in West Africa and Brazil, where it became a basic seasoning.

Ginger is also preserved in brine or sugar syrup (stem ginger), or crystallized in sugar. Dried ginger may be available in whole form or, more commonly, as a powder with a spicy, more peppery, and less floral flavor than the fresh form.

Season: Fresh ginger is available year-round, with peak season in spring through early fall. Powdered, dried whole, candied, and other forms of preserved ginger are available year-round.

Purchase and Avoid: Because of its fleshy, knobby shape, fresh ginger is sold by the "hand." Choose plump, rock-hard ginger, heavy for its size, with smooth, taut skin; a light sheen; and fresh, spicy fragrance. Stay away from very

knobby, wrinkled, or shriveled roots; any root with
green mold or broken-off tips will deteriorate quickly.
Dry ginger is found in eight grades ranging from
peeled (top grade) to ratoons (bottom grade). Choose
soft, plump candied (or crystallized) ginger. Asian
markets are good places to buy candied ginger.

Storage:

To store fresh ginger, first wrap it in a paper towel,
then place in a zip-top plastic bag and refrigerate. To
preserve ginger longer, cover it with rice wine before
storing in the refrigerator. Fresh ginger can be frozen
up to 6 months. Place in a small zip-top plastic bag,
squeeze out the air, and freeze.

Preparation:

- **Trim off small knobs of ginger, then peel with a knife
  or peeler. Or use the back of a spoon to scrape off the
  thinnest layer of skin. Grate or slice thinly across the
  grain, or chop finely.**

- **If the ginger is fibrous and green rather than creamy
  inside, cut it into large chunks, then process, chop, or
  grate to a chunky paste. Squeeze out the juices
  through cheesecloth, discarding the fibers (or add
  them to Chinese chicken broth).**

- **If using frozen ginger, let the root warm up for about
  5 or 10 minutes, peel, then grate on a box grater and
  use immediately. Refreeze the remainder.**

Serving Suggestions:	Place fish on a bed of sliced scallions and shredded ginger, sprinkle with soy sauce and toasted sesame oil, and steam about 10 minutes. • Flavor apple pie, cobbler, and baked apples with ground dried ginger. • Add ground ginger to shortbread cookie doughs, to pastry dough for fruit tarts, and to the filling for pumpkin, squash, or sweet potato pie.
Food Affinities:	Almond, apple, butter, chicken, chiles, cilantro, garlic, honey, molasses, onion, pear, pineapple, scallion, seafood, sesame oil, snow peas, soy sauce, turkey, yam.

68. 📷 **GRAINS OF PARADISE**

Other Names:	Alligator pepper; *gawz as-Sudan* (Arabic); *graines de paradis* (French); *grani paradisi* (Italian); Guinea grains; *guineapfeffer* or *paradieskörner* (German); *idrifil* (Turkish); *korarima* (Amharic); *malagueta* (Spanish); melegueta pepper; *piperi melenketa* (Greek).
General Description:	*The small reddish brown seeds of grains of paradise* (Aframomum melegueta) *have a flavor like spicy, nutty black pepper, cardamom, and lemon, with woody and evergreen notes, a numbing quality, and a lingering camphor flavor.* The seeds are about the size and shape of cardamom, and both are in the Zingiberaceae (ginger) family. Most grains of paradise are imported from Ghana. In that part of Africa, the seeds are chewed on

cold days to warm the body. Grains of paradise were an important spice in fifteenth-century Europe, used as a pepper substitute. In the Renaissance, grains of paradise were common as beer flavoring. Today this spice is best known in North Africa, where it appears in the Moroccan spice mixture ras el hanout (page 286) and Tunisian gâlat dagga (page 281).

Purchase and Avoid: Grains of paradise can be purchased from specialty spice merchants.

Note: Grains of paradise must be ground before use and should be added shortly before serving. Despite its rather pungent taste, it's best used liberally.

Recipe: *Spiced Fruit Syrup with Grains of Paradise*

1. Combine ³/₄ cup sugar, ³/₄ cup dry white vermouth, ¹/₂ cup water, 2 tablespoons chopped rosemary leaves, 2 tablespoons chopped ginger, 2 teaspoons slightly crushed grains of paradise, and 2 tablespoons sherry vinegar in a large pot.

2. Bring to a boil, lower the heat, and simmer for about 10 minutes. Strain and cool. Sprinkle over fresh fruits such as strawberries, mango, melon, and peaches.

Serving Suggestions: Crush some grains of paradise with garlic and vinegar and spread over chicken, beef, or lamb before roasting.

• Brown chicken or fish fillets and top with a squeeze of lemon juice and a sprinkling of grains of paradise. • Season sautéed mushrooms with grains of paradise.

Food Affinities:
Black pepper, cinnamon, cloves, couscous, duck, eggplant, guinea hen, nutmeg, peach, plum, potato, pumpkin, red wine.

69. **HORSERADISH ROOT**

Other Names:
Armorakia or *chreno* (Greek); *barbaforte, cren,* or *rafano* (Italian); *chrzan pospolity* (Polish); *cran, cranson de Bretagne,* or *raifort* (French); *fajl haar* (Arabic); *hazeeret hagina* (Hebrew); *khren* (Russian); *khreyn* (Yiddish); *kren* or *meerrettich* (German); *mronge* (Swahili); *peberrod* (Danish); *rábanao* or *raiz-forte* (Portuguese); *rábano picante* or *taramago* (Spanish); *seiyouwasabi* (Japanese).

General Description:
Horseradish (Armoracia rusticana) *has long, large, knobby, dusty tan, pungent-hot roots used as a condiment.* Horseradish is believed to have originated in central Europe, the area where it is still most used. During the Renaissance, horseradish consumption spread from central Europe northward to Scandinavia and westward to England. By the late 1600s, horseradish was the standard accompaniment for beef and oysters in England. The hot, spicy, sinus-clearing bite

and penetrating smell of horseradish is almost absent until the root is grated or ground. As the cells are crushed, volatile oils are released by enzyme activity. Vinegar stops this reaction and stabilizes the flavor. Horseradish quickly loses its pungency after grinding. Fresh horseradish also loses flavor as it cooks, so it is best added toward the end of cooking.

Season: Fresh horseradish is harvested in early spring and late fall but is occasionally available year-round.

Purchase and Avoid: Look for a small horseradish root that is exceptionally hard and free of spongy or soft spots; very large horseradish roots may be quite fibrous. Avoid sprouting, shriveled, or green-tinged horseradish, which may be bitter. Dried horseradish flakes and powder may also be found. Prepared horseradish is mixed with vinegar and packed in small glass jars; the red kind has beet juice added to it for color and a bit of sweetness. Look for prepared horseradish in the dairy section of the supermarket.

Storage: Wrapped in slightly dampened paper towels and placed in a plastic bag, horseradish will keep in the refrigerator up to 2 weeks. Cut away any soft or moldy spots as they develop. Store prepared horseradish, whether purchased or homemade, in the refrigerator for several months.

Preparation: 1. **Scrub the root with a brush or abrasive sponge to get rid of any dirt.**

2. **Cut off only as big a piece as you'll need and pare off the outer skin.**

3. **Cut into small pieces and grind in a blender or food processor, which is less tearful than hand grating.**

4. **Immediately place grated horseradish in cold water to cover or mix it with vinegar to prevent discoloration.**

Note: The fumes are potent! Grind or grate fresh horseradish in a well-ventilated room, and avoid breathing the fumes.

Serving Suggestions: Serve with cold roast beef, corned beef, or poached salmon. • Add freshly grated horseradish to mashed potatoes. • Make seafood cocktail sauce by mixing ketchup or chili sauce and horseradish.

Food Affinities: Apple, beet, corned beef, cream, cream cheese, ham, lemon, potato, pumpernickel bread, raw seafood, roast beef, salmon, sour cream, vinegar.

70. **JUNIPER BERRY**

Other Names: *Aiteil* (Gaelic); *arar* (Arabic, Hebrew); *arkevthos* (Greek); *bayas de enebro* or *nebrina* (Spanish); *genièvre*

(French); *ginepro* (Italian); *jeneverbes* (Dutch); *junípero* (Portuguese); *mozhzhevelnik* (Russian); *mreteni* (Swahili); *wacholder* (German).

General Description:

Juniper (Juniperus communis)*, an evergreen tree, has small round berries (rightly called* cones*) that take three years to mature from pale green to fleshy blue-black; they have a piney, refreshing aroma reminiscent of gin.* The berries are the only spice from the Coniferae (evergreen) family and one of the few native to cold climates. Several species of *Juniperus* grow across temperate Europe and Asia, but the best quality berries hail from southern Europe. Picking the berries, which each contain three sticky, hard brown seeds, is no easy task, because they're nestled among needlelike foliage and are soft and easily crushed. Juniper is an important spice in many European cuisines, especially in Alpine regions, where juniper grows abundantly. The aromatic, cleansing flavor of juniper works best to cut rich, gamey, or fatty foods: reindeer in Scandinavia, wild duck in Ireland, wild boar in Italy, and hare in France.

Season:

Dried juniper is available all year, but it is most commonly used in the cold-weather months. Ripe blue-black juniper berries may be picked off the bush whenever they are found.

Purchase and Avoid:

Juniper berries are at their best when they are moist and soft to the touch. The cloudy bloom that appears on some berries is harmless. Look for whole juniper berries at specialty spice merchants and German or eastern European markets.

Note: People with kidney weakness and pregnant women
⚠   should not eat juniper.

Recipe: *Sauerkraut with Juniper*

🚰 1.   **Drain 1 pound sauerkraut (fresh bag-type is preferable to canned), rinse under cold water, and squeeze out the liquid.**

🍳🔥🔪 2.   **In a large skillet, heat 2 tablespoons bacon fat and brown 1 thinly sliced large red onion along with 3 cloves and 1 tablespoon coarsely crushed juniper berries. Add the sauerkraut, 2 tablespoons dark brown sugar, 2 tablespoons vodka, 2 tablespoons champagne vinegar, and 2 bay leaves.**

🚰 3.   **Bring to a boil, lower the heat to a simmer, and cook, stirring occasionally and adding a little water if necessary, until the sauerkraut is tender and most of the liquid has been absorbed, about 30 minutes. Serve with sausage, pork chops, or duck confit, discarding the cloves before serving.**

Serving   Braise red cabbage with apples, shallots, bacon, apple
Suggestions: cider vinegar, thyme, bay leaves, and juniper. • Roast

duck with prunes, juniper berries, and thyme. • Season roasted salmon with juniper berries, shallots, and vermouth.

Food Affinities:
Allspice, apple, bacon, black pepper, boar, duck, goose, marjoram, onion, pâté, pork, sage, shallot, red wine, thyme, venison, vermouth.

71. 📷 **KOKAM**

Other Names:
Aamsool; black kokam; brindel berry; *cocum* (French, Italian, Spanish); *kokam* (German); *kokam phool, kokam uppagi,* or *raktapurka* (India).

General Description:
Kokam, which resembles a small, dark purple plum, is the fruit of a tropical evergreen tree (Garcinia indica) *that grows only in India.* This fruit is closely related to the legendary mangosteen fruit. The dried, very dark purple, flattened rind is rather sticky and has curled edges and a fruity, balsamic aroma with tannic notes. Its flavor is sharp, acidic, and salty, with refreshing dried-fruit sweetness. Kokam fruits are harvested when ripe, and it is usually the rind, comprising about 50 percent of the whole, that is preserved, by drying in the sun. Sometimes the entire fruit is halved and dried so that the dried seeds are visible in their chambers. Salt may be rubbed onto the rind to speed up drying and help with preserving the leathery pieces.

Kokam is used in India as a souring agent like tamarind or amchur. Big glasses of *kokam sharbat* (a cold beverage) are drunk to counteract the blazing heat. Kokam butter, extracted from the seeds, is used for cooking in some regions; it's sold in pale gray or yellow slabs. The closely related *asam gelugor*, or fish tamarind (*G. atroviridis*), is traditionally eaten with fatty foods to prevent weight gain and is rubbed on fatty meats to dissolve the fat in dishes such as the *rendang* of Sumatra.

Purchase and Avoid:
Kokam is sold whole or in small leathery pieces. The deeper the color, the better the quality. Look for kokam at Indian markets and buy in small quantities, as the soft, pliable rinds dry out and lose their flavor. Any crystallized white powder is likely the result of excess salt used in the drying process.

Storage:
Store in an airtight jar.

Note:
Before using, rinse kokam under cold water to remove excess salt. Kokam will color everything it touches, imparting a beautiful pinkish purple color to foods. It will also stain your clothes, so handle with care.

Recipe:
Kokam Sharbat (Cooling Indian Drink)

1. **Soak ½ cup dried kokam in hot water to cover until soft. Using a blender or food processor, puree with**

1 teaspoon toasted and ground cumin seeds. Strain the puree, discarding the solids.

 2.   Boil 4 cups water with 2 cups sugar to make a syrup. Add the strained puree to the cooled syrup and mix well.

 3.   Add ¼ cup of the mixture to a large glass of ice-cold water and mix well. Serve chilled with ice.

Serving Suggestions: Add 3 or 4 whole dried kokam skins to an average-sized dish of coconut-based fish or shrimp curry.

Food Affinities: Asafetida, coriander, cumin, fish curry, ginger, lentils, okra, potato, shrimp, tomato, turmeric.

72. 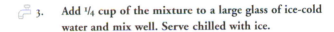 LICORICE

Other Names: *Alcaçuz* (Portuguese); black sugar; *glykoriza* (Greek); *jethimadh* (Hindi); *kan ts'ao* (Chinese); *kanzou* (Japanese); *lakrichnik* (Russian); *lakrids* (Danish); *lakritze* or *sussholz* (German); *liquirizia* or *regolizia* (Italian); *liquorice, orozuz,* or *ragaliz* (Spanish); *réglisse* (French); *shush kireah* (Hebrew); Spanish juice; *sus* (Arabic); *susu* (Swahili); *zoethout* (Dutch).

General Description: *Licorice (Glycyrrhiza glabra) is used for its root and the juice extracted from it; both have a powerful aroma reminiscent of anise or fennel but considerably stronger and a sweet, warm, rather medicinal taste.* Licorice root, especially the root bark, contains about 4 percent glycyrrhizin, which is about 50 times sweeter than sucrose (cane sugar). Licorice was known to the Greeks, Egyptians, and Romans as a remedy for coughs and colds. The black juice extracted from the roots was taken as a refreshing drink by the Greeks and Romans. German and Russian licorice is extracted from wild licorice (*G. echinata*). Chinese licorice (*G. uralensis*), widely cultivated in China, is grown for export and also to flavor Chinese master sauces, in which a strongly salted and spiced broth is used and reused as a cooking liquid.

In northern Europe, especially Holland, northern Germany, and Scandinavia, licorice is the base of traditional candies made from evaporated licorice juice plus flavorings like lemon or, more traditionally, salmiac (sal ammoniac, or ammonium chloride), and usually no sugar. The Dominican monastery at Pontefract, England, which first cultivated licorice in the sixteenth century, later became the center of the English licorice candy industry. In Mongolia, licorice leaves are called *nakhalsa* and used as a tea. Licorice root is added for flavor, body, and black color to porter and stout, Turkish raki, and Italian Sambuca, as well as snuff and chewing tobacco. It is widely used as a flavoring for candies, baked goods, ice cream, and soft drinks. Licorice-based sweets are suspected to cause high blood pressure, but it is unclear whether consumption of a few licorice candies has any significant effect. The sweetness in licorice root is safe for diabetics.

Purchase and Avoid: Licorice may be found dried in root form; as a gray-green, very fine, talcumlike powder, especially in natural foods stores; and in a liquid extract from Italian and other Mediterranean groceries.

Recipe: *Licorice Ice Cream*

1. In a large bowl, whisk 6 egg yolks with ¾ cup sugar. In a nonaluminum saucepan, combine 1½ cups milk, 1¼ cups heavy cream, and 10 (1 inch long) soft black licorice candies and bring to a boil over medium-high heat, stirring frequently so the licorice melt. (If the licorice resists melting, puree it with some hot milk.)

2. Beat a little of the hot milk mixture into the eggs and then, in a steady stream, slowly whisk in the rest of the hot milk. Return the mixture to a pan over medium-low heat and cook, stirring constantly, until it thickens visibly and registers 165°F on a candy thermometer. Do not boil.

3. Remove from the heat and stir in 2 tablespoons Pernod liqueur and 1 tablespoon vanilla extract. Strain through a fine sieve into a bowl, discarding any solids. Cool, then chill in the refrigerator. Freeze as directed in an ice cream maker.

Serving Suggestions:	Flavor custard and panna cotta with licorice. • Add a little licorice extract to fruit salads. • Season roast pork or chicken with a few melted licorice candies.
Food Affinities:	Allspice, cardamom, cinnamon, cloves, coriander, fennel seed, ginger, ice cream, pepper, poached fruit, pork, poultry, Szechuan pepper.

73. 📷 **MAHLAB**

Other Names:	*Abrunheiro-bravo* or *esgana-cão* (Portuguese); *agriokerasia* or *machalepi* (Greek); *cerezo de Santa Lucía* (Spanish); *cerisier de Sainte-Lucie* (French); *ciliegio canino* or *ciliegio di Santa Lucia* (Italian); English cherry; *habbul malan* (Farsi); *idrisağacı* or *mahlep* (Turkish); rock cherry; St. Lucie cherry; *steinweichsel* or *türkische kirsche* (German); *tunda la mahaleb* (Swahili); *vishnya makhalebka* (Russian).
General Description:	*The stones of St. Lucy's cherries* (Prunus mahaleb) *contain small beige kernels called* mahlab, *which are about the size of a large peppercorn.* Native to southern Europe, the small tree grows wild in the Mediterranean region across to Turkey. Mahlab has an aroma reminiscent of cherry, almond, flowers, and rose water, with a nutty yet surprisingly bitter aftertaste. First used for perfumes and medicine, mahlab later became a popular culinary spice, especially for flavoring breads. Mahlab

is used in Middle Eastern and eastern Mediterranean cooking to give an intriguing fruit flavor to sweet pastries, cookies, confectionery, and Nabulsi cheese (a white, brined cheese from Jordan). In Greece, the kernels go into *tsoureki*, a briochelike braided sweet bread eaten only at Easter time. Iran is the most important grower of mahlab, followed by Turkey and Syria.

Season: Mahlab may be easiest to find around Easter.

Purchase and Avoid: Look for mahlab in Greek, Turkish, Lebanese, or Arabic markets. Buy whole mahlab kernels and crush them just before using. Although mahlab may sometimes be bought ground, once powdered it goes from creamy white to yellow and loses its flavor and aroma rapidly.

Storage: Store in an airtight container to prevent the aroma from penetrating other foods, or freeze.

Preparation: • **Grind mahlab by mixing the kernels with a little of the sugar or salt called for in a recipe. Use a mortar and pestle or clean coffee grinder to grind the two together; the salt or sugar granules will help break the mahlab seeds into powder.**

Recipe: *Mahmoul (Syrian Filled Cookies)*

 1. **Combine 4 cups fine semolina, 1 cup all-purpose flour, 1 tablespoon freshly crushed mahlab, and 1 1/4 cups**

melted unsalted butter. Let the mixture stand, covered, for 1 hour. Knead in about ½ cup water, just enough to make a soft but not sticky dough.

2. Make the filling by processing together 1 pound walnuts or pistachios, 1½ cups granulated sugar, 1 teaspoon orange flower water, and about 2 tablespoons water, or enough to make a thick paste.

3. Preheat the oven to 375°F. Roll a walnut-size piece of dough into a ball and, holding it in your cupped palm, make a deep depression in its center with your finger. Press in 1 teaspoon of filling and pinch the edges of the dough firmly together to fully enclose the filling. Continue forming cookies in the same manner, arranging them seam side down and 1 inch apart on 2 greased baking sheets.

4. Bake until pale golden, about 25 minutes. Transfer to racks to cool, then dust with confectioners' sugar. Makes about 30.

Serving Suggestions: Add ½ to 1 teaspoon freshly ground mahlab per cup of flour in recipes for sweet yeast breads like brioche. • Add ground mahlab in small quantities to rice pudding and other creamy desserts.

Food Affinities: Butter, honey, milk puddings, pastry dough, pistachio, rose water, semolina, sugar, Turkish rice, walnut.

74. **MASTIC**

Other Names: *Aza* (Arabic); Chios Greek mastic; gum mastic; *mastic* (French); *mastice* (Italian); *mastikha* (Greek); *mastique* (Spanish); *mastix* (German); tears of God.

General Description: *Mastic is a resin obtained from* Pistacia lentiscus *var.* chia, *a tree related to the pistachio that grows only on Chios, a Greek island in the Aegean Sea that is the reputed birthplace of Homer.* The immeasurably ancient mastic tree is a slow-growing evergreen with shiny, dark green leaves and a rough, gnarled trunk. When tapped or hurt, as the process is called, the trunk yields a clear resin that hardens into brittle, crystalline pieces referred to as *tears*. If broken, the tears have a shiny quartzlike surface with a faint piney aroma and a bitter mineral-like flavor. After a few minutes of chewing, mastic becomes beige and takes on the texture of chewing gum. In cookery, mastic contributes to flavor but is just as important for smooth texture and as a binding agent.

Among its many uses, culinary and medicinal, mastic is deemed an aphrodisiac in southern Morocco and Mauritania. Mastic was an important commodity in the Middle Ages, but is now almost exclusively used in Greek cooking, where it goes into specialties like mastic candy, *loukoumi* (Turkish delight), liquors like ouzo and raki, and *tsoureki*, a brioche-type braided Easter sweet bread. There is also a local Chios mastic liqueur.

Season: Mastic production occurs between June and
September and is finished in December. The crystals
may be purchased any time of year.

Purchase
and Avoid: The purest crystals are called *dahtilidopetres* (flintstones)
and the soft ones with spots are called *kantiles* (blisters). Mastic is available from online specialty producers
and may occasionally be found at Greek groceries.

Storage: Store in an airtight container away from humidity.

Recipe: ***Kaimaki Ice Cream with Mastic***

1. **Pound ½ teaspoon mastic to a powder with 2 tablespoons sugar. Mix with 1 tablespoon cornstarch and stir in ½ cup milk.**

2. **Mix 1 cup milk, ½ cup heavy cream, and 1 cup sugar in a saucepan and heat to scalding.**

3. **While constantly whisking, pour a little of the hot milk mixture into the mastic mixture. Scrape back into the pot and heat, stirring constantly, until thick and bubbling.**

4. **Transfer the mixture to a metal bowl and stir in 1 teaspoon orange blossom water. Place the bowl in a larger bowl of ice and water to cool the mixture quickly. Chill, then freeze as directed in an ice cream maker.**

Serving Suggestions:	Pound mastic with a little sugar and mix with rose or orange blossom water; use to flavor pound cake, pastry dough, meringues, or puddings (¼ teaspoon of crushed mastic is enough for 4 servings). • Pound mastic with salt, olive oil, lemon juice, and spices to bind the lamb mixture for Turkish doner kebab.
Food Affinities:	Almond cake, breads, lemon, olive oil, pastries, pistachio, puddings, rose water, semolina pudding.

75. MSG

Other Names:	Accent (trade name); *Ajinomoto* (Japanese trade name); *sapore* (Italian); *wei jing* (Chinese).
General Description:	*MSG (monosodium glutamate), a chemical compound in the form of a white, coarse powder with very little flavor of its own, acts as a flavor enhancer that seems to make the tongue more receptive to savory and salty tastes.* For more than a thousand years, the Japanese have been using the brown seaweed kombu as the base for soup stocks. In 1908, a Japanese chemist, Kikunae Ikeda, found that kombu is an especially rich source of monosodium glutamate. He also found that MSG provides a unique, savory taste, which he named *umami* (meaning "savory" or "delicious"), and added it to the other four basic tastes: sweet, sour, salty, and bitter. A year after Ikeda's discovery, the Japanese

company Ajinomoto began selling pure MSG, extracting it from wheat gluten proteins.

The unfortunate aspect of MSG is that it has been exploited to provide a cheap, one-dimensional substitute for more complex flavors by industrial food manufacturers and less-than-stellar restaurants. Beginning in the late 1960s, MSG was blamed for "Chinese restaurant syndrome," which afflicts susceptible people with sensations of burning, pressure, and chest pain.

Purchase and Avoid:	Purchase MSG under the trade name Accent in America, or Ajimonoto in Asian markets.
Serving Suggestions:	Add a pinch of MSG to soups, stocks, meat, vegetables, poultry, and fish to enhance natural flavor, not as a substitute for flavor.
Food Affinities:	Most savory foods, especially fish, meat, poultry, seafood, soups, and vegetables.

76a–b.

MUSTARD SEED

Other Names: **White mustard:** *Bach gioi tu* (Vietnamese); *chieh* (Chinese); *gorchitsa belaya* (Russian); *hardal lavan* (Hebrew); *khardal* (Arabic); *mostarda branca* (Portuguese); *mostaza silvestre* (Spanish); *moutarde blanche* (French); *netch senafich* (Amharic); *senape biancha* (Italian); *sinapi agrio* (Greek); *weisser senf*

(German). **Black mustard:** *Cai den* (Vietnamese); *gai lat* (Chinese); *haradali* (Swahili); *hardal shahor* (Hebrew); *khardal aswad* (Arabic); *mostarda* (Portuguese); *mostaza negra* (Spanish); *moutarde noire* (French); *rai* (Hindi); *schwarzer senf* (German); *shiro-karashi* (Japanese); *sinapi mauro* (Greek); *tikur senafich* (Amharic). **Brown mustard:** Indian mustard; *Indischer senf* (German); *mostaza de Indias* (Spanish); *moutarde brune* (French).

General Description:

There are three main types of mustard, all in the Brassica (cabbage) family and all with small, rounded seeds. Relatively mild though still pungent, white mustard (*Sinapis alba*) originated in the Mediterranean and has pale yellow to gold seeds used mostly for prepared mustard and pickling spices. Pungent black mustard (*Brassica nigra*), which originated in Asia Minor, has smaller dark brown seeds; it's important in Indian cooking. Easier to cultivate and less pungent, brown mustard (*B. juncea*), which originated in the Himalayas, has larger seeds and is widely used in Europe for prepared mustard.

Mustard has been cultivated since ancient times and has been an important spice in Europe since Roman times because, unlike many spices, it could be grown locally. Medieval European courts often employed a *mustardarius,* an official in charge of growing and preparing mustard. The first mustard companies date back to the mid-fourteenth century around Dijon, France. In 1804 in England, Jeremiah Colman developed a way (still used today) to make surprisingly hot powdered mustard from the oily seeds.

Mustard is second only to peppercorns as a spice in the United States, where most of it goes into mild, bright yellow ballpark mustard colored with turmeric. In France, mild Bordeaux mustard is brown, slightly sweet, and often tarragon flavored; strong Dijon mustard is smooth and pale yellow; mild *moutarde de Meaux* is made from coarsely crushed mustard seeds. In Düsseldorf, Germany's mustard capital, *löwensenf* (lion's mustard) is a pungent mustard similar to Dijon made from black mustard seeds. Sweet Bavarian mustard is made from coarsely ground white mustard seeds, honey, and herbs. In Italy, mustard flavors *mostarda di frutta*, a spicy fruit relish, but is rarely used on its own.

Whole white mustard seeds are used to season pickles, sausage, and sauerkraut in Europe and North America. In India, black mustard seeds are commonly toasted or fried in a little oil until they pop and acquire a grayish hue. Frying changes the character of the seeds so they are nutty and mild. Though black mustard seed oil is used as a flavoring and for cooking in India, it may contain harmful compounds, so it's illegal to sell it for food use in most Western countries. Indian food shops often sell mustard oil labeled "for external use only." As is done in India, mustard oil should be heated to a high temperature then cooled before further cooking, a process that is thought to be useful for detoxification.

Purchase and Avoid: Buy yellow mustard seeds for pickling mixtures, black mustard seeds for Indian cooking, or mustard powder to make English- or Chinese-style prepared hot mustard. Buy prepared mustard to use as a condiment.

Recipe: *Creole Mustard Sauce*

1. **Whisk together 2 cups mayonnaise, 1 finely diced celery stalk, 1 diced roasted red bell pepper, ½ cup chopped Italian parsley, ½ cup thinly sliced scallions, 4 tablespoons whole-grain mustard, 2 tablespoons sherry vinegar, 2 tablespoons paprika, 1 tablespoon dry mustard, 1 tablespoon prepared horseradish, and 2 teaspoons hot sauce.**

2. **Store in the refrigerator. Serve with grilled seafood, fish, chicken, and steak.**

Serving Suggestions: Mix Dijon mustard, whole-grain mustard, garlic, olive oil, chopped thyme, salt, and pepper and use to coat rack or leg of lamb before roasting. • Make pork curry vindaloo with toasted mustard seeds and mustard oil.

Food Affinities: Apple, asparagus, beans, chicken, chutney, corned beef, curry, dal, Gruyère cheese, hot dogs, ketchup, lamb, lentils, pork, potato, roast beef, sausage, shrimp.

77. **NIGELLA SEED**

Other Names: Black caraway; *charnushka* (Russian); *cheveux de Vénus*, *nigelle*, or *poivrette* (French); *cominho-preto* or *nigela* (Portuguese); *çörek oto* or *siyah kimyon* (Turkish); *grano nero* (Italian); *habba sauda* or *sanouz* (Arabic); *jinten hitam* (Indonesian); *kalonji* or *munga reala* (Hindi); *ketzah* (Hebrew); *neguilla* or *pasionara* (Spanish); nutmeg flower; onion seed; Roman coriander; *schwarzkümmel* or *zwiebelsame* (German); *siah daneh* (Farsi); *tikur azmud* (Amharic).

General Description: *Nigella* (Nigella sativa) *has small, matte black, hard, sharp-cornered seeds with an oregano-like scent; they're used for their hauntingly aromatic, acrid, smoky flavor.* Nigella probably originated in western Asia but today is cultivated from Egypt to India. Though it's sometimes called *black cumin*, it's unrelated to cumin; the black cumin mentioned in the Old Testament may actually be nigella, which has been found in the Giza pyramid and in the tomb of King Tutankhamen. Confusingly, nigella is also known as onion (or wild onion) seed because the two look similar, although only nigella is used as a spice. In eastern Europe, nigella tops Russian black and Jewish rye breads. Turkish and Indian naan are frequently sprinkled with the seed. It enhances Turkish, Lebanese, Iranian, and Indian vegetable dishes, pickles, chutneys, and breads. An Arab proverb says, "Nigella seed is a remedy for every disease except death."

Purchase
and Avoid:
Whole nigella seeds should be jet-black. Poor quality seeds will have bits of husk mixed in with the seeds.

Recipe: ***Indian Naan with Nigella Seeds***

 1. **Place 1 tablespoon nigella seeds and ½ cup cold water in a small saucepan and bring to a boil.**

 2. **Remove from the heat, transfer to a large bowl, and allow the mixture to cool until lukewarm, then sprinkle in 1 teaspoon dry yeast; add 1 cup plain, unsweetened yogurt; and stir well. Add 2 cups all-purpose flour and mix until well combined. Cover and leave in a warm place for 30 minutes, or until partially risen.**

 3. **Knead in 1 teaspoon salt, 1 tablespoon vegetable oil, and 2 cups all-purpose flour, kneading until the dough is smooth and elastic. Cover again and leave in a warm place until the dough has doubled in size, about 2 hours. Knead the dough briefly. Divide it into 6 portions, shape into balls, then roll out into rounds. Pull the rounds into long teardrops.**

4. **Preheat the oven to 450°F, preferably with a pizza stone in place. Lay 3 of the breads directly onto the stone (or a lightly oiled baking pan) and bake 5 minutes or until lightly browned. Repeat with remaining breads.**

5.   **Serve warm, brushed with butter.**

Serving
Suggestions:
Spread whole-grain mustard on rolled-out pizza dough, spread with caramelized onions, and sprinkle with nigella seeds before baking. • Sprinkle nigella seeds over bread doughs before baking.

Food
Affinities:
Allspice, black-eyed peas, black bread, chickpeas, cilantro, coriander, cumin, eggplant, fenugreek, ginger, lemon, string cheese, turmeric, white beans.

78a–b.   NUTMEG AND MACE

Other Names:
Nutmeg: *Basbasa* (Arabic); *chan thet* (Thai); *djus hendi* (Farsi); *egoz musqat* (Hebrew); *gabz* (Amharic); *hindis-tancevizi* (Turkish); *jaiphal* (Hindi); *jou tou kou* (Chinese); *moschokarido* (Greek); *muskatnuss* (German); *muskatny oryekh* (Russian); *noce moscata* (Italian); *noix de muscade* (French); *noz-moscada* (Portuguese); *nuez moscada* (Spanish); *pala* (Indonesian). **Mace:** *Besbase* (Turkish); *dok chand* (Thai); *fleur de muscade* or *macis* (French); *fuljan* (Arabic); *javatri* (Hindi); *macis* (Spanish, Portuguese); *muskatblomme* (Danish); *muskat-bluete* (German); *muskatnyi tsvet* (Russian); *sekar pala* (Indonesian).

General
Description:
Nutmeg is the large, light grayish brown, speckled, wood-hard kernel that grows inside the apricot-like fruit of a

tropical tree (Myristica fragrans). Surrounding nutmeg in the fruit is a web of mace, called the *aril*, that is brilliant scarlet when harvested but changes to a dull reddish orange after drying. Both spices are strongly aromatic, with a warm and slightly musky flavor. Nutmeg is a bit spicier with a sharper aroma, while mace is gentler, fresher, and more rounded in flavor. Nutmeg quickly loses its fragrance when ground, so it's best freshly grated. Whole nutmeg, though hard on its surface, is easy to grate by hand. Note that the myristicin contained in nutmeg and mace is narcotic and may be harmful if ingested in large quantities.

Europeans believed that nutmeg originated in India, though actually it came from the famed Spice Islands (the Moluccas) in eastern Indonesia. In the sixteenth century, Portuguese ships sailed to India and further, bringing back large quantities of the hugely popular nutmeg. For 150 years starting in the seventeenth century, the Dutch monopolized the nutmeg trade, as they did with cloves. In the eighteenth century, the French smuggled nutmeg trees out from the Banda Islands and broke the monopoly.

In the Arab world and northern India, nutmeg and mace flavor delicate meat dishes. In Europe and North America, these spices flavor cakes, crackers, poached fruits, and cheese sauces. The Dutch favor nutmeg, using it to season cabbage, potatoes, meat, soups, stews, and sauces. Mace complements seafood and lighter meat dishes as well as pickles and ketchup.

Many spice mixtures contain nutmeg and mace. Nutmeg and mace can be used interchangeably in many dishes.

Purchase and Avoid: Whole nutmeg is preferable. Good quality whole nutmegs will be hard and heavy for their weight with no tiny holes, a sign of insect damage. Buy powdered nutmeg in small quantities, because it quickly loses flavor. Mace is more expensive than nutmeg because it takes 400 pounds of nutmeg to make 1 pound of mace. Whole blade mace is the most expensive form; mace is most often found ground.

Storage: Whole nutmeg and mace will keep quite well. Powdered nutmeg and mace are more perishable.

Recipe: *Classic Eggnog*

 1. **Beat 8 egg yolks with ¾ cup sugar until light. Meanwhile, scald 2 cups milk and 2 cups heavy cream.**

 2. **Beat a little of the hot cream mix into the yolks to temper them, then add rest of the cream to the yolks. Heat in a nonreactive pot until the mixture visibly thickens at about 165°F. Do not boil.**

 3. **Remove from the heat and whisk in 1½ teaspoons freshly ground nutmeg, ½ teaspoon ground mace, a**

pinch of ground cloves, ¼ cup bourbon, and ¼ cup dark rum. Serve in small punch cups and top with a grating of fresh nutmeg.

Serving
Suggestions:
Grate fresh nutmeg into creamed or buttered spinach. • Grate nutmeg over steamed potatoes, winter squash, carrots, or cauliflower. • Flavor pumpkin pie, sweet potato pie, and gingerbread with nutmeg. • Sprinkle mace on seafood before grilling or pan-frying. • Season stock with mace and use it to steam shellfish. • Sprinkle mace over applesauce and baked apples.

Food
Affinities:
Nutmeg: Apple, butter, carrot, cream, parsnip, pear, ricotta cheese, sage, spinach. **Mace:** Cabbage, chicken, curry, fish, pâté, shellfish, spice cakes, terrines, veal.

79a–c.

ONIONS AND SHALLOTS

Other Names:
Onion: *Basal* (Arabic); *bawang merah* (Indonesian); *bazal* (Hebrew); *cebola* (Portuguese); *cebolla* (Spanish); *chung* (Chinese); *cipolla* (Italian); *hanh* (Vietnamese); *key shinkurt* (Amharic); *kitunguu* (Swahili); *kremmidi* (Greek); *løg* (Danish); *luk* (Russian); *oignon* (French); *piaz* (Farsi, Hindi); *soğan* (Turkish); *ton hom* (Thai); *tsibele* (Yiddish); *tsong* (Tibetan); *zwiebel* (German). **Shallot:** *Ascalonia, chalota,* or *escalma* (Spanish); *aschlauch, klöben,* or *schalotte* (German); *askalonio* (Greek); *chalota das cosinhas* (Portuguese); *chaloto*

(Provençal French); *ciboule* or *échalote* (French); *horm lek* (Thai); *kitunguu kidogo sana* (Swahili); *scalogno* (Italian); *shalot* (Russian); Spanish garlic.

General Description:

The onion (Allium cepa), *a member of the lily family, has round to elongated bulbs with white, yellow, or red skin; they're sharply pungent when raw and sweet when cooked.* The bulb may be used as a vegetable (served whole or in large pieces) or as an aromatic vegetable for seasoning. Onions may also be found dried, as either bits, slices, flakes, or powder. Onions are an indispensable ingredient in nearly every cuisine.

Raw onions ground with spices are used to marinate meat, poultry, and seafood in Indonesian *bumbu* and Jamaican jerk seasoning. In India, onions are fried slowly with spices until they turn brown before adding other vegetables or meat. Crisp fried onion rings are popular in central Europe and Vietnam; in Indonesia they top the fried rice dish *nasi goreng*. Onion powder is used in chili powder and Cajun seasoning (both page 279), and dehydrated onions are the main ingredient in most herbal substitutes for salt.

The closely related shallot (*A. ascalonicum*) is smaller and denser than the onion. Shallots are much favored by chefs because of their sweet aromatic yet pungent flavor and because they hold their firm texture even through long cooking. They're quite popular in northern France, where they are essential for red wine sauces, béarnaise sauce, and flavored mayonnaise. They may also be found in intensely flavored freeze-dried bits. Asian shallots, also called Thai pink or purple shallots, are used extensively in Southeast Asian cooking. They are often slow-fried until crispy.

Season: 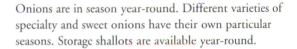 Onions are in season year-round. Different varieties of specialty and sweet onions have their own particular seasons. Storage shallots are available year-round.

Purchase and Avoid: Look for onions that are dry, firm, and shiny with a thin skin. The necks should be tightly closed with no sprouts emerging. Avoid onions with dark patches and soft spots. Onions with green sprouts will taste bitter. Dehydrated onion flakes, onion powder, granulated onion, and onion salt are found in the spice section. Choose large, plump, firm, well-shaped shallots that are not sprouting. Peeled shallots are sometimes available in supermarkets, though the quality of these is not high. Avoid shallots that are wrinkled or sprouting or show any signs of black mold. Specialty spice merchants carry freeze-dried or dehydrated shallots and onions.

Storage: Store shallots and storage onions in a cool, dry, well-ventilated place up to 1 month. Store sweet onions in the refrigerator up to 2 weeks. Dried onions and shallots may be stored unrefrigerated up to 6 months.

Recipe: ***Tandoori Onion Salad***

1. **Thinly slice 3 red or sweet onions, sprinkle with 1 tablespoon kosher salt, and drain in a colander for 1 hour. Rinse and pat dry.**

2. **Dissolve 2 tablespoons dark brown sugar into the juice of 1 lemon and a little hot water and mix with the onions.**

3. **Add 3 thinly sliced tomatoes, 1 thinly sliced green pepper, 1 thinly sliced green or red chile, 1 tablespoon grated ginger, 2 tablespoons chopped cilantro, and salt to taste. Serve as a relish with naan, papadam, and other Indian breads or with tandoori dishes.**

Serving Suggestions: Add onion powder to creamy vegetable soups, vegetables, chowders, stews, casseroles, dips, salad dressings, cheese sauce, hamburger mix, and egg dishes. • Sprinkle onion flakes on beef, pork, lamb, chicken, fish, and veal before roasting. • Sauté minced shallots in butter, toss with wilted spinach or other greens, and sprinkle with nutmeg. • Add freeze-dried shallots when making salad dressings, hamburger mixes, or sautéed vegetables.

Food Affinities: Onions are used in almost every savory dish imaginable worldwide. Shallots pair well with French, Belgian, Vietnamese, Thai, and Indonesian dishes.

80a–d. 📷 **PAPRIKA**

Other Names:

Paprika: *Boia de ardei* (Romanian); *deghi mirch* (Hindi); *édes paprika*, *fiszerpaprika*, or *piros paprika* (Hungarian); *fulful halou* (Arabic); *paprica* (Italian); *paprika de Hongrie* or *piment doux d'Espagne* (French); *papryka* (Polish); *perets krasnyj* (Russian); *pimentão doce* (Portuguese); *pimento* (Spanish); *piperia* (Greek); *tian jiao* (Mandarin); *tihm jiu* (Cantonese); *yafranj karya* (Amharic). **Espelette pepper:** *Ezpeletako bipera* (Basque); *piment d'Espelette* (French).

General Description:

Paprika, the name for a wide range of aromatic powdered red peppers from various strains of Capsicum annuum, *ranges in flavor from sweet to hot, depending on the variety of pepper and whether the hotter seeds and spongy tissue (or placenta) were included.* Paprika is equally valued for its taste and its bright red color, derived from capsanthin. Although all *Capsicum* species originated in the New World, the particular varieties used to make paprika were developed in Europe, especially Hungary. The national spice of Hungary, paprika comes in grades ranging from sweet and mild to quite hot. The Hungarian "national dish" is *gulyás* (goulash), a thick and spicy soup well seasoned with paprika, made from beef, vegetables, and *tarhonya*, a special pasta. Sweet Spanish paprika from Murcia is made from small, round, intensely flavored and sweet-fleshed ñora peppers that are sun-dried and hand ground; the smoked paprika powder called *pimentón* also hails from Spain.

Espelette pepper, France's only native pepper, comes from the Basque region. The peppers are hand harvested, hand sorted, dried on the sunny side of the houses, and then oven-dried and crushed hot.

Purchase and Avoid:	The highest grade of Hungarian paprika, *különleges*, (exquisitely delicate) consists of only the flesh of fully ripe, flawless peppers and has a mild, delicate flavor, brilliant red color, and silky texture. *Édesnemes* (noble-sweet), the most widely exported grade, has subtle pungency and bright red color. *Rosza* (rose) is less colorful and has more heat because it's ground with some seeds. Spanish pimentón is sold in three forms: *dulce* (sweet and mild), *agridulce* (bittersweet), and *picante* (hot). French espelette peppers can be purchased in paste or puree form to flavor sauces; in powder form to sprinkle on foods before serving; as a mild cream to use instead of mayonnaise; and in brine to serve as a garnish.
Storage:	Paprika will keep well for 2 years if stored in a cool, dark place.
Recipe:	***Hazelnut Romesco Sauce***

  I.   **Puree 2 roasted red bell peppers and their juices in the bowl of a food processor. Without washing the**

bowl, transfer the puree to a small pot and cook slowly until it's thick enough to hold its shape, about 10 minutes.

 2. Place 6 cloves garlic and ½ cup olive oil in a small pot and cook together until the garlic is lightly browned, about 10 minutes. Add 1 thick slice French bread cut into rough cubes and cook 2 minutes longer, or until lightly browned.

3. Place the pepper paste, ¼ pound lightly toasted and skinned hazelnuts, and the garlic, bread cubes, and their cooking oil back into the food processor. Process to a chunky paste, then add 1½ teaspoons pimentón and ½ cup olive oil and process again until a thick, rose-colored paste the consistency of mayonnaise is obtained. Serve the sauce with seafood or vegetables.

Serving Suggestions: Add paprika to barbecue rubs for meat and poultry. • Sprinkle paprika on fish or chicken before broiling. • Season deviled eggs with paprika and sprinkle some on top for garnish. • Add pimentón to Spanish rice for extra flavor.

Food Affinities: Beef, cabbage, caraway, chicken, cream, eggs, fish, garlic, goulash, onion, paella, potato, pork, rice, sausage, seafood, veal.

81a–g. **PEPPERCORNS**

Other Names: *Biber* (Turkish); *cây tiêu* (Vietnamese); *fefer* (Yiddish); *felfel* (Farsi); *fulful* (Arabic); *gol mirch* (Hindi); *hu jiao* (Mandarin); *koshou* (Japanese); *kundo berbere* (Amharic); *merica* (Indonesian); *pepe* (Italian); *perets* (Russian); *pfeffer* (German); *pili-pili* (Swahili); *pilpel* (Hebrew); *pimenta* (Portuguese); *pimienta* (Spanish); *piperi* (Greek); *poivre* (French); *prik thai* (Thai); *wuh jiu* (Cantonese).

General Description:

Peppercorns, the small, highly pungent and aromatic dried fruits of the pepper plant (Piper nigrum)*, are found in four different versions: black, white, green, and red.* Black and white pepper were known in antiquity, but green pepper and the even newer red pepper are more recent inventions. After Alexander the Great crossed central Asia in the fourth century B.C., new trading routes brought pepper to the West. Within a short time, pepper's growing popularity made it a highly valued spice. In spite of, or perhaps because of, its astronomical price, pepper was much used by the Romans, and in the early Middle Ages it became a status symbol for fine cookery. Arab traders established a monopoly in trading pepper to European customers, from whom they kept secret their knowledge of its origin in India. Increasing demand for pepper led to the European age of exploration in an effort to reach India to obtain pepper directly. By the end of the fifteenth century, the Portuguese explorer Vasco da Gama reached India and founded several Portuguese outposts, followed later by Dutch and then English explorers.

Black pepper, widely used in almost all cuisines of the world and cultivated in tropical regions worldwide, is produced from nearly ripe berries that are sun-dried so an enzyme contained in the outer portion (the pericarp) oxidizes and turns them black. White pepper consists of only the inner seed with the pericarp removed by soaking and rubbing or by decorticating when dry. More expensive white pepper is less aromatic and hotter than black because it contains more piperine, the volatile oil that gives pepper its characteristic flavor. It is preferred in Europe, especially France, for light-colored foods and is now popular in Japan for sukiyaki.

Green peppercorns, hand picked when full-sized but not yet ripe, are highly aromatic and less pungent than the black type. To keep them green, the enzyme they contain is kept from activating, either by brining, by boiling and then oven-drying, or by freeze-drying. Green pepper is used mostly in European and American cooking, where it seasons mustard, pepper steak, and pâtés. Red peppercorns are picked when fully ripened and red and then dried. They combine the aromatic pungency of black pepper with the fresh notes of green pepper. Rare and not to be confused with the unrelated crushed red pepper flakes (page

157) and pink peppercorns (page 232), they combine the spicy, mature flavor of black pepper with the freshness of green pepper.

Long pepper, resembling a small, narrow pinecone, may come from either *P. longum* or *P. retrofractum*. It has a sweet, fragrant, and musky aroma and a hot, lingering, and numbing flavor. Much used in classical and medieval times, long pepper has fallen out of use in Europe, though it is popular in India and Asia. Cubeb pepper (*P. cubeba*) resembles black peppercorns with small stalks protruding from one end and has a peppery aroma similar to juniper berries and hot, pungent flavor. Native to Java, it was valued by the Romans; today it's used mostly in India and North Africa. The aromatic leaves of betel (*P. betle*) are used in India to make mouth-reddening pan, chewed as a stimulant. Taiwan's native peoples have grown and chewed betel nut for centuries, and the habit has become a distinctly Taiwanese custom.

Purchase
and Avoid:

Indian Malabar and Tellicherry peppercorns are highly regarded. Dark brown Tellicherry pepper, made from nearly ripe berries, has excellent flavor and aroma and fetches a high price. Lemony flavored Indonesian peppercorns, such as the hot Lampong black from Sumatra and milder Muntok white, tend to be smaller in size and lower in price; they are most popular in Asia, Australia, and New Zealand. Grayish Malaysian Sarawak pepper with milder fruity aroma and less pungency is commonly used for supermarket-grade ground black pepper. Sarawak white peppercorns from Malaysia are reputed to be the finest, due to careful handling and processing. Milder Brazilian black and white peppers are named after their main port, Belém. Green peppercorns may be found brined, oven-dried (firm enough for a pepper mill), and freeze-dried. True red peppercorns are rare and hard to find.

Avoid purchasing preground pepper, because its volatile aromatic notes quickly dissipate and what's left is single-dimensional hotness. Also, poorer quality peppercorns are commonly preground. Pepper may be purchased in many forms: whole, cracked, coarsely ground, medium ground, finely ground (fine as powder), pericarp only, and table or shaker grind.

Recipe: **_Chef's Salt and Pepper Mix_**

1. **Using a clean coffee grinder or mortar and pestle, grind or crush black (and/or white) peppercorns to a fine powder.**

2. **Mix 1 part pepper with 12 parts kosher salt or 8 parts fine or flake sea salt. Store in a metal spice can or glass jar away from the light.**

3. **Transfer a small amount to a ramekin or small bowl and keep on the countertop for seasoning, using your fingers to measure.**

Serving Suggestions:	Make swordfish, tuna, or beef steak au poivre by spreading with crushed peppercorns. • Make mignonette sauce for raw oysters by combining red wine vinegar with chopped shallots, grated lemon zest, sea salt, and finely crushed white and black pepper.
Food Affinities:	Most savory foods, especially balsamic vinegar, beef, brandy, curry, fish, goose, lamb, lemon, pork, rabbit, red wine, red wine vinegar, seafood, shallot, venison.

82. PINK PEPPER

Other Names:	*Aroreira* (Brazilian Portuguese); *ba sai wuh jiu muhk* (Cantonese); *ba xi hu jiao mu* (Mandarin); Brazil pepper; Christmas berry; *kurisuma-beri* or *sansho-modoki* (Japanese); *pepe rosa* (Italian); *pimenta-rosa* (Portuguese); *pimienta roja* (Spanish); *poivre rose* (French); *rosa pfeffer* (German); Schinus pepper.
General Description:	*Pink pepper* (Schinus terebinthifolius) *is a bright pink to scarlet, easily crushed berry usually sold dry.* Pink peppercorns have an intensely sweet and aromatic flavor similar to juniper berry, though much stronger. Similar in size to peppercorns and native to Brazil, they have only been produced commercially since the late 1980s. Pink pepper trees are related to mastic trees, and their sap is similarly used as chewing gum. The similar but larger Peruvian pepper (*S. molle*) is

used as a condiment in Peru but isn't available else-where. Pink peppercorns often show up in the mixed peppercorn blends. Pink pepper should not be con-fused with rare ripe red peppercorns (page 229). Pink pepper is best used in small amounts for its lovely color and slight crunchy texture.

Purchase and Avoid: The brightest dried whole pink pepper is dried in the shade to maintain its color and is preferable. Pickled pink peppers are dull in color and less desirable.

Note: Too much pink pepper can irritate the intestines because of the cardinol it contains. For most people, eating the small amount used for flavoring food will cause no more irritation than chiles or peppercorns. However, children and people who are more sensitive should avoid eating the berries.

Recipe: ***Salmon with Pink Pepper and Red Wine–Butter Sauce***

 1. **Combine 1 cup red wine, 2 tablespoons red wine vinegar, and 4 tablespoons chopped shallots in a small nonreactive saucepan. Bring to a boil, then lower the heat and simmer until syrupy.**

 2. **Separately, boil 3/4 cup heavy cream until reduced by half, about 15 minutes. Stir the cream into the wine mixture and cook together for several minutes, until lightly thickened.**

3. **Firmly press 4 teaspoons each crushed pink pepper-corns and minced ginger into the flesh side of 4 salmon fillets and sprinkle with kosher salt to taste. Cook the salmon in clarified butter, flesh side down, over medium-high heat until browned, about 4 minutes; turn over and cook until barely cooked through, about 4 minutes more. Keep warm.**

 4. **Reheat the sauce, whisk in 4 tablespoons butter, and season to taste with salt and black pepper. Spoon the sauce over the salmon and serve.**

Serving Suggestions: Add crushed pink peppercorns to breadcrumb mixtures and use as a coating for veal or chicken cutlets. • Add pink peppercorns to browned butter with chopped shallots and serve over steamed asparagus or green beans.

Food Affinities: Asparagus, Belgian endive, butter, game, ginger, grapeseed oil, green beans, salads, salmon, shallot, tuna, veal, white pepper, vinaigrettes.

83. **POPPY SEED**

Other Names: *Adormidera* (Spanish); breadseed poppy; *dormideira* (Portuguese); garden poppy; *haşhaş tohumu* (Turkish); *keshi* (Japanese); *khashkhash* (Arabic); *mak snotvornyj* (Russian); maw seed; *mohn* (German); *mon* (Yiddish);

paparouna (Greek); *papavero* (Italian); *papi* (Amharic);
papoula (Brazilian Portuguese); *pavot somnifère*
(French); *pereg* (Hebrew); *post* (Hindi); *ton fin* (Thai);
valmue-frø (Danish); *ying suhk hohk* (Cantonese).

General Description:	*Poppy seeds are gathered from the same plant from which opium is produced; bluish black seeds come from* Papaver somniferum *and creamy white seeds from* P. somniferum *var.* album. Poppies originated in the eastern Mediterranean, where 3,500 years ago the Sumerians called it "plant of joy." The ancients valued poppy seed for its oil, though its narcotic and painkilling powers were also well-known. Poppy seeds have virtually no narcotic content, although people who eat them may test positive for opium in drug tests. Growing decorative poppy flowers and purchasing large amounts of poppy seeds for such things as topping bagels may be illegal in some countries. Poppy-seed oil is cold-pressed in small quantities for the table or heat-extracted for use in artist's paints.

Both the slightly larger, oilier, bluish black poppy seeds (Hungarian or Dutch) and the smaller, creamy white poppy seeds (Persian or Indian) have a sweet, pleasant aroma and mild, nutty taste. Blue poppy seeds are stronger in flavor, especially after toasting, and are popular in eastern Europe, Holland, Germany, and Austria, where they appear in stollen, tortes, dumplings, Bohemian kolache, and noodle casseroles. In Ashkenazi Jewish cookery, poppy seeds top breads such as challah, bagels, and bialys. They are crushed to make *mohn*, a poppy seed filling for *hamentaschen* cookies and Hungarian strudel. Mild white poppy seeds are prized for their thickening properties, especially for creamy Moghul-style Indian korma sauces. They flavor breads, cakes, and cookies in Scandinavia and appear in Japan's subtly flavored dishes and the Japanese spice mixture shichimi toga-rashi (page 286).

Purchase and Avoid:	Look for white poppy seeds in Indian, Middle Eastern, and Scandinavian food stores. Look for blue poppy seeds and *mohn* (ground poppy) in German, Russian, and central European markets. Buy small quantities of poppy seeds, and only from stores with high turnover or from specialty spice purveyors.
Storage:	Because they are high in oil, poppy seeds are prone to rancidity. They also tend to get infested with insects, so they are best stored in the freezer.
Preparation:	• **Because poppy seeds are extremely hard, a special poppy seed grinder is used to grind the seeds; if soaked first to soften, the special grinder isn't needed.**
Recipe:	*Jewish Purim Hamentaschen with Poppy Seed Filling*

 1. **To make the filling: Pour 2 cups boiling water over ½ pound blue poppy seeds to cover and soak overnight.**

Drain well. Grind finely using the finest blade of meat grinder, a special poppy seed grinder, or a coffee grinder.

 2. Cream ½ cup butter and ½ cup honey, then add 2 tablespoons heavy cream, 1 cup coarsely ground walnuts, ½ cup golden raisins, 2 teaspoons grated orange zest, and the ground poppy seeds. Chill before using.

 3. To make the dough: Cream 1 cup butter and 2 cups sugar, then beat in 1 egg. Sift 4 cups all-purpose flour with 4 teaspoons baking powder and ½ teaspoon salt. Stir half the flour mix into the creamed mixture. Beat in 4 tablespoons orange juice, 4 teaspoons orange zest, and 2 teaspoons vanilla, then beat in the remaining flour mixture. Chill the dough until firm.

 4. Preheat the oven to 350°F. Roll the dough out slightly more than ¼ inch thick. Reroll the dough scraps if desired. Cut into 3-inch rounds, dot each with a teaspoonful of poppy seed filling, and fold up the edges on three sides to form open triangles.

5. Place on baking sheets and bake until delicately browned, about 15 to 20 minutes.

Serving Suggestions: Sizzle blue poppy seeds in butter and toss with egg noodles, spaetzle, or steamed potatoes. • Flavor muffins with lemon juice and zest and plenty of poppy seeds. • Toss asparagus with browned butter

and blue and/or white poppy seeds. • Use white
poppy seeds to thicken Indian lamb korma.

Food
Affinities:

Almond, butter, cream, fruit salad, honey, lamb,
lemon, raisin, strawberry, vanilla, walnut, yogurt.

---

84. 📷 **SAFFRON**

Other Names:

Açafrão (Portuguese); *azafrán* (Spanish); *fan hong hua*
(Chinese); *kesar* (Hindi); *safran* (French, German,
Hebrew, Turkish); *safrani* (Greek); *safuran* (Japanese);
shafran (Russian); *za'afaran* (Farsi); *zafferano* (Italian);
zafraan (Arabic).

General
Description:

*Saffron is the orange-red stigmas attached to the base of
the autumn-flowering crocus (Crocus sativus), in the
Iridaceae (iris) family.* Saffron has a pungent, earthy,
bittersweet flavor and a unique, acrid, haylike aroma.
The saffron crocus is sterile and is propagated by
dividing the corms (small underground bulbs). Saffron
is legendarily the most expensive spice in the world by
weight. However, because it's so concentrated, a few
threads can flavor an entire dish. Seventy thousand
flowers, gathered and cleaned by hand the same day
that they open—usually by the smaller fingers of
women—are needed to make one pound of dried saffron. Spain and Iran together account for more than
80 percent of world production of about 300 tons

annually. Saffron is cultivated on a much smaller scale in Italy, Crete, Turkey, and Kashmir.

Saffron is essential for Mediterranean fish and seafood dishes such as bouillabaisse, *paella Valenciana*, and *risotto alla Milanese*. It flavors northern Indian *biriyanis*, Persian rice pilaf, and some Indian milk-based sweets. Cornish saffron cake is a traditional spiced yeast-raised cake replete with dried fruit; a similar bread is made in Sweden. Note that in large quantities (far more than is used in cooking), saffron is toxic.

Unlike most spices, saffron is soluble in liquid. To extract the most color and flavor, soak it in warm water, milk, broth, or white wine until the liquid turns bright yellowish orange, then add the liquid to a dish. Saffron loses its aroma with prolonged cooking, though the threads may be briefly toasted in a dry pan to enhance the aroma.

Season:

Saffron flowers in autumn, but the spice is always used dry. When purchasing 1-ounce tins, check the harvest date, which should be of the current year, or at the latest, the past year.

Purchase and Avoid:

Look for saffron in Indian, Iranian, and Spanish markets. Saffron should be bought whole from a reputable spice dealer as powdered saffron can be easily adulterated. Avoid cheap "saffron," which may come from safflower, turmeric, or marigold. The best saffron, that of Kashmir and Iran, includes only the deeply colored red-orange stigmas; less expensive saffron is bulked up with flavorless yellow stamens.

Storage: Saffron may be kept in the freezer for 1 to 2 years with little loss of flavor. Otherwise, purchase saffron in small quantities and store in a cool, dark place.

Recipe: ***Steamed Mussels with Saffron, Leeks, and Tomato***

1. **Soak ¼ teaspoon saffron threads in 1 cup dry white wine for 10 minutes, or until the liquid turns bright yellow.**

2. **Clean 2 pounds cultivated mussels, checking to ensure they're tightly closed.**

3. **In a large, heavy soup pot with a lid, sauté 3 sliced, washed leeks in 2 tablespoons olive oil for 2 minutes, or until bright green. Stir in 1 tablespoon chopped garlic and sprinkle with crushed red pepper flakes. Cook 1 minute, or until the aromas are released.**

4. **Add the saffron-infused wine, the mussels, and 2 cups purchased or homemade tomato sauce. Cover tightly and steam, shaking frequently, until the mussels open, about 5 minutes. Discard any mussels that don't open, sprinkle in 2 teaspoons chopped marjoram and ¼ cup chopped Italian parsley, and shake to combine. Serve in heated bowls and top with crostini.**

Serving Suggestions:	Soak saffron in a little milk and use along with cardamom and cinnamon to flavor Indian-style rice pudding. • Soak saffron in water or broth and add to risotto alla Milanese. • Soak saffron in milk and add to dough for brioche, challah, or fresh pasta.
Food Affinities:	Almond, artichoke, cardamom, chicken, cinnamon, cream, currant, fennel, fish, garlic, honey, lemon, rose water, seafood, thyme, tomato, white wine.

SALT

Other Names:	*Melah* (Hebrew); *melh* (Arabic); *sel* (French); *sal* (Spanish); *sale* (Italian); *salz* (German); *shio* (Japanese); *sol* (Russian).
General Description:	*Salt (sodium chloride) is a mineral composed of chlorine and sodium, the latter of which is essential to life.* The only mineral, nonbiological food humans regularly eat, salt is one of the four basic tastes, along with sweet, sour, and bitter (five including "umami," or savory). Throughout human history salt has been essential to the preservation of foods. Humans and other animals have an inherent taste for salt, which brings out natural flavors, retards food spoilage, regulates fermentation rates, strengthens gluten in bread, and is essential for preserving meats and sausages. Salt is also an effective carrier of flavor, thus celery salt,

onion salt, and garlic salt are common in the kitchen, and many chefs prepare their own flavored salts.

The word *salt* probably originates from the ancient town Es-Salt, close to one the world's best-known salt sources, the Dead Sea. Roman soldiers were given money to purchase salt, the *salarium argentum*, from which we get the word *salary*. The Romans also liked to salt their greens, which led to the word *salad*. The expression "He is not worth his salt" can be traced back to ancient Greece, where salt was traded for slaves.

Salt was integral to preserving the vast catches of cod and other fish discovered by European fishermen in the Grand Banks of Newfoundland at the end of the fifteenth century. Salt taxes have had profound impacts on world history, being a significant factor in the French Revolution, contributing to the toppling of China's imperial government in the early twentieth century, and galvanizing Mahatma Ghandi's resistance to British colonial rule in India. The Erie Canal, opened in 1825, was known as "the ditch that salt built" because salt was its main cargo.

Salt, in the form of the mineral halite, is obtained from underground mines such as the famed Wieliczka Salt Mine in Poland and the mines near Salzburg, Austria. The Bonneville Salt Flats in Utah are the dried-up residue of ancient seas. Sea salt, prized by connoisseurs, is made by evaporating seawater, which averages 2.6 percent salt. Although much sea salt is evaporated artificially, in places where the ratio of rainfall to temperature is low enough, seawater in shallow basins is evaporated naturally by the heat of the sun. Sea salt typically contains traces of other minerals, including iron, magnesium, calcium, potassium, manganese, zinc, and iodine.

Table salt comes in very fine crystals and is treated so it will pour easily. It usually derives from salt mines and is refined until it is pure sodium chloride. Iodine, a trace element lacking in some diets, is often added. Popcorn or flour salt is superfine salt designed especially to adhere to popcorn and other snacks. Pretzel salt, large-grained salt that doesn't melt quickly, is used for pretzels and salted breadsticks.

Kosher salt comes in large, irregular crystals and is used to prepare meat according to Jewish dietary guidelines (where meat must be salted to remove the blood before cooking), as well as on the rims of margarita glasses. With a large surface area due to the hollow pyramid shape of its crystals, kosher salt readily absorbs moisture. It's preferred by American chefs because it's light and easy to pinch and crush with the fingers, so it can be sprinkled evenly, doesn't make salad watery, and, unlike table salt, isn't prone to be confused with sugar in the kitchen.

Canning or pickling salt is fine-grained and does not include iodine or anticaking agents, which would cause darkened pickles and cloudy brine. It may form lumps in humid weather or if exposed to moisture.

Alaea salt or Hawaiian sea salt contains a small amount of volcanic clay (alaea) that colors the salt with red iron oxides and also imparts a subtle flavor. Hawaiian black lava salt is evaporated with black lava rock, and charcoal is added. Black salt (kala namak or sanchal) from India is an unrefined mineral salt that is actually a pearly pinkish gray and has a strong, sulfuric flavor. French gray sea salt is a naturally moist, sandy-textured, unrefined salt harvested from the Atlantic off the coast of Brittany. Flake sea salt, a light crystal reminiscent of snowflakes, is made by evaporating seawater with sun and wind, then heating the brine until delicate crystals of salt appear. The town of Maldon, England, has produced quality flake sea salt since the Middle Ages. Australian flake sea salt is produced by evaporating saline water in arid northwestern Victoria. *Fleur de sel* is a highly esteemed salt comprised of "young" crystals that form naturally on the surface of salt evaporation ponds in the Guérande region of France. Prized by chefs for sprinkling on foods just before serving, this high-priced salt contributes crunchy texture and bold, explosive flavor. *Sel gris* is gray from trace minerals in the water. Italian sea salt is produced along the coast of Sicily, where salt pans, low-lying depressions, are filled with the seawater in spring and left to evaporate by sun and wind. To make Japanese *uni no houseki* (jewel of the ocean), named for its gemlike appearance and utmost quality, surface seawater is combined with deep water for a rich balance of minerals. Peruvian pink salt comes from an ancient ocean now underground high in the Andean mountains. The shimmering flakes of South African sea salt come from the country's dry, windy west coast.

Smoked sea salt is smoked over wood fires using a method dating back to the Vikings to infuse the salt crystals with smoke flavor from woods like juniper, cherry, elm, beech, and oak. Korean roasted salt is pearl gray and almost powdery, with a distinctive flavor from its mineral concentration, accentuated by roasting.

Rock salt's large crystals are grayish because it's less refined than table salt. It's mixed with ice to lower the temperature of water when making ice cream and used as a bed for serving seafood items like baked oysters. It is not eaten.

Purchase and Avoid: Table salt is the most common variety; more obscure types may be found at specialty grocery stores.

Use:
- **In cooking, salt added to raw ingredients will draw out moisture. For example, when making cucumber salad, first tossing the sliced cucumbers with a little salt and allowing them to drain will keep the salad from being watery.**

- **A very small amount of salt will enhance sweetness in baked goods and even very sweet fruit, such as watermelon or peaches. Add a pinch of salt to your favorite cookie and cake recipes for best flavor.**

- Salt that's added to a liquid, such as stock, that will later be reduced will concentrate as the water evaporates, so it's best to wait to salt stocks, sauces, and the like until they've already reached ideal consistency.

- Salt can impede some foods, such as beans and whole grains, from becoming tender, so it's best to add it once they're half cooked.

- Salt tames the action of yeast, so it's important to add salt to bread dough to keep it from rising too much.

- Use flake salt or kosher salt when seasoning whole fish or meat for the grill, not only for seasoning, but also to make a light crust that will resist sticking to the grill.

- Sprinkle specialty salt on food just before serving or at the table rather than while cooking.

86a–b. ## SESAME SEED

Other Names: *Ajonjolí* or *sésamo* (Spanish); *benne* (Wolof); *gergelim* (Brazilian Portuguese); *gingelly* (Hindi); *kae* (Korean); *sesam* (Turkish); *sésame* (French); *sesamo* (Italian); *sésamo* (Portuguese); *shumshum* (Hebrew); *simsim* (Arabic); *sousami* (Greek); *ufuta* (Swahili); *vanglo* (German); *wijen* (Indonesian). **Black sesame:** *hak chi* *mah* (Chinese); *kuro-goma* (Japanese). **White sesame:** *chi mah* (Chinese); *muki-goma* (Japanese).

General
Description:

Sesame seeds (Sesamum indicum) *are small, thin, tear-shaped black or tan seeds with a pleasing nutty flavor that's intensified by toasting.* Black and tan sesame seeds are similar in flavor, while white sesame seeds are more delicate. Used as a seasoning and for their oil, they are about 50 percent oil by weight. Popular the world over, sesame probably originated in Africa and is now grown mostly in India, China, Mexico, and the Sudan.

In India, the seeds are sprinkled on baked goods and added to rice dishes, sauces, and stuffings. In China, they coat small deep-fried tidbits and sweets and are toasted and ground to make the potent Chinese sesame paste *zhi ma jiang*. In Japan, where sesame is used extensively, the seeds are always lightly toasted. They are mixed with salt as a condiment (*gomasio*), ground and made into sesame tofu (*goma-dofu*), and mixed with dressings and dipping sauces.

In the Middle East, sesame seeds are ground and compressed with sweet syrup and honey to make halva, or ground into tahini, a paste used in making hummus and baba ghanouj. Sesame seeds are sprinkled on *simit*, ring-shaped Turkish breads sold by street vendors. The seeds were introduced to America by West African slaves, who called them *benne*, still their name in the American South.

Cold-pressed sesame oil is gently heated to preserve natural aromas; hot-pressed sesame oil yields greater quantities of less flavorful oil and is the preferred frying oil in southwest India and Burma. Asian sesame oil extracted from toasted seeds is called "fragrant oil" in China; it's a common flavoring in Korea, Japan, and the Chinese province of Sichuan, where it's seasoned with crushed dried chiles. Japanese tempura is made by deep-frying battered vegetables in a mixture of one part toasted sesame oil and ten parts soy oil.

Purchase and Avoid:
Look for white sesame seeds, sesame oil, and cold-pressed sesame oil in supermarkets and natural foods stores. Asian toasted sesame oil, roasted sesame paste, natural sesame seeds, and black sesame seeds can be found in Asian markets and spice shops. Tahini can be found in Middle Eastern groceries and natural foods stores.

Storage:
Store sesame seeds in the refrigerator since their high oil content can lead to rancidity. Store toasted sesame oil, roasted sesame paste, and tahini in the refrigerator once opened.

Recipe:
Asian Sesame-Cucumber Salad

1. **Peel and seed 3 cucumbers and cut on the diagonal into thin slices. Toss the cucumber pieces with 1**

tablespoon kosher salt, transfer to a colander, and let
drain for 1 hour.

2. **Toast 2 tablespoons white sesame seeds in a dry skillet until they're golden brown. Whisk together 2
tablespoons rice wine vinegar, 2 tablespoons toasted
sesame oil, 1/2 teaspoon sugar, and 1/4 teaspoon
crushed red pepper flakes.**

3. **Rinse the cucumber slices thoroughly under cold
running water and pat dry with paper towels. Toss
the cucumbers with the dressing and toasted sesame
seeds and serve.**

Serving
Suggestions:
Sprinkle white sesame seeds on breads, crackers, and
cookies before baking. • Lightly toast white or tan
sesame seeds in a dry skillet, shaking so the seeds toast
evenly, and sprinkle on salads, stir-fries, and sautés.

Food
Affinities:
Almond, beef, bok choy, broccoli, butter, caramel,
cheese, chicken, cilantro, corn, duck, honey, lamb,
lemon, miso, olive oil, orange, rice, scallion, shrimp,
tofu, watercress.

87. **STAR ANISE**

Other Names:
Anasphal or *badayan* (Hindi); *anice stellato* (Italian);
anis estrellado (Portuguese); *anis de la Chine* or *anis*

étoilé (French); *anís estrellado* (Spanish); *anison* or
glikaniso asteroeides (Greek); *ba jiao* (Mandarin); *baat
gok* (Cantonese); badian anise; *cay hoi* (Vietnamese);
Chinese anise; *daiuikyou* or *hakkaku* (Japanese);
Indian anise; *pok kak bua* (Thai); *sternanis* (German).

General
Description:

Star anise (Illicium verum) *has mahogany-colored, star-
shaped fruit with an aroma similar to, but more potent
than, anise.* Star anise is always used dried. The essential oil of star anise resides in the pericarp (fruit
walls), not the seeds, and is pungent and lingering
like licorice, with warm sweet spice notes of clove and
cassia. Star anise commonly has eight points (though
it may be found with as many as twelve); in Chinese,
its name means "eight corners." Individual sections of
dried star anise will often split, revealing the shiny,
light brown, pointy seed within, which is nutty and
mild. Most star anise comes from China, but it's also
grown in Laos, the Philippines, and Jamaica.

Star anise is popular in Chinese cuisine, especially
for braised pork and roast chicken, and it's essential to
Chinese five-spice powder (page 279). In northern Vietnam, star anise flavors beef soups. In northern Thailand,
it goes into stews; in the tropical south, it flavors iced
tea. Star anise is used occasionally in Persian and Moghul
Indian *biriyani* rice dishes and in succulent meat curries.
In Europe, star anise is mainly used as a substitute for
the more expensive anise; although the two species are
unrelated, both contain the essential oil anethole.

| Purchase and Avoid: | Buy whole star anise pods with as few broken pieces as possible. Look for star anise in Asian markets, but be aware that a bin of Chinese star anise may possibly be contaminated with or confused with the closely related and similar-looking but poisonous Japanese star anise (*I. anisatum*). This type, which can be identified by its lack of anise aroma and turpentine-like flavor, is often used for potpourri. |

Storage: In whole form star anise keeps well for 1 year or more.

Recipe: *Thai Iced Tea with Star Anise*

1. **Bring ½ gallon of cold water to a boil. Add 8 finely crushed star anise pods, 1 teaspoon orange blossom water, the scrapings of 1 vanilla pod or 1 tablespoon vanilla extract, a pinch each ground clove and ground cinnamon, and ½ cup Chinese black tea leaves.**

2. **Boil for 3 to 5 minutes, stirring occasionally. Remove from the heat and stir in 1 cup sugar and a few drops of red food coloring (optional, though traditional). Cover, steeping until tepid.**

3. **Strain and pour the tea over plenty of crushed ice. Top with half-and-half or sweetened condensed milk.**

Serving Suggestions: Boil carrots with water, butter, and star anise. •
Simmer sections of pork tenderloin in a sauce made

from sautéed ginger, rice wine, soy sauce, hoisin
sauce, sugar, and star anise. • Add 2 or 3 star anise
pods to the liquid for poaching fruit.

Food
Affinities:
Asian pear, beef, black cardamom, carrot, chiles, cinnamon, fig, garlic, ginger, honey, pear, pork, port
wine, rhubarb, scallion, soy sauce, Szechuan pepper,
white chocolate.

88a–j. 📷 **SUGAR**

Other Names:
Açúcar (Portuguese); *azúcar* (Spanish); *sucre* (French);
sukkar (Arabic); *tsuker* (Yiddish); *zucchero* (Italian);
zucker (German).

General
Description:
*Sugar is the refined juice extracted from the sugarcane
plant* (Saccharum officinarum)*, which resembles bamboo and has sappy, sweet pulp-filled stems, or from the
sugar beet* (Beta vulgaria). Sugarcane, a plant native to
eastern or southern Asia, was cultivated from early
times in India and China. Once, all sugar came in the
form of large, tan-colored, solid loaves, which had to
be broken apart and crushed before use. Today, dark
brown cakes of unrefined sugar known as *kurozato* are
sold in Japan; in Mexico, cone-shaped loaves are
called *piloncillo*; and in Colombia, loaf sugar is called
panela. Cones of unrefined dark palm or cane sugar
called *jaggery* or *gur* are used in India and Southeast

Asia. The core of fresh sugarcane stems may be chewed or used as an edible skewer for grilling shrimp. Fresh sugarcane juice, called *guarapo*, is popular in Latin America and the Caribbean.

All partially refined sugar products have special flavors due to residual plant substances or substances created by the manufacturing process. Fully refined white sugars have virtually no flavor apart from their sweetness and differ only in crystal size. Both beet and cane sugars are 99.95 percent sucrose, but many bakers claim that the remaining .05 percent of trace minerals and proteins makes a difference, and that cane sugar performs better. Some manufacturers don't specify whether their product is beet sugar or cane sugar.

In sugar refining, molasses is separated from the sugar crystals after each of three or more boiling or extraction processes. The highest grade of molasses is made from clarified, reduced, and blended sugarcane juices without any sugar extracted. Bitter-tasting blackstrap molasses (black treacle in Great Britain), obtained from the last boiling, contains the lowest sugar content but the most vitamins, minerals, and trace elements. In Britain, light cane sugar syrups (treacle, golden syrup, or invert sugar syrup) are popular; similar syrups are popular in Louisiana. Note that only sugarcane is used to make molasses for the table, whereas sugar beets, palm, corn, maple, and sorghum may all be used to make syrups and crystallized sugars.

Granulated or regular sugar has medium-sized crystals and is the most common type. Lump sugar is granulated sugar moistened with sugar syrup and pressed into cubes. Sanding sugar has large crystals with carnuba wax added to keep the crystals separate; it's sprinkled on top of baked goods so that they sparkle. Superfine or bar sugar is finely crystallized and known in Great Britain as caster or castor sugar. Baker's special sugar, with a crystal size between granulated and superfine, is used to produce fine crumb texture in cakes and for sugaring doughnuts and cookies. Confectioners' sugar or powdered sugar is granulated sugar ground to a powder, sifted, and then mixed with 3 percent cornstarch to prevent caking.

Rock sugar is made by growing large crystals, often on strings, in a strong sugar solution. It may be found in either brown or white crystals and is often served with coffee. Yellow or clear Chinese rock sugar may be found in Asian groceries. Coarse sugar (or preserving sugar) has large crystals and is processed from the purest sugar liquor so as to be resistant to color change or inversion (natural breakdown to fructose and glucose) at high temperatures.

Brown sugar consists of sugar crystals coated in molasses syrup. Dark brown sugar is moister and has a stronger molasses flavor than light brown sugar. Muscovado or Barbados sugar, popular in Great Britain, is very dark brown and has a strong molasses flavor and coarse, sticky crystals. Raw or turbinado sugar is blond colored with relatively hard crystals and mild molasses flavor. It's similar to Demerara sugar, originally made in Demerara (Guyana) and popular in Great Britain.

Purchase and Avoid: The type of confectioners' sugar most commonly available in supermarkets, 10X, is the finest; 6X and 4X are progressively coarser.

Use:

- **Use rock sugar in Chinese savory dishes for its subtle, mellow flavor and to give a translucent finish to braised or "red roasted" dishes.**

- **Use preserving sugar for best results when making fruit preserves or jellies.**

- **Sprinkle sanding sugar, colored or plain, over holiday cakes and cookies such as biscotti.**

- **Rub sugar cubes over the surface of citrus fruits to absorb the essential oils, then crush the cubes for use in making desserts.**

- **Use superfine sugar to sweeten iced tea and berries. For smooth, silky texture, use it for making meringues, soufflés, and mousses.**

- **Use confectioners' sugar to make icings, hard sauce, and whipped cream.**

- Use muscovado sugar in sticky toffee pudding and dark fruit and chocolate cakes to produce a deep, rich molasses flavor.

- Use light brown sugar for butterscotch pudding, cookies, and glazes; use dark brown sugar for ginger-bread, baked beans, and barbecue sauce.

- Sweeten tea, coffee, and hot chocolate with turbinado or Demerara sugar, or sprinkle it on hot cereals.

89.   **SUMAC**

Other Names: Elm-leafed sumac; *gewürzsumach* (German); *kankras-ing* (Hindi); shumac; Sicilian sumac; *somagh* (Farsi); *sommacco* (Italian); *soumaki* (Greek); *sumac* (French); *sumak* (Turkish); *sumaq* (Hebrew); *summaq* (Arabic); *zumaque* (Spanish).

General
Description: *The dried fruits of sumac* (Rhus coriaria) *are burgundy red and quite tart, with resinous, woody, and citrus notes.* Sumac berries, which are not true berries, have a thin outer skin and flesh surrounding an extremely hard seed. Dried sumac is usually sold ground into a deep purplish red powder that is coarse-textured and moist with a fruity, tangy aroma and a salty aftertaste from the salt added as a preservative. Sumac trees grow wild in the Mediterranean and are found in much of the

Middle East. Sumac is a popular condiment in Turkey and Iran, where it's liberally sprinkled on kebabs and rice or mixed with onions as an appetizer or salad. In Lebanon, Syria, and Egypt, sumac is cooked with water to a thick sour paste, which is added to meat and vegetable dishes; this method was also common in Roman times. Sumac appears in the Jordanian spice mixture za'atar (page 288) and is also used in North Africa. In North America, native tribes made a sour drink from related species called lemonade sumac, squash berries, or sugar bush.

Season:
Sumac may occasionally be sold fresh in late summer, but usually it's found dried.

Purchase and Avoid:
The best sumac will have deep brick red to burgundy color, coarse uniform texture, and a high ratio of flesh to pulverized stem and seed. Purchase sumac from a Middle Eastern grocery or a spice dealer.

Note:
Several related plants of the genus *Rhus* are used as ornamentals in Europe and in North America. While these are mostly harmless, they may be mildly toxic and are not the same as the sumac used as a spice. The closely related New World genus *Toxicodendron*, formerly *Rhus*, contains highly toxic plants that are often referred to as sumac, including poison ivy, poison oak, and poison sumac. The fruits of *Toxicodendron* species are white to pale gold, not red.

| Recipe: | ***Beef Shawarma in Pita Bread*** |

 1. **Whisk together 2 tablespoons red wine vinegar, 1 tablespoon lemon juice, 1 teaspoon ground allspice, and salt and pepper to taste. Marinate 1 pound beef or lamb stir-fry strips in the mixture at least 2 hours and up to overnight, refrigerated.**

 2. **Prepare tahini sauce by blending 1 cup tahini with ½ cup fresh lemon juice, 2 to 3 cloves garlic, the leaves of ½ bunch Italian parsley, and about 1 cup water, enough to make a thin, creamy consistency.**

 3. **Prepare an onion relish by combining 1 diced sweet or red onion, ½ cup coarsely chopped Italian parsley, and 1 tablespoon ground sumac.**

 4. **Drain the meat, then grill or broil it and serve in pita breads, topped with the tahini sauce and onion relish.**

| Serving Suggestions: | Sprinkle sumac on lamb or beef kebabs. • Garnish hummus, baba ghanouj, or tomato, parsley, and onion salad with a sprinkle of sumac. • Put crushed garlic cloves inside a chicken, dust all over with sumac, season with salt and pepper, and roast. |

| Food Affinities: | Almond, cucumber, eggplant, garlic, lemon, mint, olive oil, pine nut, red onion, scallion, sesame, tomato, winter squash, yogurt, zucchini. |

90.   ## SZECHUAN PEPPER

Other Names: *Andaliman* or *intir-intir* (Indonesian); aniseed pepper; Chinese pepper; *chopi* or *sancho* (Korean); *dang cay* (Vietnamese); *emma* (Tibetan); *faa jiu* or *hua chia* (Cantonese); fagara pepper; Indonesian lemon pepper; Japanese pepper; *ma lar* or *mak kak* (Thai); *mullilam* or *tilfda* (Hindi); Nepal pepper; *pepe di anis* (Spanish); *poivre du Sichuan* (French); *sansho* (Japanese); *hua jiao* (Mandarin); Sichuan pepper; sprice pepper; *Szechuan-pfeffer* (German); *timur* (Nepali).

General Description: *Szechuan peppercorns are the small dried fruits of a prickly ash tree* (Zanthoxylum simulans). Usually reddish brown, the fruits have rough walls that split open, exposing tiny black seeds, a small tough stem, and, often, thorns. The aroma and pungency reside in the pericarp (fruit wall), not in the seeds. Szechuan peppercorns impart a tingly numbness to the mouth that is lingering and somewhat "fizzy." The aroma is lemonlike with warm and woodsy notes. The peppercorns are lightly toasted and crushed before being added to food, generally at the last moment.

Szechuan pepper is most important in central China and Japan, but related species are known in parts of India, the Himalayas, Indonesia, and Southeast Asia. The characteristic "biting" pungency of Szechuan pepper, or *ma*, is indispensable for Sichuan (formerly spelled Szechuan) cookery, often in combination with fiery chiles. A local species called *yerma* (*Z. armatum*) is important in Tibetan cookery because it's one of the few spices that can be grown in the Himalayas.

In Japan, the dried and powdered leaves of *sancho* (*Z. piperitum*) flavor noodle dishes and soups, while the fresh leaves, called *kinome*, flavor vegetables, especially bamboo shoots. The plant's berries produce shiny black seeds that are traditionally ground in a mortar made from prickly ashwood. This pungent, lemony spice is sprinkled on unagi (broiled eel) and it flavors nanami and shichimi togarashi. Korean *sancho* (*Z. schinifolium*) has a mild, aromatic flavor; its aromatic seeds are used for pickles and hot sauces. Several types of Szechuan pepper grow wild in Indonesia; one milder type from Sumatra is called *andaliman*, or Indonesian lemon pepper.

Purchase and Avoid:
It's best to buy whole Szechuan pepper from an Asian market. If you're buying the ground spice, purchase it from a high-quality spice dealer. Though previously banned in the U.S. (to prevent the spread of plant canker), heat-treated Szechuan peppercorns may now be legally imported.

Note:
Szechuan pepper often contains bits of pointy thorns that can be harmful if swallowed, so be vigilant. The seeds are usually also removed because they have an unpleasant, gritty texture.

Recipe: **Szechuan Roasted Salt and Pepper Mix**

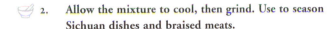

1. **Heat 1 tablespoon cleaned and trimmed Szechuan peppercorns and 3 tablespoons sea salt in a heavy frying pan over medium-low heat, shaking the pan occasionally, until wisps of smoke appear and the mixture is fragrant, about 10 minutes.**

2. **Allow the mixture to cool, then grind. Use to season Sichuan dishes and braised meats.**

Serving Suggestions: Crush 1 teaspoon Szechuan peppercorns with 1/2 teaspoon each white and black peppercorns and 1/4 teaspoon allspice berries and use to coat steak or pork chops. • Season spareribs before cooking with a mixture of Szechuan Roasted Salt and Pepper Mix (recipe above), minced ginger and garlic, and toasted sesame oil.

Food Affinities: Barbecue ribs, duck, garlic, ginger, mushroom, onion, peanut, rice wine, snow peas, soy sauce, star anise.

91. **TAMARIND**

Other Names: *Asam jawa* (Indonesian); *asam koh* (Chinese); *cay me* (Vietnamese); *imli* (Hindi); *indische dattel* (German); *mak kham* (Thai); *sampalok* (Tagalog); *tamarindo* (French, Italian, Japanese, Portuguese, Spanish); *tamr al-hindi* (Arabic); *ukwaju* (Swahili).

General
Description:

Tamarind (Tamarindus indica) *has a brittle, easily cracked fruit pod filled with hard seeds surrounded by tangy edible pulp.* Native to tropical Africa, tamarind had already spread to India by prehistoric times; it's long been established in Southeast Asia and now grows throughout tropical and subtropical regions. The cinnamon-brown pods, each containing up to ten dark brown seeds, grow in clusters that may be left to hang on the tree up to six months before they are picked. As the pods mature, the pulp turns reddish brown and dehydrates naturally to a tangy, sticky, somewhat stringy paste; its flavor is slightly woody, with prune and orange overtones, like tangy raisins. Tamarind is highly popular in the Middle East, India, Indonesia, the Caribbean, and Latin America, where it is used for its citric, sweet-sour flavor in chutneys, cooling drinks, candies, sauces, and frozen fruit pops, much as lemon is used in European and American cuisines. It goes well with chiles and is widely used with spicy foods. It is a characteristic flavor in Worcestershire and Pickapeppa sauces and many prepared chutneys.

Purchase
and Avoid:

Fresh tamarind may be found sporadically in Asian, Indian, Caribbean, and Latin American markets and well-stocked supermarkets. Dried tamarind paste, frozen tamarind pulp, and tamarind concentrate may also be found in Asian, Indian, Caribbean, and Latin American markets. For fresh tamarind, select clean, relatively whole pods. Prepared tamarind is commonly sold in blocks of mashed paste that includes the large seeds, and the blocks must be soaked in warm water to rehydrate, then strained. Pure tamarind paste without seeds is also available. Prepared tamarind is also sold in jars as a salted concentrate, as strained and frozen pulp, and in powder form.

Storage: Store fresh tamarind pods refrigerated up to 1 month. Store soaked and strained tamarind paste up to 1 week refrigerated, or freeze up to 3 months. Store tamarind concentrate in the pantry.

Recipe: **Date-Tamarind Chutney**

1. **Soak 1 cup pitted dates and ½ cup seedless tamarind pulp in cold water to cover for 30 minutes.**

2. **Blend the mixture with the soaking liquid, strain, and stir in 1 teaspoon ground coriander, 2 tablespoons brown sugar, and salt to taste. Serve with Indian foods and breads.**

Serving Suggestions: Combine boiling water with tamarind pulp, add sugar or honey to taste, cover, and soak. Strain and flavor with lime juice, cinnamon, or grated ginger. Dilute with more water, chill, and serve over ice. • Season salmon, tuna, or other firm fish fillets with tamarind before broiling.

Food
Affinities: Almond, chipotle peppers, cilantro, cinnamon, coconut,
cumin, duck, eggplant, ginger, honey, lamb, mango,
mint, orange, star anise, sweet potato, tomato, tuna.

92a–b.

TRUFFLES

Other Names: **Winter black truffle:** Black diamond; Perigord truf-
fle; *tartufo nero pregiato* (Italian); *truffe noir du
Périgord* (French). **White truffle:** Alba truffle;
Piedmontese truffle; *tartufo bianco di Alba* (Italian).
Summer truffle: Grey truffle; March truffle; red-
grained black truffle; *scorzone* (Italian); *truffe de la
Saint-Jean* (French).

General
Description: *Truffles are a highly aromatic, underground-fruiting
fungus species in the genus* Tuber. These mysterious,
costly, and delicate fungi may be eaten whole, but
normally, because of their high cost and concentrated
flavor, they're used as a seasoning. Both white and
black truffles range from marble to fist sized and are
warty and rounded, though irregular in shape. Truffles
are hunted by female pigs in France or dogs in Italy.

The prized winter black truffle (*Tuber melanospo-
rum*), found in France's Perigord region, is dense and
shiny with an enticing and unmistakable earthy
aroma. Their flavor is enhanced by gentle cooking,
and they are essential to *pâté de foie gras truffé*. The
Italian winter black truffle (*T. magnatum Vitt.*) has

blackish wrinkled skin that is less rough than that of its French cousin. Its flesh is deep violet scored with fine white veins and tinged reddish brown at the edge. It is spread on crostini and is essential to *spaghetti alla Norcina*.

The rare white truffle (*T. magnatum Pico*), found in Italy's Piedmont and Umbria regions, has a pungent, ineffable, somewhat garlicky aroma. Its skin is smooth and yellowish and its interior ranges from cream to fawn with white veins, according to its maturity. This white "diamond of the table" grows at great depth and is always expensive. Normally walnut to orange size, in exceptional cases white truffles can be much larger. Their potent flavor is fragile and best enjoyed by shaving paper-thin slices raw onto eggs, pasta, and risotto just before serving.

Summer black truffles (*T. aestivum*), popular in French and Italian cooking, are found in abundance, and while not as highly prized as the winter truffle, have resinous flavor and good aroma with thicker, less fragile skin. They're commonly used to produce truffle oils, pasta, creams, pâté, cheeses, and liqueurs.

Bianchetti truffles (*T. albidum Pico*) are the smallest of the truffles and grow under pine trees. Their sharp taste is mellowed when mixed with oil or butter. Desert truffles (*Terfezia boudieri*) are a seasonal delicacy found and eaten after winter rains in North Africa and the Middle East. Small and light, they are sliced and fried, made into soup, or added to lamb stew. Oregon truffles (*T. gibbosum*) are small white truffles that grow in association with Douglas fir trees. Chinese truffles (*T. himalayensis*) may be passed off by unscrupulous dealers as the black French truffles they resemble in appearance but not flavor.

Season: Truffle seasons vary from year to year. All but summer truffles are generally available in colder months.

Purchase and Avoid: Because of their high price and the potential for fraud, always purchase truffles, especially fresh ones, from reliable dealers. Choose firm, aromatic winter black truffles with thin white veins running throughout. Summer black truffles will be less expensive and less aromatic, though firmer and less perishable. Choose white truffles that are light in color, fairly smooth, and hard, never soft or sticky. White and black truffle oils vary greatly in quality; the best is made by cold infusion. Truffles may also be found bottled in many forms, frozen, as a paste, sliced, as a flour, in vinegar, and in flavored oils, though some of these may be flavored artificially.

Storage: Fresh truffles are quite perishable and are best kept refrigerated in a closed container, immersed in brandy if desired, to help preserve the truffle. White truffles are very delicate and should be used within 10 days of harvest. Wrap in a paper towel, place in a closed jar, and refrigerate, changing the towel every day. Summer truffles will keep for 3 weeks after harvest if refrigerated. Store truffle oil in a cool, dark place, or refrigerate; avoid repeated chilling and warming. Truffles can be frozen, though they lose their firmness after thawing.

Preparation: • **To clean truffles, use a soft brush and carefully clean off any mold or dirt and pat dry with a paper towel. Cut away any moldy or soft bits. Black truffles are often peeled, with the peelings saved for sauces. Don't wash white truffles; simply rub them clean.**

Recipe: *Spaghetti alla Norcina*

1. **Bring a large pot of salted water to a boil. Grate or mash 1 to 2 ounces winter or summer black truffles.**

2. **Warm 4 tablespoons extra virgin olive oil in a skillet. Remove from the heat, add the truffles, and mix well. Place over low heat and add 1 smashed clove of garlic and 2 rinsed, cleaned, and chopped salt-packed anchovies and cook until the garlic sizzles.**

3. **Boil 1 pound spaghetti in the water until al dente, drain, and mix with the sauce. Serve immediately. Enhance the truffle flavor by sprinkling with truffle oil just before serving.**

Serving Suggestions: Insert thin wedges of black truffle under the skin of a chicken and store it overnight in the refrigerator

before roasting. • Serve beef carpaccio dressed with
fine olive oil and shaved truffles. • Garnish risotto
with shaved fresh white truffles or a drizzle of white
truffle oil.

Food
Affinities:

Anchovy, artichoke, beet, brandy, butter, cardoon,
celery, foie gras, garlic, haricots verts, mushroom,
olive oil, veal.

93a–b.

TURMERIC

Other Names:

Açafrão da terra (Portuguese); *azafrán arabe* (Spanish);
curcuma (Italian); *gelbwurz* (German); *haldi* (Hindi);
Indian saffron; *ird* (Amharic); *khamin* (Thai); *kunyit*
(Indonesian); *kurkum* (Arabic, Hebrew); *manjano*
(Swahili); *nghe* (Vietnamese); *safran des Indes*
(French); *ukon* (Japanese); *yu chin* (Chinese).

General
Description:

Turmeric (Curcuma longa) *is a rhizome (swollen underground root) that's brilliant golden orange inside with
orange-tinged tan skin.* Indigenous to Southeast Asia,
fresh, pleasantly mild, and aromatic turmeric is preferred in that region, especially for Thai cooking,
because it's sweeter and more aromatic. In Thailand,
it's grated and added to curry dishes, soups, stir-fries,
fried foods, snacks, and desserts; in eastern Indonesia
it goes into stews and curries. Dried turmeric is earth-
ier and slightly bitter, with notes of mustard and

horseradish and a medicinal powdery aftertaste, especially if overused. Turmeric has been valued for almost four thousand years in India, where it's essential for curry dishes but is also used as a cosmetic, as a dye, in traditional remedies, and in religious ceremonies.

Americans are most familiar with turmeric in yellow ballpark mustard, bread-and-butter pickles, and the chow-chow relish especially popular among the Pennsylvania Dutch. There are two main types of turmeric powder: Light yellow Madras turmeric is most commonly available and is used primarily for curries, pickles, and mustard; Alleppey turmeric is darker in color due to a higher portion of curcumin (turmeric's coloring agent) and is noted for its fine flavor and earthy aroma with delicate notes of lemon and mint.

Season: Turmeric is harvested from February to April and may be found sporadically during the warmer months.

Purchase and Avoid: Look for fresh turmeric in Korean and Southeast Asian markets. Choose plump, firm, clean "fingers" of turmeric with no signs of shriveling or wilting. Purchase high-quality powdered turmeric, as cheaper types may be unpleasantly acrid. Note that turmeric's color will fade if stored too long.

Storage: Fresh turmeric can be stored in the refrigerator up to 2 weeks. Pat dry with paper towels, wrap in a paper towel, then place in a zip-top plastic bag.

Note: Turmeric will dye your clothes, hands, tableware,
         and almost anything else upon contact. The stains
         are difficult to remove, though they generally fade with
         repeated washing.

Recipe: ***Indian New Potatoes with Turmeric***

1.   Cut 1½ pounds of unpeeled new potatoes into small
     dice. Heat 6 tablespoon vegetable oil in a wok or fry-
     ing pan over medium heat.

2.   When hot, quickly add a pinch of asafetida (optional),
     then 1 tablespoon black mustard seeds and 1 teaspoon
     cumin seeds, then stir in the potatoes. Sprinkle in
     1 teaspoon turmeric, and cook, shaking often, for
     about 15 minutes, or until lightly browned and
     almost cooked through.

3.   Just before the potatoes are done, sprinkle in 1 tea-
     spoon ground coriander, 1 teaspoon ground cumin,
     ½ teaspoon cayenne, and salt to taste. Drain any
     excess oil in a colander before serving.

Serving   Add turmeric to couscous dishes and homemade may-
Suggestions: onnaise for bright color and light flavor. • Make yellow
             rice: For every cup of uncooked rice, add ½ teaspoon
             turmeric powder, 1 soft cinnamon stick, 3 cloves, and
             4 green cardamom pods.

Food Affinities:	Almond, beef, cardamom, cauliflower, chicken, chiles, cilantro, coconut, couscous, cumin, dal, garlic, ginger, lemon, lentils, mint, onion, peas, scallops.

94. **VANILLA BEAN**

Other Names:	*Baunilha* (Portuguese); *lavani* (Swahili); *paneli* (Indonesian); *vainilla* (Spanish); *vaniglia* (Italian); *vanille* (French, German); *wahn nei la* (Chinese); *wanilya* (Arabic).

General Description:	*Vanilla* (Vanilla planifolia) *is the only orchid that produces edible fruit, in the form of long thin seed pods.* Native to Central America, vanilla has a long history of use in that region, especially for flavoring Mayan and Aztec spiced drinking chocolate. Vanilla is difficult to grow, requiring hand pollination. The tasteless green pods must be cured and fermented, either in the air or over fire, to develop their vanillin content. This complex and expensive process lasts about six months. The result is shriveled, though pliable, brownish black, oily, smooth pods with delectable fragrance and flavor. Most of the fragrance resides in the miniscule black seeds and the oily liquid surrounding them. Vanilla flavors Western sweet baked goods, custards, puddings, ice cream, drinks, and liqueurs, as well as savory creations of inventive chefs, such as lobster with vanilla. Look for tiny black seeds of real

vanilla speckling desserts like crème brûlée, panna cotta, and ice cream.

Bourbon vanilla pods, from the islands of Réunion and Madagascar, have full-bodied, creamy, rich, deep, dark flavor. Mexican vanilla beans are lower in cost, with sweet, spicy, woody flavor and pronounced vanilla notes, but for people accustomed to artificial vanilla, they may seem weak. The deep, full-bodied flavor of Indonesian vanilla is appreciated in America, though quality may be mixed. Highly fragrant Tahitian vanilla, from a closely related species (*V. tahitensis*) is rarer and has strong fruit and floral notes. Vanillons (*V. pompona*), produced mainly on the island of Guadeloupe, is quite floral and low in vanillin; it's mainly used in perfumes.

Purchase and Avoid:

Choose dark, supple, oily vanilla pods, avoiding those that are brittle or dried-out. Use only all-natural vanilla extract, choosing one with aromatic, concentrated flavor from a high-quality manufacturer. Vanilla may also be purchased as ground vanilla bean powder or as vanilla sugar. Vanilla paste is a relatively new product in which vanilla seeds are suspended in a vanilla-flavored gel. Many vanilla-flavored products are made from cheap synthetic vanillin, extracted from wood. Coumarin, extracted from the potentially toxic tonka bean and now outlawed in the United States, is sometimes added to Caribbean and Mexican vanilla extract.

Storage: Store vanilla beans in an airtight container in a cool, dark place up to 18 months. Store vanilla extract in the pantry up to 1 year.

Preparation: • **To make vanilla extract: Split several vanilla beans lengthwise, place in a clean glass jar, and cover completely with vodka or brandy, shaking well. Seal the jar and let stand in a cool, dark place for 4 to 6 months, shaking occasionally.**

Recipe: *Vanilla Bean–Ricotta Cheesecake*

1. **Prepare graham cracker crust: Preheat oven to 350°F. Mix together 2 cups graham cracker crumbs, 1 cup finely ground almonds, 1/2 cup melted butter, 1/2 cup dark brown sugar, and 2 teaspoons cinnamon. Press mixture into the bottom of a 9-inch by 2-inch springform pan. Bake 15 minutes, or until lightly browned. Cool.**

2. **Prepare ricotta filling: Reduce oven temperature to 325°F. Sift together 3 tablespoons each flour and cornstarch and set aside.**

3. **Using an electric mixer, beat 1 pound room temperature cream cheese and 1 1/2 cups sugar until smooth. Beat in 1 15-ounce container whole milk ricotta cheese. When smooth, beat in 4 eggs, one at a time.**

4. Beat in 1½ tablespoons lemon juice; 1 tablespoon lemon zest; the scrapings from inside 1 vanilla bean, split lengthwise; 1 tablespoon vanilla extract; ½ cup melted and cooled butter; and 2 cups sour cream. Beat in the flour mix just long enough to combine.

5. Pour batter over prebaked graham cracker crust. Surround the cake pan with heavy-duty aluminum foil. Place the pan in a larger pan filled with hot water to about 1-inch up the sides. Bake the cake 1 hour or until barely set in the center. Turn off the oven, leaving the cake inside for 1 hour longer. Cool on a rack and then refrigerate before removing from the pan and slicing into 12 portions.

Serving Suggestions: Boil vanilla beans in water until soft and tender. Simmer in sugar syrup until shiny, then bake at 300°F for 15 minutes, or until crisp. Serve as a garnish for desserts.

Food Affinities: Almond, banana, blueberry, brandy, chestnut, chocolate, citrus, coffee, cream, hazelnut, honey, lobster, mango, pecan, ricotta cheese, strawberry, walnut.

---

95. **WASABI**

Other Names: *Bergstockrose* or *Japanischer kren* (German); Japanese horseradish; *raifort du Japon* (French); *saan kwai* (Chinese).

General Description:	*Wasabi* (Wasabia japonica) *has a fleshy rhizome, resembling but not related to horseradish, which is grated and prepared in a fresh green paste that is the essential condiment for sashimi and sushi.* This native Japanese plant is an evergreen that grows in wet, cool mountain river valleys along streambeds and on sandbars. Wasabi, which has found widespread popularity in Western cuisine, has a short-lived hotness that subsides into a pleasant, mild vegetable flavor. The pure, clean pungency of wasabi is especially valued in Japanese cuisine because it produces an enzyme action that helps kill germs and parasites when eating raw fish and is said to help digestion. Wasabi is one of the rarest vegetables in the world because it's among the most difficult to grow. In Japan, fresh wasabi, which like horseradish will induce tears, is preferred, and its leaves are often used as an aromatic decoration. Elsewhere, wasabi is most commonly sold either dried as pale green powder or as a green paste.
Purchase and Avoid:	Fresh wasabi is occasionally available in Asian and specialty markets; expect it to be expensive. Choose whole, firm roots and avoid any that are slimy or deteriorating. Many widely available brands of wasabi powder and wasabi paste consist mainly of colored horseradish, mustard, and cornstarch, or may include parts of the plant other than the prized root. Frozen prepared true wasabi paste, sold by Japanese specialty suppliers, is of high quality.

Storage:	Store fresh wasabi in the refrigerator up to 1 month, wrapped in damp paper towels. Rinse in cold water once a week. Refrigerate opened wasabi paste.

Preparation: 1. **Trim off any dark edges from fresh wasabi root and scrub with a soft brush, peeling if desired.**

2. **Grate wasabi in a circular motion using a fine grater or nutmeg grater. Sushi chefs use a sharkskin grater because it gives the wasabi a smooth, soft, and aromatic finish. After grating, mash the fresh wasabi with the back side of a knife to release more flavor.**

3. **Compress the fresh wasabi into a ball and let stand for 5 to 10 minutes at room temperature to develop its flavor.**

Serving Suggestions: When eating sushi, spread a little wasabi paste on the fish, then dip the rice side of the sushi into soy sauce so the sauce doesn't touch the wasabi. • Top tofu and tempura vegetables with soy sauce and wasabi paste. • Season Bloody Marys and mashed potatoes with grated wasabi.

Food Affinities: Asparagus, beef, cod, cucumber, ginger, potato, salmon, sashimi, scallops, sesame oil, sesame seed, shiitake mushroom, soba noodles, sushi, tuna.

Spice Mixtures

All around the world, herbs and spices are mixed in time-honored proportions and combinations. In this section, a worldwide collection of spice mixes is detailed, including recipes to make your own versions of these shortcuts to authentic international cooking.

96. Achiote Paste

Achiote paste, a thick, deep red seasoning also known as *recado colorado*, originated in the Yucatán region of Mexico. It is best rubbed on chicken, pork, fish, or seafood, to which it imparts a deep red color and warm, mild flavor. Ready-made achiote paste is sold under several brand names and need only be mixed with bitter orange juice, lime juice, or vinegar before use.

Crush 1/2 cup annatto seeds in a mortar or use 3 tablespoons annatto powder. Toast 10 cloves garlic on a griddle until charred, then peel. Process the garlic and 1 cup bitter (Seville) orange juice (or 1/2 cup each orange juice and lime juice) to a fine paste. Using a mortar and pestle or spice grinder, grind 2 tablespoons coriander seeds, 1 tablespoon kosher salt, 1 tablespoon cumin seeds, 1 tablespoon black peppercorns, 6 allspice berries, and 3 cloves. Stir the annatto and the spices into the garlic paste. Transfer to a glass jar and store refrigerated up to 2 months. Makes 2 cups.

Adobo Seasoning

Adobo seasoning exists in many forms in Mexico, the Caribbean, and, with the same name but different flavors, in the Philippines. Use adobo to season guacamole, tacos, chili meat, or beans. Commercial adobo usually contains MSG.

Combine 1/4 cup sweet paprika, 3 tablespoons ground black pepper, 2 tablespoons onion powder, 2 tablespoons dried oregano (preferably Mexican), 2 tablespoons ground cumin, 1 tablespoon chipotle chile powder, and 1 tablespoon garlic powder. Makes about 1 cup.

Apple Pie Spice

Apple pie spice, a mixture of sweet spices made in many versions, is used to season apple pie and other apple-based desserts, such as dumplings and cobblers.

Combine 1/4 cup ground cinnamon, 4 teaspoons ground allspice, 2 teaspoons ground nutmeg, 2 teaspoons ground mace, and 1 teaspoon ground cloves. Makes about 1/2 cup.

97. ◻ **Baharat**

Derived from the Arabic word for black pepper, *baharat* simply means "spices" in Arabic. Baharat usually contains hot spices (such as paprika, chiles, and black pepper), sweet spices (such as allspice, cloves, cinnamon, nutmeg, and cardamom), warm spices (such as cumin and coriander), and resinous herbs (such as savory and mint). In North Africa, crushed dried rose petals may appear in the mix. It flavors lamb, beef dishes, and tomato sauce.

To make Turkish baharat: Grind together 1/4 cup pickling spice (page 285), 2 tablespoons ground black pepper, 2 tablespoons dry savory, 4 teaspoons dry mint, 4 teaspoons ground cumin, 2 teaspoons ground cinnamon, and 2 teaspoons ground nutmeg. Makes about 3/4 cup.

To make Tunisian baharat: Combine equal amounts ground cinnamon, crumbled dried rose petals, and ground black pepper.

98. ◻ **Barbecue Seasoning Rub**

A rub is a spice and herb mixture that's spread over foods, especially meat and poultry, before slow cooking. Rubs are most often used in grilling and smoking because they stick to meat during the process. To use rubs, work a generous amount into the meat up to 24 hours before cooking; cover and refrigerate the meat until ready to use. Apply a second coat just before grilling or smoking.

To make a spicy barbecue rub: Combine 1/4 cup pure red chile powder (preferably New Mexico or ancho), 1/4 cup dark brown sugar, 1/4 cup kosher salt, 2 tablespoons paprika, 2 tablespoons garlic powder, 1 tablespoon ground cumin, 1 tablespoon dry mustard, 1 tablespoon oregano, and 1 tablespoon ground black pepper. Makes 1 1/4 cups.

To make a sweet-hot barbecue rub: Combine 1/4 cup paprika, 1/4 cup mild or medium-hot chili powder, 1/4 cup dark brown sugar, 2 tablespoons ground black pepper, 1 tablespoon cayenne, 1 tablespoon garlic powder, 1 tablespoon onion powder, and 1 tablespoon kosher salt. Makes about 1 cup.

99. ◻ **Berberé**

Berberé, the highly aromatic and extremely hot national spice mixture of Ethiopia, is a blend of Arabic and Indian flavors and has a coarse, earthy texture. It seasons Ethiopian stews called wats, meat, fish, chicken, and vegetables.

In a dry skillet, toast 2 tablespoons coriander seeds, 1 tablespoon cumin seeds, 2 teaspoons fenugreek seeds, 2 teaspoons ajwain seeds, 2 teaspoons black peppercorns, and

6 to 8 allspice berries until the spices are fragrant and lightly browned. Cool, then grind coarsely. Mix with 1 tablespoon fine sea salt, 1 tablespoon ground ginger, 2 teaspoons ground cardamom, 1 teaspoon ground nutmeg, 1 teaspoon ground cinnamon, $1/2$ teaspoon ground cloves, and 2 crushed bird's-eye chiles. Makes about $3/4$ cup.

100. Bouquet Garni

The French term *bouquet garni* refers to a small bundle of herbs simmered in various dishes, gently infusing mild, aromatic flavor into the food. Add bouquet garni to soups, stews, or braises and remove before serving.

Tie 4 sprigs thyme, 4 sprigs flat or curly parsley, and 1 bay leaf with kitchen string.

101. Cajun Seasoning

Hot, peppery Cajun seasoning is essential for Cajun-style blackened fish or chicken.

Combine 6 tablespoons paprika, $1/4$ cup kosher salt, 2 tablespoons ground black pepper, 2 tablespoons ground white pepper, 2 tablespoons garlic powder, 2 tablespoons onion powder, 1 tablespoon dried thyme, and 1 tablespoon cayenne. Makes about $1 1/4$ cups.

Chili Powder

Preblended chili powder was first invented to season the iconic Texas dish chili con carne. There's much disagreement about the first recipe for chili powder. In 1890, DeWitt Clinton Pendery of Fort Worth, Texas, supplied his blend of chiles and spices to cafés and hotels under the name Mexican Chili Supply Company. Around the same time, William Gebhardt, in New Braunfels, Texas, started making what he called Tampico Dust, later changing the name to Eagle Brand Chili Powder. Use 1 to 2 tablespoons chili powder per quart of chili con carne, or use it as a rub for slow-cooked beef brisket, pork ribs, chicken, or beans.

Combine $1/4$ cup ancho chile powder, $1/4$ cup red New Mexico chile powder, 2 tablespoons toasted and ground cumin seeds, 2 tablespoons onion powder, 2 tablespoons Mexican oregano, 1 tablespoon chipotle chile powder, 1 tablespoon garlic powder, and 1 teaspoon ground allspice. Makes about 1 cup.

102. Chinese Five-Spice Powder

Highly aromatic Chinese five-spice powder enhances stir-fried vegetables, chicken, and especially fatty meats like pork and duck. Five-spice powder isn't hot but is quite concentrated, so use it in small quantities. (Heat-treated Szechuan pepper may now be legally imported to the United States.)

Combine 2 tablespoons ground star anise, 2 tablespoons ground fennel seeds, 2 teaspoons crushed cassia, 2 teaspoons crushed Szechuan pepper, and 1/4 teaspoon ground cloves. Makes about 1/3 cup.

103. ▣ Cinnamon Sugar

Cinnamon sugar is simply that: a mixture of ground cinnamon and sugar that can be sprinkled on buttered toast, Mexican sopapillas (fried dough) and *bunuelos* (batter fritters), German snickerdoodle cookies, French toast, and coffee cake.

Combine 1/2 cup sugar with 2 tablespoons ground cinnamon. Use true (soft-stick) cinnamon for mild, aromatic flavor; use cassia cinnamon for bolder, spicier flavor. Or crush 1 cinnamon stick and grind in a spice grinder with 1/4 cup sugar until a fine powder is formed, then mix in 1/4 cup more sugar. Makes about 1/2 cup.

104a–c. ▣ Curry Powder

British manufacturers developed curry powders in an attempt to provide a ready-made spice mixture equivalent to the kari podi (*podi* means "powder") that British colonists became accustomed to in southern India. Essential to the fiery cooking of southern India, sambar podi is the combination of spices that evolved into British-style curry powder. Poudre de Colombo was brought to the French West Indies by Sri Lankans who were brought there to work on the sugar plantations. Japanese curry powder, under the S&B brand, has been produced since 1923, when Minejiro Yamazaki began blending a well-balanced and sweetly aromatic curry powder especially suited to Japanese tastes. For all curry powders, starting with whole spices and lightly toasting them before grinding yields a more fragrant, fresher mixture.

To make sambar podi: Combine 3 tablespoons ground coriander; 3 tablespoons *besan* (chickpea) flour; 1 tablespoon ground cumin; 1 1/2 teaspoons coarsely ground black pepper; 1 teaspoon each salt, ground fenugreek seeds, amchur powder, dry mustard, and hot red chile powder; 1/2 teaspoon each ground cinnamon and turmeric; 8 crumbled dried curry leaves; and 1/4 teaspoon asafetida. Makes about 2/3 cup.

To make a basic curry powder: Combine 5 tablespoons ground coriander seeds, 2 tablespoons ground cumin seeds, 1 tablespoon ground turmeric, 2 teaspoons ground ginger, 2 teaspoons dry mustard, 2 teaspoons ground fenugreek seeds, 1 1/2 teaspoons ground black pepper, 1 teaspoon ground cinnamon, 1/2 teaspoon ground cloves, 1/2 teaspoon ground cardamom, and 1/2 teaspoon ground chile peppers. Makes about 3/4 cup.

To make poudre de Colombo: Toast 1/4 cup white rice in a dry skillet over medium heat, shaking frequently, until light brown, about 5 minutes. Remove and cool. In the same skillet, toast $1/4$ cup cumin seeds; $1/4$ cup coriander seeds; 1 tablespoon each black mustard seeds, black peppercorns, and fenugreek seeds; and 1 teaspoon whole cloves until lightly toasted and fragrant, about 2 to 3 minutes. Cool the spices, combine with the rice, and grind to a fine powder. Stir in 2 teaspoons turmeric. Makes about 1 cup.

105. Dukkah

An Egyptian blend of toasted nuts and spices, dukkah is used as a seasoning for lamb stew. Pita bread is also dipped in olive oil and then in dukkah. Use dukkah as a crunchy coating for chicken and fish, or sprinkle it over salads along with a little sumac.

In a dry skillet, lightly toast $1/4$ cup each blanched hazelnuts and pistachio nuts. Remove from the pan, cool, and chop finely. In the same pan, lightly toast $3/4$ cup white sesame seeds until fragrant, nutty, and golden brown. Cool, then combine with the nuts, 5 tablespoons ground coriander, 3 tablespoons ground cumin, and salt and black pepper to taste. Makes about $1 3/4$ cups.

106. Fines Herbes

Popular in French cuisine, fines herbes is a classic blend with a delicately balanced bouquet of fresh tender herbs. Use fines herbes to season mildly flavored dishes, such as omelets, fish, and vegetables.

Using only fresh herbs, combine 2 tablespoons chopped Italian parsley, 2 tablespoons chopped chervil, 1 tablespoon finely chopped thyme, 2 tablespoon snipped chives, and 4 teaspoons chopped tarragon. This mixture should be chopped just before use, as it deteriorates quickly. Makes about $1/2$ cup.

Gâlat Dagga

Gâlat dagga, a moderately hot southern Tunisian mixture of five spices, is well suited to vegetable dishes, tagines, and rich stews, especially those made from lamb.

Grind 2 tablespoons black peppercorns, 2 tablespoons grains of paradise, 1 crushed cinnamon (not cassia) stick, and 1 tablespoon whole cloves. Add 1 whole freshly ground nutmeg. Makes about $1/3$ cup. Store in an airtight container for 3 to 4 months.

107. Gomasio

A simple mix of sesame seeds and salt, gomasio is used mostly in Japan and Korea. Traditionally, it is made using a *suribachi*, a Japanese grooved ceramic mortar with a wooden pestle.

Toast 3 tablespoons fine sea salt in a cast-iron skillet until it turns gray. Remove from the pan and set aside. In the same pan, toast 2 cups unhulled sesame seeds over low heat until crisp and browned, stirring often. Process the salt and seeds in pulses in a food processor. The gomasio should be light and sandy-textured, not mushy or pasty. Makes about 2 1/2 cups. Store in an airtight glass jar in a cool, dry place up to 1 month.

108. Harissa

Harissa, the basic seasoning paste of Tunisia, is served with kebabs and couscous, and appears on the table in a small dish. It is also delicious on crusty bread spread with hummus. It is to be used sparingly as a condiment. Harissa is sold ready-made in tubes or small cans; the best comes from Tunisia.

Combine 1 1/2 pounds roasted, seeded, and peeled red bell peppers; 1/4 pound fresh hot red chiles, seeded and trimmed; 1 cup sweet Spanish paprika; 1/2 cup extra virgin olive oil; 6 to 8 cloves peeled garlic; and 1/4 cup ground caraway seed. Puree in the bowl of a food processor until smooth and thick, adding salt to taste. To use as a sauce, whisk 1 tablespoon harissa with 1/4 cup extra virgin olive oil, 1 tablespoon chopped flat parsley, and enough water to make a pourable sauce. Makes about 3 cups.

Hawaij

Hawaij is essential to the cuisine of Yemen and is also very popular in Israel, due to the large Yemenite community there. The currylike mixture is used liberally as a rub for grilled meat, poultry, seafood, and vegetables like eggplant, and may also be sprinkled into soups, stews, sauces, and rice.

In a dry skillet, combine 6 tablespoons black peppercorns, 1/4 cup cumin seeds, 2 tablespoons coriander seeds, 1 tablespoon green cardamom pods, and 1 teaspoon whole cloves, and toast over medium heat, shaking often, until fragrant. Cool and then grind. Stir in 3 tablespoons ground turmeric. Makes about 1 1/4 cups.

109. Herbes de Provence

Composed of the vigorous, resinous herbs that grow on hillsides throughout Provence, herbes de Provence is a traditional blend of herbs found in French, and especially Provençal, cooking.

Combine 2 tablespoons dried thyme, 2 tablespoons dried tarragon, 1 tablespoon dried summer savory, 1 tablespoon crumbled dried orange zest, 2 teaspoons crushed fennel seeds, 1 teaspoon celery seeds, 1 teaspoon dried and crushed lavender buds, 1/2 teaspoon ground white pepper, and 1 crushed bay leaf. Makes about 1/2 cup.

Khmeli-Suneli

Georgia is well-known for the subtle blends of herbs in its khmeli-suneli, which is used liberally to flavor *kharchio*, a thick stewlike soup made from beef, lamb, or chicken. In Georgia, the pale gold to light brown mix can be purchased in many variations.

Combine 2 tablespoons dried marjoram, 2 tablespoons dried dill, 2 tablespoons dried summer savory, 2 tablespoons dried mint, 2 tablespoons dried parsley, 2 tablespoons ground coriander, 1 tablespoon dried fenugreek leaves, 2 teaspoons dried ground marigold petals, 1 teaspoon ground black pepper, 1 teaspoon ground fenugreek seeds, and 2 crushed bay leaves. Makes about 1 cup.

110a-b. 📷 ## Masala

The basic mixtures of spices essential to Indian cookery are called *masala*, from an Arabic word meaning "seasonings." Garam masala, the best known, comes from northern India's Persian-derived Moghul cuisine. It's mostly used with meat dishes, similar to the use of baharat (page 278) in the Arab world, and goes well with onion-based sauces. Chaat masala is a tart and salty spice blend used to flavor the enormously popular snack concoctions called *chaat*. Chai masala is added to a boiling pot of black tea, which is steeped, strained, mixed with milk, and sweetened with sugar or honey to make a fragrant, warming, and invigorating beverage.

To make garam masala: In a dry skillet, toast 2 crushed cinnamon (not cassia) sticks, 3 crushed Indian bay leaves (or substitute bay laurel), 1 tablespoon fennel seeds, 1 tablespoon green cardamom pods, 1 tablespoon black peppercorns, 2 teaspoons coriander seeds, and 1 teaspoon whole cloves until the spices are fragrant and lightly smoking. Cool and then crush. Stir in 1 teaspoon ground mace or nutmeg. Makes about 1/3 cup. Store in an airtight jar for 3 to 4 months.

To make chaat masala: In a dry skillet, toast 2 tablespoons cumin seeds, 2 tablespoons fennel seeds, and 2 tablespoons coriander seeds until lightly browned and fragrant. Cool and crush in a mortar and pestle or in a spice grinder. Combine with 2 tablespoons sea salt, 2 tablespoons black salt, 1 tablespoon amchur powder, 2 teaspoons ground ginger, 1 teaspoon ground hot chiles, 1 teaspoon ground black pepper, and 1 pinch asafetida. Makes about 1 cup.

To make chai masala: In a dry skillet, combine 4 star anise pods, 4 teaspoons green cardamom pods, 4 teaspoons black peppercorns, 1 crushed cinnamon stick (not cassia), and 1 teaspoon cloves. Toast until fragrant, shaking often. Cool and then grind. Stir in 1 tablespoon ground ginger. Makes about 1/2 cup.

111. 📷 **Montreal Steak Seasoning**

Montreal steak seasoning combines the British love of beefsteaks with the French flair for seasoning. It's excellent on steaks and potatoes.

Combine 2 tablespoons paprika, 2 tablespoons crushed black pepper, 2 tablespoons kosher salt, 1 tablespoon granulated garlic, 1 tablespoon granulated onion, 1 tablespoon crushed coriander, 1 tablespoon dill, and 1 tablespoon crushed red pepper flakes, and mix well. Makes about ³/4 cup.

112. 📷 **Old Bay® Seasoning**

Old Bay Seasoning is a mixture of herbs and spices traditionally used in Baltimore to steam hard-shell crabs. Today Old Bay is used on grilled fish, steamed shrimp, fried chicken, French fries, and potato salad, and for vegetable dips. The exact recipe is a secret, but this is a close approximation.

Combine 2 tablespoons ground bay leaves, 2 tablespoons celery salt, 1 tablespoon dry mustard, 2 teaspoons ground black pepper, 2 teaspoons ground ginger, 2 teaspoons sweet paprika, 1 teaspoon ground white pepper, 1 teaspoon ground nutmeg, 1 teaspoon ground cloves, 1 teaspoon ground allspice, ¹/2 teaspoon crushed red pepper flakes, ¹/2 teaspoon ground mace, and ¹/2 teaspoon ground cardamom. Makes about ¹/2 cup.

113. 📷 **Panch Phoron**

Panch phoron is a five-seed mixture from Bengal, India, a region famous for its distinctive cuisine. Panch phoron is most common in northern India, where the majority of seed spices are grown. Grind coarsely and use as a coating on roasted meat, or sprinkle on Indian breads, potato dishes, and vegetables, especially eggplant and cauliflower.

Combine 2 tablespoons each whole black mustard seeds, whole nigella seeds, whole cumin seeds, whole fenugreek seeds, and whole fennel seeds. Makes about ²/3 cup.

Pastrami Seasoning

Pastrami is a Romanian specialty adapted from Turkish *basturma*—spiced, pressed, and dried meat—brought to the United States by immigrants in the late nineteenth century.

Combine ¹/2 cup kosher salt, ¹/2 cup molasses (not blackstrap), ¹/2 cup chopped garlic, ¹/4 cup finely chopped fresh ginger, ¹/4 cup sugar, 2 tablespoons crushed coriander, 2 tablespoons crushed fennel seeds, 1 tablespoon each coarsely ground black and white pepper, 2 teaspoons allspice, and ¹/2 teaspoon ground cloves. Blend in a food processor until a wet, chunky paste is obtained. Use to cure and smoke beef brisket for pastrami.

Store the pastrami seasoning refrigerated in an airtight container up to 2 weeks. Makes about 2 cups.

114. Pickling Spice

Pickling spice is a mixture of spices used for pickling meats such as corned beef and sauerbraten; vegetables such as cabbage, onions, and mushrooms; and fish such as salmon and herring. Pickling spices are best left whole so the flavor cooks in without leaving any powdery residues that would make the liquid cloudy and unappealing. Tie pickling spices in a cheesecloth bag for easy removal. Use about 1 tablespoon pickling spice for each quart of liquid.

Combine 1/4 cup broken cassia bark, 2 tablespoons yellow mustard seeds, 2 tablespoons black mustard seeds, 2 tablespoons coriander seeds, 2 tablespoons allspice berries, 2 tablespoons black peppercorns, 1 tablespoon dill seeds, 1 tablespoon fennel seeds, 2 teaspoons whole cloves, 2 teaspoons celery seeds, 2 teaspoons crushed mace blades, 8 crushed bay leaves, 1 (1-inch) section dried ginger, and 1 small dried hot red pepper. Makes about 1 1/4 cups.

115. Poultry Seasoning

It probably comes as no surprise that poultry seasoning is used for seasoning poultry, especially roast chicken and turkey. This recipe makes a basic American-style blend.

Combine 2 tablespoons rubbed sage, 1 tablespoon dried thyme, 1 tablespoon dried marjoram, 1 tablespoon dried savory, 1/2 teaspoon ground black pepper, and a pinch of cloves. Makes about 1/4 cup.

116. Pumpkin Pie Spice

A favorite American spice mixture, pumpkin pie spice is used in autumn's pumpkin, sweet potato, and squash pies and is a Thanksgiving tradition. Use 1 to 2 teaspoons of the mix for each pie.

Combine 2 tablespoons ground cinnamon, 1 tablespoon ground ginger, 2 teaspoons ground nutmeg, 1 teaspoon ground cloves, and 1/4 teaspoon salt. Makes about 1/4 cup.

117. Quatres Épices

Meaning "four spices" in French, quatres épices is a combination of white pepper with aromatic spices that dates back to prerevolutionary France. It is often used in charcuterie to season pâtés and terrines and is suited to rich meat dishes such as beef braised in red wine or venison stew.

Combine 2 tablespoons ground white pepper, 1 tablespoon ground nutmeg, 2 teaspoons ground ginger, and 1 teaspoon ground allspice or 1/2 teaspoon ground cloves. Makes about 1/4 cup.

118. 📷 Ras el Hanout

Ras el hanout, which means "head of the market" in Arabic, is a complex mélange of many spices and is basic to the cooking of Morocco, Tunisia, and Algeria. In Morocco, ras el hanout seasons *mrouziya*, a lamb stew with honey, raisins, and almonds. Ras el hanout goes well with lamb, game, tagines, and couscous dishes.

Combine 1 tablespoon allspice berries, 1 tablespoon black peppercorns, 1 tablespoon mace blades, 1 tablespoon cardamom seeds (removed from their pods), 1 teaspoon saffron (not packed), 2 crushed sticks cinnamon or cassia, and 1 crushed nutmeg. Toast in a dry skillet, shaking often, until the spices are fragrant and lightly browned. Cool and grind, then mix in 1 tablespoon ground ginger and 2 teaspoons turmeric. Makes about 1/2 cup.

119. 📷 Shichimi Togarashi and Nanami Togarashi

Togarashi, the Japanese word for chiles, is a group of condiments always including chiles that bring out the clean, simple flavors of Japanese food. Shichimi togarashi is also called seven spice (*shichi* is "seven" in Japanese) because seven ingredients are generally used. It works well with fatty foods such as *unagi* (broiled eel), tempuras, *shabu shabu* (small bits of food cooked in rich broth), noodle dishes, and *yakitori* (grilled dishes). Nanami togarashi is a close cousin, with a slightly different proportion of ingredients emphasizing citrus zest.

To make shichimi togarashi: Combine 2 tablespoons sansho (or 1 tablespoon black peppercorns), 1 tablespoon dried tangerine peel, 1 tablespoon ground red chile pepper, 2 teaspoons flaked nori, 2 teaspoons black sesame seeds, 2 teaspoons white poppy seeds or black cannabis seeds, and 2 teaspoons minced garlic. Grind together to a chunky consistency. Store refrigerated in an airtight container up to 1 month. Makes about 1/2 cup.

Shrimp or Crab Boil

Popular along the southeast coast of the United States and especially in Louisiana, shrimp or crab boil is used, not surprisingly, for boiling shrimp and crabs. The mixture may also be ground and used to season fish or seafood.

Combine 1/4 cup pickling spice, 3 tablespoons sliced fresh chives (or 1 tablespoon freeze-dried chives), 2 tablespoons yellow mustard seeds, 2 tablespoons black peppercorns, 2 tablespoons crushed red pepper flakes, 1 tablespoon celery seeds, 1 tablespoon sliced fresh ginger, 2 teaspoons dried oregano, and 5 crushed bay leaves. Tie the spices in a muslin bag and add to the boiling liquid with sea salt to taste. Makes about 1 1/4 cups.

Tabil

Tabil, pronounced "table," is a word in Tunisian Arabic meaning "seasoning" that once referred to ground coriander, this blend's main ingredient. Tabil is used together with harissa (page 282) to season stews with meat, chicken, fish, or preserved lamb. On its own, it seasons cooked vegetable salads and stuffings for vegetables.

Combine 1/4 cup coriander seeds, 2 tablespoons chopped fresh garlic, 1 tablespoon caraway seeds, and 1 tablespoon crushed red pepper flakes and grind. Spread out onto a baking tray and dry in a low oven (200°F) for about 1 hour. Cool, then grind again to a fine powder. Add 1/2 teaspoon ras el hanout (page 286; optional). Store in an airtight jar up to 4 months. Makes about 1/2 cup.

120. Thai Curry Pastes

These pungent, aromatic, and hot seasoning pastes are basic to the cooking of Thailand. Red curry paste, made with dried red chiles, seasons soups and stir-fries. For the hotter green curry paste, fresh green chiles are substituted. Masaman curry paste, brought to Thailand by Muslim immigrants from India, is used in masaman curry soup. Vegetarian yellow curry paste is used to make yellow curry soup. The pastes can be purchased in small cans in Thai and Asian grocery stores.

To make Thai red curry paste: Trim and seed 6 each whole dried red New Mexico chiles and whole dried small hot red chiles. Soak in water to cover until soft and pliable, about 30 minutes. In a dry skillet, toast 1 tablespoon coriander seed, then grind and reserve. Wrap 1 tablespoon Thai shrimp paste in aluminum foil and heat the packet in the same skillet, flipping frequently, until aromatic, about 5 minutes, then remove from heat and reserve. Still using the same skillet, dry-roast 1 cup sliced pink Asian shallots and 1/2 cup sliced garlic until softened and lightly browned, about 5 minutes, and reserve. Mince together 2 teaspoons wild lime or lime peel, the sliced heart of 2 large stalks lemongrass, 6 tablespoons finely chopped ginger, 1 tablespoon chopped cilantro root (optional), and 1 slice peeled fresh turmeric or 1/4 teaspoon turmeric powder. Drain the chiles, reserving the liquid. Puree the chiles to a chunky paste in a food processor, then scrape in the shrimp paste from the foil and add the ground coriander, roasted shallots and garlic, and the lime peel mixture, adding some of the reserved chile soaking liquid as needed, pureeing until smooth. Store in the refrigerator for up to 2 weeks.

121. 📷 Za'atar

Za'atar is an Arabic word used to describe both a specific herb (page 63) and a tangy blend of herbs and spices that varies according to region but includes the resinous herb za'atar, tart brick red ground sumac, and toasted sesame seeds. Use za'atar to season grilled lamb or mix with plain yogurt and drizzle with olive oil for a vegetable dip.

Combine 2 tablespoons dried crushed za'atar leaves (or crushed thyme, summer savory, oregano, marjoram, or a mixture), 2 tablespoons toasted sesame seeds, and 1 tablespoon ground sumac. Grind to a chunky paste and season with salt to taste. Store at room temperature. Za'atar's flavor will begin to fade after 2 months. Makes about ⅓ cup.

122. 📷 Zhoug

Yemen's fiery hot green spice paste, zhoug, can be added to salads and used as a sauce for meat, fish, and poultry dishes. Yemenites believe that eating zhoug daily keeps away illness and strengthens the heart.

Trim, seed, and coarsely chop 1 pound jalapeño or serrano chiles. In the bowl of a food processor, combine the chiles with 1 cup each chopped Italian parsley and cilantro including the tender stems, 2 tablespoon coarsely chopped garlic, 2 teaspoons salt, 1 teaspoon ground cumin, and ½ teaspoon ground black pepper. Process to form a rough, chunky paste. Pour in ¼ cup extra virgin olive oil and process again briefly. Pack into a glass jar, cover the top with olive oil, and store in the refrigerator up to 3 months. Makes about 3 cups.

Table of Equivalencies

Volume

U.S.	Metric
$1/4$ tsp	1.25 ml
$1/2$ tsp	2.5 ml
1 tsp	5 ml
1 tbsp (3 tsp)	15 ml
1 fl oz (2 tbsp)	30 ml
$1/4$ cup	60 ml
$1/3$ cup	80 ml
$1/2$ cup	120 ml
1 cup	240 ml
1 pint (2 cups)	480 ml
1 quart (2 pints)	960 ml
1 gallon (4 quarts)	3.84 liters

Weight

U.S.	Metric
1 oz	28 g
4 oz (1/4 lb)	113 g
8 oz (1/2 lb)	227 g
12 oz (3/4 lb)	340 g
16 oz (1 lb)	454 g
2.2 lb	1 kg

Length

Inches	Centimeters
1/4	0.65
1/2	1.25
1	2.50
5	12.5
10	25.5

Oven Temperature

Degrees Fahrenheit	Degrees Centigrade	British Gas Marks
200	93	—
250	120	1/4
275	140	1
300	150	2
325	165	3
350	175	4
375	190	5
400	200	6
450	230	8
500	260	10

Recipes Index

Index

Numbers in **bold** (for example, **96**) can be used to locate herbs and spices in the photograph section. All other numbers are page numbers.

Sources: Books

Andrews, Jean. *Peppers: The Domesticated Capsicums*. Austin: University of Texas Press, 1995.

Boxes, Arabella, Jocasta Inners, Charlotte Parry-Crooke, and Lewis Esson. *The Encyclopedia of Herbs, Spices and Flavorings*. New York: Crescent Books, 1984.

Bremness, Lesley, and Jill Norman. *The Complete Book of Herbs and Spices*. New York: Viking Penguin, 1995.

Dampney, Janet, and Elizabeth Pomeroy. *All About Herbs*. New Jersey: Charwell Books, 1977.

Davidson, Alan. *The Oxford Companion to Food*. Oxford: Oxford University Press, 1999.

Facciola, Stephen. *Cornucopia II: A Source Book of Edible Plants*. Vista, California: Kampong Publications, 1988.

Goldstein, Darra. *The Georgian Feast*. New York: HarperCollins, 1993.

Hemphill, Ian. *Spice Notes: A Cook's Compendium of Herbs and Spices*. Sydney: Pan Macmillan, 2000.

Kowalchick, Claire, and William H. Hylton, eds. *Rodale's Illustrated Encyclopedia of Herbs*. Emmaus, Pennsylvania: Rodale Press, 1987.

McGee, Harold. *On Food and Cooking*. New York: Scribner, 2004.

Miloradovich, Milo. *The Art of Cooking with Herbs & Spices*. Garden City, New York: Doubleday, 1954.

Rosengarten, Frederick, Jr. *The Book of Spices*. Wynnewood, Pennsylvania: Livingston Publishing, 1969.

Sahni, Julie. *Classic Indian Cooking*. New York: William Morrow, 1980.

Sodsook, Victor, with Theresa Volpe Laursen and Byron Laursen. *True Thai*. New York: William Morrow, 1995.

Stella, Alain. *The Book of Spices*. Paris: Flammarion, 1998.

Tainter, Donna R., and Anthony T. Grenis. *Spices and Seasonings: A Food Technology Handbook*. New York: John Wiley & Sons, 1993.

Tsuji, Shizuo. *Japanese Cooking: A Simple Art*. Tokyo: Kodansha International, 1980.

Turner, Jack. *Spices: The History of a Temptation*. New York: Alfred A. Knopf, 2004.

Sources: Web Sites

http://botanical.com/botanical/mgmh/mgnh.html
www.caviarassouline.com
www.foodsubs.com/HerbsHisp.html
www.g6csy.net/chile/database.html
www.historicfood.com/Hippocras%20Spices.htm
www.ibiblio.org/herbmed/index.html
www.iisr.org/spices/index.htm
www.indianspices.com/html/s0620cge.htm
www.kalustyans.com
www.mastic.gr
www.ozevillage.com.au/herbies/index.html
www.patch-work.demon.co.uk/elder.htm
www.penzeys.com
www.richters.com
www.salttraders.com/StoreFront.bok
www.saltworks.us/salt_info/si_gourmet_reference.asp
www.seasonedpioneers.co.uk
www.silk.net/sirene/spicefin.htm
www.thaiherbs.com
www.thechilewoman.com
www.thespiceshop.co.uk
www.uni-graz.at/~katzer/engl
www.vannsspices.com
www.waitrose.com/food_drink/wfi/ingredients/herbsspicesseasonings
    andcondiments.asp
www.wellsweep.com
http://whatscookingamerica.net/EdibleFlowers/EdibleFlowersMain.htm

Acknowledgments

A complex book like this is a collaboration between some very talented and dedicated people. Erin Slonaker, my hard-working editor with the able assistance of Kevin Kosbab, helped make sense of the fascinating world of herbs and spices with her incisive comments and questions. Steve Legato, photographer extraordinaire, took on the challenge of photographing everything from angelica to za'atar. Art director Karen Onorato kept everything in order and lent the book her superb design sense. We all worked together with patience, humor, and enthusiasm to produce all 240 herb and spice photos with over 300 individual items.

I could never have written this book without the help of some extraordinarily knowledgeable and helpful people in the spice business. My special thanks go to Ann Wilder, founder and owner, and Courtney Nathan, sales director, of Vann's Spices (www.vannsspices.com) in Baltimore, who supplied me with many of the spices pictured in the photos and used for testing the recipes. My longtime friend, Joel Assouline, owner of Caviar Assouline (www.caviarassouline.com) came through for me with truffles, vanilla beans, exotic salts, and more. His willingness to help and to answer all my questions made this a better book. Gernot Katzer's Spice Pages (www.uni-graz.at/~katzer/engl), an incredibly thorough and meticulously researched Web site, made my job not only easier, but helped insure the accuracy of the book. Ian "Herbie" Hemphill's wonderful book *Spices Notes*, along with his Web site www.herbies.com.au, helped me to learn about native Australian seasonings.

Two dedicated local farmers that I have been working with for over 20 years brought me exquisite fresh herbs and blossoms: Mark and Judy Dornstreich of Branch Creek Farm in Perkasie, Pennsylvania, and Glenn and Karen Brendle of Green Meadow Farm in Gap, Pennsylvania. The people of Chios, Greece, were generous in providing me with information and examples of native mastic resin, available from their Web site, www.mastic.gr. Many of the unusual herb plants shown came from Well Sweep Herb Farm (www.wellsweep.com) in Port Murray, New Jersey.

More Quirk Field Guides

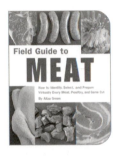

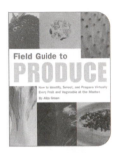

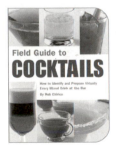

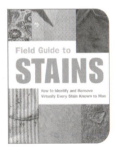

Available Wherever Books Are Sold